Neurodiversity and the Twice-Exceptional Student

Written for busy teachers, this practical manual defines terms, shares examples and provides evidence-based information and strategies to support the teaching of twice-exceptional students.

Providing a comprehensive blueprint in an easy-to-use format, this book explains classroom techniques for differentiation with tips and advice based on research and teacher experience. The topics covered include learning disabilities, gifted and high potential education, talent development and general classroom pedagogy involving curriculum differentiation and individualised programming. It also explains, in more depth, the varying presentations of neurodiversity in the form of specific learning disabilities, autism and attention deficits in the gifted/high potential student to enable teachers to acquire more knowledge of the nuances evident in each twice-exceptional student. Case studies capture the perspectives of twice-exceptional young people who have thrived, and the book provides weblinks to a very comprehensive list of helpful, freely available resources.

This essential, practical resource will serve teachers and educators in both primary and secondary schooling, as well as pre-service educators. It will also be of interest to parents and carers.

Rhonda Filmer is currently the Board Chair at the Specific Learning Difficulties Association of NSW. After spending her early working life in mainstream classrooms and teaching gifted groups Rhonda spent the last 20 years presenting professional development in schools, speaking at conferences and seminars, consulting on case management in schools and privately tutoring 2e students.

T0391553

Neurodiversity and the Twice-Exceptional Student

A Comprehensive Resource for Teachers

Rhonda Filmer

with
Geraldine Townend and Trevor Clark

Routledge
Taylor & Francis Group

LONDON AND NEW YORK

Designed cover image: © Getty Images

First published 2024
by Routledge
4 Park Square, Milton Park, Abingdon, Oxon OX14 4RN

and by Routledge
605 Third Avenue, New York, NY 10158

Routledge is an imprint of the Taylor & Francis Group, an informa business

British Library Cataloguing-in-Publication Data
A catalogue record for this book is available from the British Library

ISBN: 9781032520322 (hbk)
ISBN: 9781032520315 (pbk)
ISBN: 9781003404972 (ebk)

DOI: 10.4324/9781003404972

Typeset in Bembo
by Newgen Publishing UK

Contents

Acknowledgements

The impetus for this work came from the burgeoning scientific knowledge in the fields of neurodiversity, learning difficulties, psychology, behavioural sciences and classroom teaching that was simply not filtering through into our classrooms. Empathy for my colleagues working in underperforming schools was a motivation to produce this resource composed from the unique instruction I received over 20 years working with families and twice-exceptional young people. Thank you to each and every one of you who shared so generously your lived experiences. To the young adults who wrote of their sad memories of past struggles in order to illustrate and contribute, I am deeply grateful.

Other unintended tutors were the staff and students of St Andrew's Cathedral School, Sydney, members of the GLD Australia Support Group led by Carol Barnes and my voluntary work at SPELD NSW where matters of teaching literacy are palpable. I am indebted to my Gifted/High Potential Students chapter co-author, Dr Geraldine Townend, whose knowledge, currency and support have been invaluable. Thank you, too, to Dr Trevor Clark, my co-author on the Autism chapter, to Cheryl McArthur for her expertise in gifted education and diverse learning conveyed in excellent feedback and to Vilija Stephens at Routledge/Taylor & Francis for her prudent advice throughout this project.

Thank you to my colleagues, wonderful family and friends for their encouragement in my endeavours and to the community of St John's Anglican church, Ashfield, for upholding me in prayer and celebrating the milestones toward completion.

To my husband, Colin, I appreciate enormously your incisive, quiet advice, your forbearance and your cute artwork. You are a stalwart in my life.

The Author's story …

Twenty years ago when I was working as a Gifted and Talented Co-ordinator in a large primary and secondary independent school, the critical mass of students assigned to me who were intellectually gifted or very bright, creative and articulate, but who were not gaining the levels of academic excellence that would reasonably be expected, reached such a number that I felt compelled to find out more about how these students think and why they were so different. It was clear that most of them were not lazy or unmotivated or purposely oppositional to authority but that they were different. The term 'neurodiversity' ("the individual differences in brain functioning regarded as normal variations within the human population" from Merriam-Webster, online) was still only lurking in the research and had not hit the literature that I was reading.

A few of these students qualified for places in the school's inter-school debating teams that came under my role as Master of Debating and Public Speaking but generally there was little overlap between the high achievers and the students who were low achievers despite their oral precocity. Why?

Looking deeper, I found that some of these underachieving students had poor literacy, inadequate understanding of mathematics to allow them to progress, poor concentration levels, sensory sensitivities at a very high level and were sometimes, despite their bravado and attempts to disguise it, quite dispirited and disinterested. Their low self-confidence often prevented them from attempting to join the debating teams or other school provisions that would be appropriate for their interests and abilities.

My office became the refuge for the 'out-of-synch' secondary students who wanted to offload about everything that was wrong with school. I listened (when I could do so ethically) and I learned. Much of the protestation was legitimate. They were misunderstood and in need of help.

After the students were sent home, their parents would begin phoning me with their questions. I listened and felt increasingly inadequate for the task of intervention and extension. Out-of-school provisions such as Tournament of Minds, Future Problem Solving and so on were not an answer but merely a temporary amelioration.

Staff were not purposely prohibiting students' access to the curriculum. They did not understand how to change their practice and I only had intuition and a sketchy knowledge to assist them.

Interestingly, it took me back to an earlier time …

My first year of teaching had been a disaster.

As a young child who loved school all I wanted to be was a teacher. I was a successful student who had the benefit of education in an excellent public primary school where I was Dux in Year 6 and a high achiever at a selective public high school in NSW.

Summoned by my first posting, in the third week of Term 1, I tootled off down the Hume Highway to meet the Principal of Goulburn Primary School. He had a particular surprise waiting for me: a Year 3/4 composite class of 17 children who had failed to pass foundational reading and mathematics standards in their K–2 years. He allocated me an empty room and I was to meet the class the following day. The classroom had no books, stationery or ornamentation. Of course, it was only when I met and began working with the students that I realised their very low levels of achievement. I could see that several of them had undiagnosed 'special needs'. I only survived that year because I am so determined and from a long line of hardy country folk reared with the motto 'just get on with it'. I scoured the storerooms and begged, borrowed and bought whatever I could find as resources. A phone call to a colleague who worked in learning support saw me heading up the highway that weekend to fill my little car with every resource she could offer me.

I learned more than any of the children that year and we had quite a good time but my very poor Initial Teacher Education (ITE) that did not instruct graduate primary teaching students how to teach reading … a fact I will never come to grips with … nor the learning diversity of children, left me unable to give those students what they needed. They all made progress, but it was insufficient despite my best efforts.

Perhaps that experience stayed with me, haunting me, about how to meet the wide range of students' learning needs when we are totally unprepared by our training or professional learning opportunities. It caused me to 'look even deeper'.

This time, even though I was armed with a Masters' degree from UNSW composed 50% of gifted education subjects, an excellent working relationship with the Head of Learning Support and over twenty years of classroom experience I could not see how to advise staff nor assist them to address the complexity and accumulated challenges of these students in an ordinary timetable and workload.

And each student was unique.

I made a decision to take time out of my professional teaching role to investigate the phenomenon of 'twice-exceptionality'. It was a very 'left-of-field' decision to leave my wonderful teaching job to research this enigmatic segment of the student population. There was no clear path to knowledge via a PhD topic as this population is too complex and too broad. I took an 'unpaid sabbatical' while I researched every question I had about this group of students. I joined courses, spent 'professional hours' with psychologists and paediatricians, attended webinars and conferences.

I embarked on a whole new phase of my life as a teacher and consultant.

I want to share it all with my profession, the members of which constitute some of the most dedicated, skilled, unsung heroes of our time. What other profession enters the working life so poorly prepared and rehearsed and what profession's work has such long-reaching consequences in the lives of our population? I want to share my conclusions of what to do and how to do it.

I want to share it with parents who have a difficult time trying to find the answers they need for the poor academic outcomes of their bright and articulate children.

And for the children who spend so much time in school feeling like they are failures with a sense of guilt that they should be able to 'get it together'.

I have been working in this field long enough to have seen a succession of talented, articulate, self-efficacious, twice-exceptional, young people thrive in life so that I have a full caseload to share with you. You will meet some of them in the pages of this book.

The first student was Tom

Tom is a kind and helpful, empathic Year 6 student who befriends new students to the school even though he has many friends himself.

When Tom is doing a written exercise, it is a difficult experience for him. He tries hard to write neatly but the work always looks very untidy and illegible and every exercise is begun with a sentence or two with evidence of inspiration but fizzles out before the 7th line. His spelling contains many errors and yet is quite 'phonetic'. It is very difficult to get homework from him and he is never far from frustration which is expressed in an occasional refusal to do set work. He cannot manage to complete a test, particularly if it is a timed one, so there are very inadequate results from which to evaluate his progress.

In oral discussions, however, Tom is the fastest, sharpest and most knowledgeable student in the class. He has a store of amazing facts in his head and makes interesting connections between seemingly disparate ideas. Tom has a twin sister who is identified as moderately gifted and a high achiever at school.

Tom's mother worries about him and wants to know which professional practitioner may be able to help him. Despite having engaged in remedial spelling programmes and Occupational Therapy, Tom was still struggling with written communication.

And soon I met Cassie, James, Julia and Eleni and all the others ...

About this book ...

The scope of this book is potentially immense; any one topic could be used to formulate multiple topics for research theses or whole volumes in themselves.

This book will describe the component parts of 2e profiles and the importance of carefully assessing the impact of the co-existing conditions on not only the learning but also the well-being and lived experience of the child. Often lurking beneath the complexities is a very sensitive, confused young person whose self-esteem is wavering.

In Section 1, in the Introduction, you will meet the concept of twice-exceptionality, its complexities and peculiarities along with the framework that I am advocating. The terminology used in the literature is defined and discussed. Chapter 2 discusses how to identify the twice-exceptional student and presents estimates of their prevalence in Australia. Chapter 3 summarises the legislative requirements of educational institutions regarding the education of children with disability.

In Section 2, Chapter 4 will define and describe Giftedness/High Potential Learners while Chapters 5 to 8 present the detail of each of the more commonly occurring component parts in a 2e learning profile/neurodevelopmental disorders, set out in each chapter in this reader-friendly way:

- Vignette
- What it is (Definition/s)
- What you will see in the classroom
- What do I do about it?
- Going Deeper
- 'Go to' Resources
- References
- Case studies are used to illustrate teacher practice, student responses and outcomes

From the research and literature in the learning difficulties fields you will gain an understanding of the entirety of each condition so you can:

■   recognise any student who presents with that condition

■   see the nuances of these impacts and have definitional lists of characteristics to draw upon

■   understand how giftedness and the neurodevelopmental disorders impact the learning of the twice-exceptional (2e) student.

Section 3 activates the use of this knowledge and advises how to implement recommended practice into the classroom through **executive function coaching** and **differentiated curriculum practice** in the mixed ability classroom, at any stage of schooling.

Several longitudinal case studies detailing the individual profiles of several students, their struggles and successes, with reflections from the students themselves about what worked for them during their school years follow in Chapter 12. It is a rather unique opportunity, and a privilege, to take a longitudinal look into the lived experiences of 2e young people whose lives were shaped by the families into which they were born and the teachers they encountered. I believe their stories have intrinsic value for you in your quest for greater understanding.

Everything that has been written in this book is validated in research or, in the absence of definitive research, from accepted best practice in the field or from my best professional advice. No research is relied upon that is older than the year 2000 unless no research is available after that year.

Overview

Introduction to the twice-exceptional student

The importance of early diagnosis and intervention within a research-evidenced framework advocated throughout this book is the way forward for educating twice-exceptional students.

In this chapter you will find:

■ Discussion around the use of the term 'twice-exceptionality'
■ The framework and underlying assumptions used
■ Definitions of the terminology used

Giftedness is described here as the characteristic of children in the ninetieth to the one-hundredth percentile of intellectual potential. Gagne's Differentiated Model of Giftedness and Talent is referenced below to show how the terminology is used. In the NSW Department of Education policy of 2019 'gifted' children are described as High Potential and Gifted Children. The policy can be downloaded here: https://education.nsw.gov.au/teaching-and-learning/high-potential-and-gifted-educat ion/about-the-policy/high-potential-and-gifted-education-policy

> The 'twice-exceptional' student is defined as one who is gifted in one or more of the domains of human ability: the intellectual, creative, social-emotional and physical domains yet has at least one co-existing disability which can be in the area of a specific learning disability or an emotional, physical or neurodevelopmental disorder. It can encompass attention deficit hyperactivity disorder (ADHD) and/or autism spectrum disorder (ASD).

You will not find 'twice-exceptionality' in the Diagnostic and Statistical Manual (DSM-5-TR), the American Psychiatric Association's handbook and the standard used in Australia for the diagnosis of disorders, as it is merely a descriptive term.

Yet, this expression serves to point the way to a student who is, for teachers, 'counter-intuitive', fascinating, and at first glance, unfathomable, in so many ways

DOI: 10.4324/9781003404972-2

that I will describe through the pages of this book (see Figure 1.1). Instead, the child may be perceived as 'lazy' or deliberately underachieving and may not receive appropriate education for either the disability or the giftedness.

The complexity of the neurological functioning of a 'twice-exceptional' (2e) student often means that the school setting cannot accommodate the range of learning needs required to build a fully functioning, self-efficacious learner and the child will underachieve in terms of her high intellectual potential. Her learning 'needs' are more than the sum of the parts. Each 2e student's profile will fit a series of diagnostic criteria yet the child is an individual for whom the effects of each assessed characteristic will manifest at an individual level.

Despite the fact that I have met many 2e students who are gifted, with SLD, ADHD and ASD.....

> Each 2e student has particular strengths and weaknesses that differ from every other child with a similar profile.

Underlying everything that is written in this book is my following statement:

> The importance of **early diagnosis and intervention** is indisputable in the literature of the fields of education, allied health and disabilities. The gifted or high potential student should be **intellectually and creatively stimulated, enriched and extended** as soon as he demonstrates his areas of greatest strength and passion. Similarly, if her verbal precocity is not developing into **expected levels of well-expressed, written language** then the reason for this should be extensively and intensively sought. In the young 2e student with poorly developing written language skills, a full picture of her current literacy levels should be assessed as early as possible in the K–2 years and then **remediation/ intervention** should be sought. Similarly for any other learning weaknesses: **learning support, assistance and adjustments** should be embedded in the child's programme along with **compacting/enrichment/extension** as early as possible so there are no barriers to the student's learning.

Terminology and the framework used

There is a wide range of terms used for this learning profile.

- *Twice-exceptional* can be 2e or 2X or 2XCEL. This variety of terms has been used extensively by researchers in the US and in Australia.
- *Gifted and Learning Disabled* or *Gifted with a Learning Disability* (GLD). The first term was famously coined by Baum, Owen and Dixon (1991) and is variously used now.

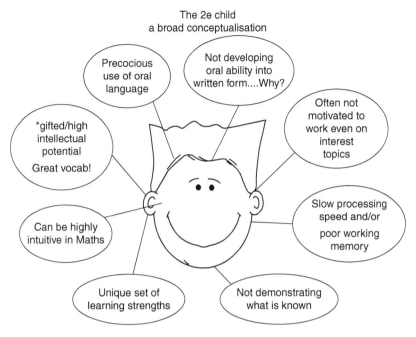

FIGURE 1.1 Some broad possible characteristics of the 2e child demonstrating inherent discrepancies in a 2e child's learning profile.

■ *High potential and gifted students with disability* (NSW Dept of Education policy) is the favoured term in NSW. Increasing use of this term will build the sense of shared language ('metalanguage') and understanding in communication about these children within schools.

Definitions

Co-morbidity – more than one co-existing condition impacting at once.

I have used the term '*twice-exceptional*' (2e) because it means we must address each presenting element in the student's profile, in particular, then we look at the functional impact of the student's learning problems on his potential school performance. The term may not be particularly clear to the novice, but it does describe a wide set of profiles that belong to neurodiverse students. The 2e News noted that even dictionary.com has an entry for 'twice-exceptional' now.

Effect Size (ES) indicates the size of an experimental effect. In comparing the results of an intervention in a research experiment the ES indicates how big the effect was on the outcome. This measure can range from a negative to a positive number. Hattie & Zierer (2019, p. 19) called anything above ES 0.4 to be in the range of 'desired effects', that is, greater than what is already happening at school and what would happen if nothing changed in the child's education but that he grew in achievement through simply growing and maturing. The relative strengths of interventions are reported using ES measures.

Cognitive load (theory), hypothesised and researched by Prof John Sweller, has led us to understand that when the brain is working with new information from the environment the working memory is limited in both capacity and duration. We can process about 3–4 items and hold new items in working memory for only about 20 seconds. We have evolved as a species to acquire new information most effectively by direct instruction rather than by inquiry learning. Instructors need to reduce unnecessary working memory load to allow the transfer of information to long-term memory.

The application of this theory is particularly relevant to students with learning difficulties and attention problems where working memory may be reduced.

The framework I am advocating

Look at the student's school performance for aspects that are inconsistent and presumably incongruous (and which raise questions for further, later diagnosis) and consider the impact these symptoms have on her capacity to thrive in the school curriculum and setting.

- Ultimately, we want to be able to mentally **map** where her strengths (intellectual, physical, creative and social-emotional) lie. They don't exist in isolation from each other but highly influence each other. This is the high potential side of the 2e student's ability.
- Then we want to understand what cognitive and other deficits are impacting on her school performance. This would be the learning difficulty/disability side and would vary in severity, causality and functional impact, all of which need to be assessed.

> The totality of a student's strengths and weaknesses can be called her *learning profile*.

There is a growing school of thought that neurodiversity does not represent weaknesses or limitations but that the neurodiverse student is simply different. I take the view that insofar as these students struggle to gain literacy and numeracy to serve their intellectual capacity then these differences require remediation in our schools. It is certain that neurodiverse individuals can have enormous creative, intellectual, physical and/or social-emotional gifts and capacities.

> The task of the teacher is to educate the student for the adult world and that will always place the acquisition of high levels of competency in literacy and numeracy as the perpetual goals of teachers in schools.

Among particular advocacy groups there is a perceived problem with the terms *intervention* and *remediation* because they imply attempts to fundamentally change or eradicate differences in a child. The terms are used in this book to modify curriculum or to correct for unsuccessful past teaching practices that failed to result in the learning that the child needs to succeed in the adult world. If there has been a failure to understand how a student learns resulting in a student's poor skills, a *remediation or intervention programme* is applied to correct those results and to bring about learning by applying more understanding of how that child learns. It is not the student's fault. It is a failure of the educators to understand how to do it better.

Students who believe they *could not* learn to read/spell/do mathematics will continue to battle low self-efficacy and self-esteem. No amount of morale boosting, interest projects, assistive technology tools or individualised programming will take away that perception. A combination of research-evidenced literacy and numeracy programmes in the K–6 years, augmented at the appropriate times by Information Technology (IT) aids in a smooth transition to success in learning. It is a pathway that is being underutilised in schools.

I believe this anti-remediation movement is a reaction to the use of ineffective methods that not only did not work but may have caused harm, being applied without respect for, or attention to, the high intellectual capacity of students so that they have been demeaned by placement into inappropriate educational settings. We have passed that stage in Australian schools. Information is available for the asking so that interesting, appropriate reading/spelling and mathematics programmes are readily available. No-one would suggest that if the early intervention 'window of opportunity' period is missed that it is easy to remediate older students' skills. But it can be done and should be attempted. (See Chapter 5.)

Applicants for disability provisions in the Year 12 final exams in NSW, the Higher School Certificate (HSC), report that it is becoming increasingly difficult for students to be granted extra time, the use of a scribe/reader or a computer for these exams. Until the Higher School Certificate, our final Year 12 exams, is administered on computer, then equity cannot be applied to all students in this state. This is a matter of urgency, in my opinion.

Author note:

■ I use the pronouns *he/she* interchangeably, allowing no implication that any characteristic is particularly manifest in a female or male student unless indicated by research findings.

■ I have not referenced the needs of First Nations students nor those of language backgrounds other than English. A student who is twice-exceptional can come from any background; from socio-economic advantage or disadvantage, of any race, creed or gender. It is assumed that those differences are addressed in an informed and caring school environment and I long for the time when we live in a truly multicultural nation that effectively respects, cares for and educates all its people.

■ I have not addressed vision, hearing or speech disorders for classroom attention.

    NSW Health offers all four-year old children free vision screening through the StEPS programme so that all children can be screened before starting school. Doctors can be asked to test the hearing of young children from 2–2.5 years if there is evidence of slow development of speech and responsivity.

Speech disorders are the domain of speech pathologists and a previously undetected problem noted by a teacher should be reported to the learning support teacher and the child's parents for assessment outside the school. NSW public schools do not routinely employ speech pathologists. In NSW, specialist teachers work with vision and hearing-impaired students in their classrooms.

The emotional disorders of anxiety and depression in children and adolescents need to be investigated by psychiatrists or psychologists with professional guidance offered to the teachers involved in that child's life. It is reported that the prevalence of anxiety has increased in the post-pandemic era and will be discussed in Chapter 6.

■   Behavioural disorders should be investigated for specific sources of concern in the student's life and, where possible, liaison between home and school will help teachers to understand her circumstances, early history and health conditions.

I have never met a 'lazy' or oppositional child where there were no underlying environmental, cognitive, social or emotional causation factors.

In this book I have explored the neurodevelopmental conditions for which there is a body of research to guide the teacher on how to adapt curriculum to the underlying learning needs of the student, caused by these conditions.

Reference

Hattie, J., & Zierer, K. (2019). *Visible learning insights* (1st edn). London & New York: Routledge. https://doi.org/10.4324/9781351002226

The identification and prevalence of twice-exceptional students

Rhonda Filmer

In this chapter you will find:

- How 2e students are identified
- Estimated prevalence in Australia
- What the literature says about the identification of 2e students

How are 2e students identified?

The 'gold standard' for diagnosis and understanding of a child's learning profile has traditionally been a full comprehensive assessment using a Wechsler IQ scale, WISC 5, which calculates a student's intellectual potential in the cognitive domains that affect performance and the Wechsler Individual Achievement Test 3rd edition, (WIAT 3) Australian and New Zealand norms. In addition, where a psychologist has been alerted to the symptoms of a child's difficulties with learning, he can choose further tests and checklists from a wide range of standardised materials available to collect important data. But sometimes young 2e students cannot demonstrate their full capacities in these tests so retesting at a later time may be required.

Only psychologists can administer the WISC 5, but special education teachers and some allied health professionals can use the WIAT 3 which indicates the student's current performance levels in aspects of Reading, Oral Language, Written Expression and Mathematics. The WIAT 3 gives the examiner both quantitative data (the child's performance compared to age/grade peers as indicated in Percentiles and Age Equivalent measures) and qualitative data that is very helpful for the diagnosis of perceptual and learning problems through observation of her performance during literacy and numeracy tasks. I find these testing sessions

DOI: 10.4324/9781003404972-3

enormously informative, qualitatively, as I observe her learning behaviour and her approach to test items in a clinical setting.

It is very important to caution against the use of the Ability-Achievement Discrepancy as a way of identifying a learning difficulty in the 2e child. A child with processing weaknesses and undiagnosed specific learning disabilities may not score highly on the WISC 5 regardless of his actual level of ability. If the results are low, then the likelihood of a discrepancy between the intellectual potential (ability) and performance will not be 'significant' in quantitative terms. Sometimes a child is performing in the Average category when this result actually represents significant underachievement. The child may be compensating for her disabilities by using advanced reasoning. In many settings this child will not be viewed as far enough behind grade level in his achievement to qualify him for remedial placement or curriculum adjustments.

> No child should be left on the 'waiting list' for diagnosis without the onset of interventions. As soon as difficulties have been noted, screeners and specific skills tests can be used to validate inclusion of the child in an appropriate remedial programme with challenge/adjustments for high ability.

Many psychologists are not trained in Educational and Developmental Psychology and can miss the subtle indications of conditions that are not fully evident, yet, in the early years. Any mild weaknesses should be 'flagged' for possible future investigation. Similarly, I am grateful to schoolteachers who mention issues of attention and organisation in their comments on School Reports. Sometimes, this is the only time that anyone has recorded the observation that later becomes important qualitative evidence toward understanding a student's learning profile and possible later diagnosis of a neurodevelopmental condition.

More on this later.

How many 2e students are there in Australia?

To calculate the prevalence of 2e children in Australia is highly problematic and can only be estimated simply. By definition, 'twice-exceptionality' is a complex construct that is not included in the standardised diagnostic procedures used in this country. It is not simple to extrapolate an estimate from the Australian Bureau of Statistics (ABS) data because their surveys do not contain specific questions about the elements of 2e. The Nationally Consistent Collection of Data on School Students with Disability (NCCD, 2020) does not collect information on students who are gifted. Ronksley-Pavia (2020) noted the importance of statistics for driving educational funding and planning while noting the gap in Australian research that quantifies the number of twice-exceptional learners. She carefully outlined the problems with estimation but finally settled on the range that 2–7% of Australian school students are twice-exceptional. See her article for more detail.

TABLE 2.1 An estimation of the number of twice-exceptional (2e) children in Australian schools in 2022 from authoritative sources of data

Australian Bureau of Statistics from Census 2022 Released 15 February 2023

Schools 9614   Students in Australian schools 4,042,512
Staff 307,041   FTE Average Student-Teacher Ratio: 1 teacher for every 13.2 students

Source: Australian Bureau of Statistics (2022), Schools, ABS Website, accessed 2 November, 2023

Type of Disability	% of population	Number of Children (using 2022 ABS statistics)	Source of Prevalence Rate
Autism	1 in 70 1.4%	56,595	Aspect www.autismspectrum.org.au
ADHD	8.2%	331,486	Australian Government Institute of Health and Welfare www.aihw.gov.au/reports/children-youth/ australias-children/contents/health/ children-mental-illness
Anxiety disorders	6.9%	278,933	
Specific Learning Disability (SLD)	5%	202,126	AUSPELD ULD Guide https://uldforparents.com/
Developmental Coordination Disorder (DCD) /Dyspraxia	6%	242,529	Licari, M., Williams J., and the Impact for DCD Team. (2020). *National Survey Evaluating the Impact of Developmental Coordination Disorder in Australia: Summary of Results.* Telethon Kids Institute, Perth, Western Australia
TOTAL No of Students in mainstream schools with a disability that affects learning		1,111,669	The data did not allow for the issue that most students with disability will also have other co-morbid conditions. It is assumed that the number of students in all categories is under-estimated because of under-diagnosis, survey limitations and other reasons at this time, in Australia. See discussion below.
Gifted or HPGE	10%	111,167	Gagné, F. (2010). Motivation within the DMGT 2.0 framework. *High Ability Studies.* 21. 81–99. 10.1080/13598139.2010.525341. Gagne claimed that 10% of all children are gifted (or children of high potential)

Therefore, approximately 10% of children who have disability will be twice-exceptional.

Number of students in the average-sized school	420.5	4,042,512/ 9614	
Twice-exceptional (2e) children in Australian schools	**2.75%**	111,167/ 4,042,512	Calculations using data (above)
Rate of 2e children per school in Australia	11.6	111,167 9614	Conclusion: There are *at least* 11.6 2e students in the average school in Australia.

However, there are particular problems with this estimate:

1. The ABS figures are most assuredly underestimated because of the problem with identification and diagnosis. Families in low-socioeconomic circumstances would find the cost of comprehensive assessment prohibitive so are unlikely to have diagnostically explored their children's IQs or problems with learning. School counsellors (psychologists), who test for potential diagnoses in public schools, rely on referrals from teachers who are, unfortunately, not trained to recognise the nuances of disability or giftedness.

2. The Australian Government Institute of Health and Welfare's website, last updated on 25 February 2022, found that ADHD was the most common disorder for children (8.2%) and also the most common disorder among boys (11%). There is still discrepancy between the genders as noted by Goodsell et al (2017) in their analysis of the educational outcomes from *Young Minds Matter*: the second Australian Child and Adolescent Survey of Mental Health and Wellbeing, which noted that while the reported prevalence of ADHD was 10.4% of males in the age 4–17 school-age group, it was 4.3% of females and that is a large disparity between the genders that is not supported elsewhere in the research.

    Persistent under-diagnosis of females with ADHD in Australia has reduced the above estimate of the prevalence of 2e in our school-aged population but there is no other, more current, authoritative source of Australian data to consult. See Chapter 6.

3. AUSPELD (Australian Federation of SPELD Associations) states that 5% of children have a diagnosable SLD but an additional 15% of children have a learning *difficulty* which may depress the capacity of a child to demonstrate her intellectual ability sufficiently to cause underachievement if she receives inadequate assistance. A learning difficulty may be a component of twice-exceptionality.

4. The presence of co-morbidities, that is, co-occurring conditions, is not questioned in the ABS surveys. The most dominant symptoms of disability that a child exhibits are likely to be reported, but there may be other underlying conditions that are significant and have been overlooked and therefore are not counted.

Conclusion: At least 2.75% of the population is 2e

The International Dyslexia Association (IDA) claims that 2–5% of school-age children are 2e but I am not aware of their source of data/estimation figures.

The importance of a prevalence estimate is to raise the expectations of education authorities to the presence of 2e students in their school systems for the purpose of planning Professional Learning opportunities for teachers and for planning and resourcing schools, involving staff numbers and planned interventions. It is hoped that Australian academics will research the prevalence rates of 2e students more comprehensively in the future.

What the literature says about the identification of 2e students

Barnard-Brak et al (2015) remind us that, in 1985, Whitmore and Maker wrote "gifted individuals with disabilities are the most misjudged, misunderstood, and neglected segment of the student population" (p. 74). They report from Ruban & Reis (2005) that some gifted students with disabilities are identified in middle school or high school (p.75) yet, according to Ferri, Gregg, & Heggoy (1997), approximately 41% of twice-exceptional students remain unidentified until college.

Part of the problem is that the 'map' of each student's strengths and weaknesses will vary enormously across the range of gifted areas and disabilities. Without standard procedures for identification and adequate teacher training the 2e student can escape notice and assessment.

The identification of the 2e student in the school setting is, indeed, problematic. A key issue relevant to school psychologists is the identification of high ability students with specific learning disorders (SLD). These students demonstrate talent in one or more domains and a coexisting SLD in one or more academic area. Debates about how to identify these students abound as detailed by Assouline, Foley Nicpon, & Whiteman (2010); Lovett (2011); Maddocks (2020) and no standardised manner exists, which may contribute to late identification and/or no identification at all (Reis, Baum, & Burke, 2014). Despite the use of the WISC 5 & WIAT 3 in Australia, the student's difficulty with learning, in and of itself, can impact negatively on their performance on standardised tests (Bell, Taylor, McCallum, Coles, & Hayes, 2015), which may make identification for gifted programmes challenging. Foley-Nicpon & Assouline (2020) recommend that school psychologists can use their extensive knowledge of the range of assessments to choose an appropriate regime that will identify a student's strengths and weaknesses far more than an IQ test can discern. But our school psychologists in NSW rarely have access to this wide range of tests which are generally quite expensive.

I want all undergraduate teachers to be exposed to discussions of this kind, during their Initial Teacher Education (ITE) courses. As with all matters of identification and practice in this field, if a student teacher gains even a little insight into neurodiversity, then she begins her teaching career in schools with an open mind about how children learn.

It is not possible to put every aspect of education into a 4-year course but all secondary teachers as well as K-6 teachers need a course on neurodiversity, particularly regarding issues of literacy development, in their ITE, in order to understand how a typical child learns and how children vary in the way they cognitively process information.

What may be obvious in a child in the learning support class, because she has been entitled to LD support by her low progress, may be masked entirely in the 2e child and it will be a matter of cognitive processing deficits such as poor phonological processing, slow processing speed, inattention or working memory problems. This is what I will explain throughout this resource: the meaning of each, how it looks in a child and the effects of combinations (co-morbidities) on the academic performance of gifted and high potential learners.

As a teacher, you may not have a series of standardised test results on a child's file that will give you a picture of her strengths and weaknesses along with advice on how to adjust the curriculum so she can function to her intellectual capacity in the classroom. But, every parent of a 2e child with whom I have worked will accept the inadequacies of a class or school programme if the teacher demonstrates *understanding*. That is, if you observe sufficiently to know that you do not know everything there is to know about the child, that this child has some very distinctive needs for which you have not been trained and that you trust the child and his parents to be honest, helpful and authentic. As teachers, we can work with this. With this resource, some further reading, some enquiry, some collaboration with experts and colleagues and some creative curriculum planning, teachers can work in partnership with a 2e child and his family.

The first 'pointer' to 2e is a big difference between a child's speech and his developing written language. Gifted or intellectually able children will most often be 'orally precocious' demonstrating early development in speech with advanced vocabulary. I have found that even if the child mispronounces words (sometimes a symptom of dyslexia) the word's meaning is securely understood and correctly used.

We would expect that, given quality teaching, such a student would be writing using correct spelling and grammar and increasingly using his strong vocabulary in stories, but the 2e child will probably not. Why not?

Use Chapters 4 to 9 to read about the characteristics that you see in your students and then in Chapter 11 'Putting it all together for the 2e student' I have outlined how to differentiate for the 2e student in the mixed ability class. Teacher-friendly resources are included in each chapter and an extensive reference list appears at the end of each chapter for further reading.

Bibliography

American Psychiatric Association. (2022). *Diagnostic and statistical manual of mental disorders* (5th edn, Text Revision). Washington, DC: American Psychiatric Association.

Assouline, S. G., Foley Nicpon, M., & Whiteman, C. (2010). Cognitive and psychosocial characteristics of gifted students with written language disability. *Gifted Child Quarterly, 54*(2), 102–115. https://doi.org/10.1177/0016986209355974

AUSPELD. *Understanding learning difficulties: A guide for parents.* https://uldforparents.com/

Australian Bureau of Statistics. Retrieved on November 2, 2023, from www.abs.gov.au/statist ics/health/disability/disability-ageing-and-carers-australia-summary-findings/latest-release#children-with-disability.

Australian Bureau of Statistics. (2022). *Schools.* ABS. www.abs.gov.au/statistics/people/educat ion/schools/latest-release

Australian Government Institute of Health and Welfare. Retrieved on 2 November 2023, from www.aihw.gov.au/reports/children-youth/australias-children/contents/health/children-mental-illness

Barnard-Brak, L., Johnsen, S. K., Pond Hannig, A., & Wei, T. (2015). The incidence of potentially gifted students within a special education population. *Roeper Review, 37*(2), 74–83. https://doi.org/10.1080/02783193.2015.1008661

Baum, S., Owen, S. V., & Dixon, J. (1991). *To be gifted and learning disabled: From identification to practical intervention strategies.* Melbourne: Hawker Brownlow Education.

Bell, S. M., Taylor, E. P., McCallum, R. S., Coles, J. T., & Hays, E. (2015). Comparing prospective twice-exceptional students with high-performing peers on high-stakes tests of achievement. *Journal for the Education of the Gifted, 38*(3), 294–317. http://dx.doi.org/10.1177/0162353215592500

Ferri, B. A., Gregg, N., & Heggoy, S. J. (1997). Profiles of college students demonstrating learning disabilities with and without giftedness. *Journal of Learning Disabilities, 30*(5), 552–559. https://doi.org/10.1177/002221949703000511

Foley-Nicpon, M., & Assouline, S. G. (2020). High ability students with coexisting disabilities: Implications for school psychological practice. *Psychology in the Schools, 57*(10), 1615–1626. https://doi.org/10.1002/pits.22342

Gagné, F. (1999). Gagné's Differentiated Model of Giftedness and Talent (DMGT). *Journal for the Education of the Gifted, 22*(2), 230–234. https://doi.org/10.1177/016235329902200209

Goodsell, B., Lawrence, D., Ainley, J., Sawyer, M., Zubrick, S. R., & Maratos, J. (2017). *Child and adolescent mental health and educational outcomes. An analysis of educational outcomes from Young Minds Matter: The second Australian Child and Adolescent Survey of Mental Health and Wellbeing.* Perth: Graduate School of Education, The University of Western Australia. https://youngmindsmatter.telethonkids.org.au/siteassets/media-docs---young-minds-matter/childandadolescentmentalhealthandeducationaloutcomesdec2017.pdf

Hattie, J., & Zierer, K. (2019). *Visible learning insights* (1st edn). London and New York: Routledge. https://doi.org/10.4324/9781351002226

International Dyslexia Association Fact Sheet (2020) *Gifted and Dyslexic: Identifying and Instructing the Twice Exceptional Student.* https://dyslexiaida.org/fact-sheets/

Lovett, B. J. (2011). On the diagnosis of learning disabilities in gifted students: Reply to Assouline et al. (2010). *Gifted Child Quarterly, 55*(2), 149–151. https://doi.org/10.1177/0016986210396435

Lyman, R. D., Sanders, E., Abbott, R. D., & Berninger, V.W. (2017) Translating interdisciplinary research on language learning into identifying specific learning disabilities in verbally gifted and average children and youth. *Journal of Behavioral and Brain Science, 7,* 227–246. https://doi.org/10.4236/jbbs.2017.76017

Maddocks, D. L. (2020). Cognitive and achievement characteristics of students from a national sample identified as potentially twice exceptional (gifted with a learning disability). *Gifted Child Quarterly, 64*(1), 3–18. https://doi.org/10.1177/0016986219886668

Merriam-Webster. (n.d.). *Neurodiversity.* Merriam-Webster.com dictionary. Retrieved on 11 February 2022. www.merriam-webster.com/dictionary/neurodiversity

Nationally Consistent Collection of Data on School Students with Disability. (2020). *Information notice on Nationally Consistent Collection of Data – Students with Disability.* www.legislation.gov.au/Current/F2018C00920

Reis, S. M., Baum, S. M., & Burke, E. (2014). An operational definition of twice-exceptional learners: Implications and applications. *Gifted Child Quarterly, 58*(3), 217–230. https://doi.org/10.1177/0016986214534976

Ronksley-Pavia, M. (2020). Twice-exceptionality in Australia: Prevalence estimates. *Australasian Journal of Gifted Education, 29*(2), 17–29. https://search-informit org.ezproxy.library.sydney.edu.au/doi/10.3316/informit.43329113226463

Ruban, L., & Reis, S.M. (2005). Identification and assessment of gifted students with learning disabilities. *Theory into Practice, 44,* 115–124. doi:10.1207/s15430421tip4402_6

Smith, S. R. (Ed.) (2021). *Handbook of giftedness and talent development in the Asia-Pacific.* Singapore: Springer. https://doi.org/10.1007/978-981-13-3041-4

Sweller, J. (2022). The role of evolutionary psychology in our understanding of human cognition: consequences for cognitive load theory and instructional procedures. *Educational Psychology Review, 34*(4), 2229–2241. https://doi.org/10.1007/s10648-021-09647-0

van Viersen, S., Kroesbergen, E. H., Slot, E. M., & de Bree, E. H. (2016). High reading skills mask dyslexia in gifted children. *Journal of Learning Disabilities, 49*(2), 189–199. https://doi.org/10.1177/0022219414538517

2e News is the e-newsletter of Bridges 2e Media from Bridges Academy info@2enews.com

The legislative requirements of educational institutions in Australia

Rhonda Filmer

In this chapter you will find a brief summary of the legislation that pertains to discrimination against people with disability. Then the Disability Standards for Education, 2005, legislation is summarised. This is followed by the public review of the Standards in 2020 and links to the resources that were produced at that time.

Information about the Nationally Consistent Collection of Data (NCCD) which is mandatory in Australian schools is included.

The fact that it is necessary to include this chapter on the legislative requirements of educational institutions so that you are informed about what your school should be doing for children with disability, indicates that I don't believe all teachers are updated, supported or resourced adequately to do this work, at the current time, yet the legislation requires schools to comply.

Australia is a signatory to the

> **Convention on the Rights of Persons with Disability** adopted by the United Nations General Assembly in 2006. It can be found at https://social.desa.un.org/issues/disability/crpd/convention-on-the-rights-of-persons-with-disabilities-crpd

However, protection for people with disability in NSW comes through Australian and NSW laws:

Commonwealth Disability Discrimination Act 1992 (DDA)
states that it is against the law to treat people unfairly because of a disability

Examples of *disability* include:

- difficulties acquiring and developing literacy skills
- difficulties acquiring and developing numeracy skills

DOI: 10.4324/9781003404972-4

- learning difficulties or disabilities such as dyslexia, dysgraphia and dyscalculia
- intellectual disabilities
- mental illness
- emotional and behavioural disturbances
- autism spectrum disorder
- sensory impairment
- physical disabilities such as cerebral palsy
- speech and language disorders
- chronic illness such as chronic fatigue syndrome.

A student whose learning is affected by other factors, such as school attendance, proficiency with the English language, or disrupted schooling, would not be considered to have a disability.

A short two-page Fact Sheet is available at:
www.dese.gov.au/swd/resources/fact-sheet-1-disability-discrimination-act-1992

The main points of the DDA are:

- The definition of "disability" used in the DDA is broad. It includes physical, intellectual, psychiatric, sensory, neurological and learning disabilities. It also includes physical disfigurement and the presence in the body of disease-causing organisms, such as the HIV virus.
- It is unlawful to discriminate against a person because of a disability or the disability of an associate, such as a friend, partner, carer or family member of the person.
- It is also unlawful where it occurs because a person with a disability:

  uses a palliative, therapeutic or assistive device

  is accompanied by a carer, interpreter, reader or assistant

  is accompanied by a guide or hearing dog or other trained assistant animal

- A person does not gain any special rights or benefits by coming within the definition of disability under the DDA – only the right not to be discriminated against.
- The legislation protects people with disability against discrimination in many areas of public life, including:

  employment – getting a job, terms and conditions of a job, training, promotion, being dismissed

  education – enrolling or studying in a course at a private or public school, college or university

  accommodation – renting or buying a house or unit

  getting or using services – such as banking and insurance services, services provided by government departments, transport or telecommunication services, professional services like those provided by lawyers, doctors or tradespeople, services provided by restaurants, shops or entertainment venues

accessing public places – such as parks, government offices, restaurants, hotels or shopping centres.

- The DDA also protects people against *harassment* because of their disability, in employment, education or in getting or using services.
- The Australian Government supports the right of children with disability to have the same educational opportunities as other children. All state and territory education providers, including government and non-government schools, must comply with the DDA and the relevant disability discrimination legislation of their state or territory.

Education providers must comply with the:

Disability Standards for Education, 2005

These are available at: www.dese.gov.au/swd/resources/fact-sheet-2-disability-standards-education-2005

The standards attempt to ensure that students with disability can partake in the same educational opportunities as students without disability at every level of education from pre-school to university and vocational education.

Education providers must:

- *Consult* with parents and carers in order to gain ideas for assistance, overcome barriers, receive relevant reports, communicate written plans and keep records up to date.
- *Make reasonable adjustments* to ensure that the student can access the curriculum despite his learning needs.
- *Eliminate discrimination* of students through harassment or victimisation by staff or students.

The Disability Standards for Education document was reviewed by public consultation in 2020.

The review document can be found here: www.dese.gov.au/disability-standards-education-2005/resources/summary-document-2020-review-disability-standards-education-2005

Parents and carers told the reviewers that there is a "power imbalance" between them and the educational institutions. The Commonwealth has undertaken to provide better training to all educational professionals largely through the state education authorities.

The following resource materials are well composed and may be of assistance:

Effective consultation

www.dese.gov.au/swd/resources/fact-sheet-4-effective-consultation

Exemplars of practice

Some case studies of how schools have provided assistance for students with disability are found here: www.dese.gov.au/swd/resources/exemplars-practice

The Collaborative Curriculum Planning Process in NSW

In NSW, the Education Standards Authority (NESA) has extensive resources on collaborative curriculum planning which, they advise, should involve a team of people who have "significant knowledge and understanding of the student" that is, parents/carers, teachers, significant individuals in the student's life and the student.
https://educationstandards.nsw.edu.au/wps/portal/nesa/k-10/diversity-in-learning/special-education/collaborative-curriculum-planning

Adjustments to a student's programme are determined based on the functional impact of the disability on the student's learning, rather than a particular diagnosis of disability. There is a comprehensive list of suggestions at the above link and, where staff professional learning is required, personnel from NESA will come to schools to do that. I recommend that your school undertakes this opportunity to build a shared language and understanding of the issue of educating all their students who have disability.

The use of appropriate adjustments to curriculum is explained in detail throughout this book.

Note: The *Anti-Discrimination Act 1977* (ADA) applies only in NSW and is similar to the DDA. Complaints under the ADA are handled by Anti-Discrimination NSW (ADNSW). NSW discrimination law does not apply to private schools.

The Nationally Consistent Collection of Data on school students with disability (NCCD)

In Australia, the Nationally Consistent Collection of Data on school students with disability (NCCD) ties up and informs schools of the legislative requirements of the DDA (1992) and the Disability Standards (2005) and collects data on the reasonable adjustments provided in schools. It then uses this evidence base to inform teachers about what educational adjustments are being provided in Australia. The infographic explaining its purposes can be found here www.nccd.edu.au/sites/default/files/what_is_the_nccd.pdf

Where there has been no diagnosis but there are reasonable grounds upon which to make a judgement that a child has one, then a school can 'impute' that disability. "An imputed disability is an undiagnosed disability the school team considers a student to have that is having a functional impact on their learning."

The NCCD site suggests the asking of the question: "If we were challenged to explain our decision would we feel we had reasonable grounds and documentation to support our judgement?" The infographic and short video explaining the process of imputing disability is found here: www.nccd.edu.au/tools/imputing-disability-nccd

Bibliography

Australian Government Department of Education. www.education.gov.au/swd/resources/fact-sheet-1-disability-discrimination-act-1992

NSW Education Standards Authority. https://educationstandards.nsw.edu.au/wps/portal/nesa/k-10/diversity-in-learning/special-education/collaborative-curriculum-planning

The following resource from the Australian Centre for Disability Law presents a deeper understanding of disability discrimination law in NSW with further explanation of its implications in education: https://disabilitylaw.org.au/download/acdl-using-disability-discrimination-law-2023/?wpdmdl=2510&refresh=6499f615c53a71687811605

The component parts of 'twice-exceptionality'

Gifted/high potential learners

Rhonda Filmer and Geraldine Townend

VIGNETTE

Dani ordered a coffee at a local café when the young barista looked up and said,

'Miss! Hello! Oh miss, you were the best!'

It was Amira, who in Year 6 at a multicultural, inner city primary school had been a wide-eyed, enquiring and pensive student but not particularly forthcoming with insights. She was an average to high achiever. Yet, for some intuitive reason, Dani had included her in the enrichment group within her mixed ability classroom for all subjects.

Amira did not excel that year, but she asked good questions and always listened attentively. Amira's early background was as a refugee from Lebanon during long years of conflict.

Amira went on to high school and Dani heard no more of her.

'What are you doing now, Amira, when you are not making me good coffee?'

'I have almost completed my Masters in Forensic Psychology, Miss. I had the best time in your class and thanks!'

The twice-exceptional student is gifted first. Insight into the characteristics of gifted students underpins a comprehensive knowledge of the twice-exceptional student. In order to give you that understanding this chapter will encompass the definitions of 'giftedness' found in the literature and in Australian practice contexts and refer to the history of why the education of gifted and high potential students has been problematic in Australian schools. The tools for identifying gifted students, gifted

DOI: 10.4324/9781003404972-6

education models, curriculum options and differentiation techniques are detailed with reference to the research and with accompanying resources.

Why is it important to know about giftedness or high potentiality in students?

Historically, the education of our brightest students has had some problems and debates. It was commonly believed that these students could make it on their own because they were already smart. The belief was that our resources should be focused on students who may have greater need.

Confusion within schools about the meaning of 'giftedness' often results in marginalised and less apparent students with high intellectual potential being overlooked and underserved. Evidence has shown us that giftedness can occur across all populations of students globally. There are no inherent barriers in a child's gender, ethnicity, social, economic status or geography yet these elements can very clearly be impediments to strong talent development. How easily domain-specific talent is identified has much to do with the nature of the gifts and the environment in which they are found.

Very real environmental impediments are common in Australia today that hinder the development of gifts into talent. In recent years, the definition of giftedness has expanded to include traditionally underserved populations. Scholars (such as Reis & Renzulli, 2021) are calling for a broader conception of giftedness that encompasses a diverse range of students. To achieve this, it is important that testing and identification processes consider all students, especially those from disadvantaged groups, to ensure equitable access to gifted education. In Australia these groups include First Nations populations, children from low socioeconomic backgrounds, those living in rural and remote communities, and students with disabilities. In order to address the issue of comprehensive identification, it is crucial to define the concept of giftedness. Giftedness should not be limited to academic abilities and traditional thinking. It should also include highly creative individuals, non-traditional thinkers and those who show a genuine interest in creative and productive endeavours.

The World Council for Gifted and Talented Children has released Global Principles for Professional Learning in Gifted Education (2021) as a guide to reform all Initial Teacher Education and professional development to enhance understandings and efficacy when working with these populations of students. The aim is to improve teachers' understanding of gifted students and equip them with the necessary knowledge and skills to effectively identify, teach, and support them.

By training teachers to identify giftedness and provide appropriate educational opportunities, the barriers faced by gifted students can be reduced. This will ensure that students from all backgrounds, including those from underserved and disadvantaged groups, have equal access to gifted education and can fully develop their talents.

What it is

The definitions in the literature

The most widely applied definition in Australia draws on Françoys Gagné's definitions around talent development (2009). This is a popular definition as Gagné recognises *four main domains of possible natural abilities* that can be in the *high potential or gifted range*:

- intellectual
- creative
- social–emotional
- physical

The focus for educators is how we develop these natural abilities into talent or high performance.

The NSW Government has adapted Gagné's DGMT 2.0 (2009) to illustrate the process of talent development. Figure 4.1 illustrates the model.

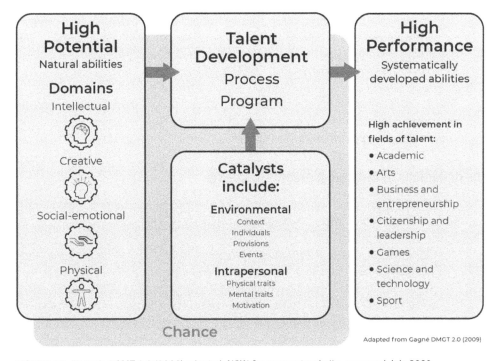

FIGURE 4.1 Gagné's DGMT 2.0 (2009) adapted, NSW Government website, accessed July 2023.

https://education.nsw.gov.au/teaching-and-learning/high-potential-and-gifted-education/HPGE-policy-information

TABLE 4.1 The domains of ability as defined in the policy document https://education.nsw.gov.au/teaching-and-learning/high-potential-and-gifted-education/HPGE-policy-information

The Intellectual Domain	Refers to natural abilities around general reasoning, logical process, understanding, ability to process information and transfer of learning (conceptual learning).
The Creative Domain	Refers to natural abilities around creative thinking, originality of thought, invention and innovation and imagination.
The Social Emotional Domain	Refers to the natural abilities to self-manage and also in relating to and interacting with others. This can include natural potential for leadership or charisma, for example.
The Physical Domain	Refers to natural abilities in muscular movement and motor control. This can often be seen with students who appear to excel in certain physical activities or sports with less practice (initially) required than their peers.

Look at these comments from two great leaders in the field:

Giftedness is an innate ability to both detect and comprehend the world in complex ways that differ significantly from age-expected norms. High academic achievement may or may not be present, but a lack of academic success does not 'disqualify' someone from being seen as gifted, according to Delisle (2021, p. 8).

*Keeping in mind that developed talent is often only recognised in adults but it can occur in younger people , a proposed definition of giftedness in children is the **potential** for becoming critically acclaimed performers or exemplary producers of ideas in spheres of activity which enhance the moral, physical, emotional, social, intellectual or aesthetic life of the community.* (Tannenbaum, 1983, p. 86)

Similar to Tannenbaum, Gagné (2009) has a focus on 'talent development' through environmental catalysts (e.g. support by teachers) and interpersonal catalysts (e.g. motivation, temperament, and volition).

The definitions in Australian practice contexts

Gifted NSW, the state not-for-profit body advocating for the needs of the gifted, on their website www.giftednsw.org.au states:

'There is no universal definition. Some professionals define 'gifted' as an intelligence test score above 130, two or more standard deviations above the norm, or the top 2.5%. Others define 'gifted' based on scholastic achievement: a gifted child works 2 or more grade levels above his or her age. Still others see giftedness as prodigious accomplishment: adult-level work while chronologically a child. But these are far from the only definitions.'

Their definition is: *Gifted and talented children are those identified by professionally quali-fied persons who by virtue of outstanding abilities are capable of high performance. These are children who require differentiated educational programs and/or services beyond those normally provided by the regular school program in order to realize their contribution to self and society.*

> There is *no generally agreed definition of giftedness*, but the NSW policy is close to encompassing the wide range apparent in gifted and high potential learners:
>
> > *High potential students are found among students of all backgrounds. Gaps in achievement, known as excellence gaps, may exist between different groups of high potential and gifted students unless specific support is provided. Such gaps further entrench inequality and disadvantage (NSW Government, 2021)*
>
> The focus is around *equity for all students to develop their potential* in school.

The NSW Government

The NSW Government High Potential and Gifted Education Policy 2019   defines the categories of giftedness as:

> **High potential students** are those whose potential exceeds that of students of the same age in one or more domains: intellectual, creative, social-emotional and physical. [Authors' note: it is important to cast 'a wide net' when searching for students with high potential. Don't overlook the possibility of high potential in any student.]
>
> **Gifted students** are those whose potential significantly exceeds that of students of the same age in one or more domains: intellectual, creative, social-emotional, and physical. This is considered to be those students whose ability is above the 90th percentile, that means the top 10% of age peers across the country.
>
> **Highly gifted students** are those whose potential vastly exceeds that of students of the same age in one or more domains: intellectual, creative, social-emotional and physical. This is considered to be those students whose ability is above the 99th percentile, that means the top 1% of age peers across the country.

The NSW Department of Education, the Catholic Education Office and a number of independent schools previously adopted the Gagné Differentiated Model of Giftedness and Talent 2.0 (DMGT) when identifying and considering the needs of gifted and talented students. Professor Gagné emphasised that giftedness is the possession of natural abilities at higher levels than would be expected across all areas of human activity. According to Gagné (2010), giftedness occurs in 10% of children across the 6 natural domains of intellectual, creative, social, perceptual, and physical (muscular & motor control). In 2023, the Australian Bureau of Statistics published data detailing that there were 4,042,512 million children in primary and secondary schools in NSW. We are therefore looking at 404,251 children who are gifted/high potential. The needs of these children vary greatly; within that 10% there is great diversity. (See Chapter 2.)

It is also very important to understand that there is a huge difference between the intellectual ability of the top percentile and that of the 90th. They require different levels of challenge.

TABLE 4.2 Classification for gifted and high potential learners from the NSW policy compared with IQ levels readily used in the research literature

NSW Policy of High Potential and Gifted Education 2019	Levels of Giftedness from literature
High Potential … exceeds that of students of the same age	Child underachieving or mildly gifted (IQ 115–130)
Gifted students …. potential significantly exceeds that of students of the same age	Moderately gifted (IQ 130–145)
Vastly exceeds that of students of the same age	Highly to Profoundly gifted (145–160 >)

What you will see in the classroom

There should definitely be indications of *some* of the following characteristics if you are looking for high potential or giftedness. (Source: generally accepted in the field as 'common characteristics' or, if not, the characteristic is referenced here.)

TABLE 4.3 Composed from the generally accepted knowledge in the field. Where a characteristic is less commonly held, it has been referenced

Observe closely for signs of one or more of the following:	**Look** for reasons why a student's innate ability may not be expressed in levels of achievement orally or in written form in the class such as:
• advanced vocabulary for chronological age • sophisticated sense of humour or even inappropriate use of humour; 'the class clown' • may prefer the company of older children or adults • outstanding memory for facts • broader base of knowledge than peers • sees endless possibilities for various situations or uses for objects • sees connections between apparently unconnected ideas, also known as conceptual thinking • develops intuitive 'theories' by linking ideas and asking further questions (Munro, 2014) • curiosity about many different things • thrives on complexity, in games, conversations and interests • invests high emotion in areas of interest • displays original ideas • shows flexibility in problem solving situations • surprising emotional depth and sensitivity for their age • possibly, achievement in the top 10% of the student age-grade population in particular subjects… or not!	• refugee or forced migration status implying possible trauma and loss of past opportunity leading to gaps in knowledge • non-English speaking background which may reduce achievement while English proficiency develops • a disjunct between the culture/values of home and that of school • low socio-economic status of parents implying possible lack of adequate formal education and a consequent lack of opportunity to practise and refine higher order thinking and associated vocabulary • lack of 'insider knowledge' by parent or carer to make judgements and decisions at crucial stages of development (Subotnik, Olszewski-Kubilius & Worrell, 2018). • undiagnosed learning or information processing difficulties

What do I do about it?

Check the student's past data records and speak with past teachers. There may be hints of ability indicated through the child's oral capacities. Giftedness/high potential can easily be missed.

Four areas when considering 'what to do':

■ Identify
■ Find the optimal intervention programme
■ Consider curriculum options
■ Be aware of social and emotional obstacles

Identifying a gifted child and suggesting appropriate educational choices are almost always the challenges of a single classroom teacher.
In the life of any child, a teacher is crucial. But for a gifted child, one teacher can open the door to an entirely new educational pathway by making sure that child is set on an appropriately challenging course.

A Nation Deceived, Vol 1, p. 51 (2004)

Identify

Traits of Giftedness

Checklist of *some* of the many qualitative characteristics

Caution is required when considering these characteristics as there will be a cluster but not all of the characteristics. In the presence of co-morbid neurodevelopmental conditions, the gifted or high potential student may be slow in developing potential characteristics or may not be able to demonstrate what they know or feel.

For example,

★★ If a child is not a 'voracious and early reader' she could be gifted but have the early signs of dyslexia demonstrated in a hesitancy to embrace the written word. Often, such a child will love the stories she encounters but be reluctant to read them independently.

♦ A gifted child with ADHD will not demonstrate 'persistent, goal-directed behaviour' nor 'independence in work and study at a young age'. The behavioural characteristics listed require some nuance to discern the difference between behaviours characteristic of young children who are gifted and those with ADHD. The presence of this behaviour does not 'rule out' giftedness nor ADHD. The child's profile requires much more investigation.

♣   A gifted child with autism may not demonstrate overtly 'unusual emotional depth and reactivity' or 'spontaneity'.

Identify a student's aptitude by collecting quantitative and qualitative data

Qualitative screeners

■   Scales for Rating the Behavioural Characteristics of Superior Students (Renzulli). The scales check for high levels of characteristics for domain-specific

TABLE 4.4 Traits of giftedness Clark, B. (2013)

Cognitive	Creative	Affective	Behavioural
Keen power of abstraction	Creativeness and inventiveness	Unusual emotional depth and reactivity♣	Spontaneity♣
	←Keen sense of humour→		
Interest in problem-solving and applying concepts	Ability for fantasy and imagination	Sensitivity or empathy to the feelings of others	Boundless enthusiasm
Voracious and early reader**	Openness to stimuli, wide interests	High expectations of self and others, often leading to feelings of frustration	Intensely focused on passions—resists changing activities when engrossed in own interests♦
Large vocabulary	Intuitiveness	Heightened self-awareness, accompanied by feelings of being different	Highly energetic—needs little sleep or down time♦
Intellectual curiosity	Flexibility	Easily wounded, need for emotional support	Constantly asks questions
Power of critical thinking, scepticism, self-criticism	♦Independence in attitude and social behaviour	Need for consistency between abstract values and personal actions	Insatiable curiosity
Persistent, goal-directed behaviour♦	Self-acceptance and unconcern for social norms	Advanced levels of moral judgment	Impulsive, eager and spirited♦
Independence in work and study♦	Extreme beliefs	Idealism and sense of justice	Perseverance, strong determination in areas of importance
Diversity of interests and abilities			High levels of frustration—particularly when having difficulty meeting standards of performance (either imposed by self or others)

ability: Learning, Creativity, Motivation, Leadership, Artistic, Musical, Dramatics, Communication (Precision), Communication (Expressive), Planning, Mathematics, Reading, Technology, Science.

Derived from research studies, they demonstrate the premise of Renzulli's three-ring model as the definition of giftedness, that is, Above Average Ability, Task Commitment and Creativity. Samples are available to view on www.google.scholar

■ Teacher Nomination form found in the public domain, developed by Caroline Merrick www.wmyc.vic.edu.au/wp-content/uploads/2015/06/Primary-Teachers-nomination-form.pdf. A sound starting point.

■ Peer nomination forms – Guess Who: Peer Nomination Form (GWPNF) – good correlation has been shown between peer nomination scores and nonverbal intelligence scores especially in the younger school grades.

■ Questions are in the form of. 'I am thinking of someone who has (enter gifted characteristic). Who am I thinking of?'

■ Self-nomination – Give students opportunities to communicate their interests and to opt for extension programmes.

Quantitative assessments

■ Cognitive Abilities Test (CogAT) is a group test, administered only by schools and is sold by the Australian Council for Educational Research (ACER) in Australia; designed to measure verbal, quantitative and nonverbal figural reasoning abilities from K–Year 12.

■ Naglieri Nonverbal Achievement Test (NNAT) version 3 is the latest. Available through Pearson Australia this group test does not require the student to read, write or speak but to demonstrate reasoning and problem-solving behaviours. It is intended to assess cognitive ability independent of linguistic and cultural background.

■ Ravens Progressive Matrices provides a nonverbal assessment of intelligence minimising the impact of language skills and cultural bias and useful for students with a reading problem.

■ The CAT4 which also includes numerical, verbal, visual and spatial reasoning

■ WISC 5 (to be completed by a psychologist) & WIAT 3 (to be completed by a specialist educator or psychologist) if available (edition numbers correct at time of writing).

Find the optimal intervention programme

Embrace the idea that gifts and talents develop in a 'multifaceted, developmentally complex' way (Dai, 2020, p. 33), placing possibilities for achievement before *all students who appear to show potential* not limiting but enabling them to thrive.

Academically gifted and high potential students need:

- advanced curriculum in content, knowledge and skills
- challenge created by tasks that engage their intellectual curiosity, their problem-solving ability and develop their skills of deductive and inductive thinking
- specific input and questioning in their areas of interest and strength.

Consider curriculum options

Curriculum for gifted students such as: compacting/acceleration/ enrichment/differentiation

Curriculum compacting: pre-test to determine what the student knows, then reduce the repetition of material that has already been mastered.

Acceleration: move at a faster pace than normal through the school grades or through subject content because of the student's assessed ability or potential.

Acceleration of content should occur in a domain of student strength (VanTassel-Baska p. 456 in Sternberg & Ambrose, 2021).

Enrichment: 'explore traditional subject matter in greater depth than is typical'… . or offer 'topics in disciplines that are not usually included in their school curriculum (Worrell et al., 2019, p. 567).'

Differentiation for the gifted: curriculum acceleration, extension and enrichment, informed by formative assessment and data collection to make the curriculum challenging and rewarding.

Be aware of social and emotional obstacles

Social-emotional development and school performance are linked for all students. Be aware of low self-confidence and low self-efficacy in students as they have been linked with underachievement (White et al., 2018, Neihart, 2016, Blaas, 2014). But the causal direction is not established. Which comes first?

Going deeper

What gifted students need

Talent development is the process by which a student's potential is developed into high achievement in a specific domain or field of endeavour (HPGE policy, 3.6, 2019) and is always the goal of school programmes for this population. As noted in the CESE resource *Revisiting gifted education,* 'Research over the last decade has shifted from referring to "gifted and talented students" to "gifted education and talent development" (p. 5).'

There has been some change in the rhetoric of gifted education literature toward recognising the broader psychosocial basis of human potential. As teachers, we see students whose determination takes them way beyond the raw potential we saw in early primary school while students who were achieving at very high levels seem to 'plateau' later in their schooling and in life. We can so seldom see the detailed nature of a child's psychosocial functioning nor the implicit factors in the child's home environment.

In a detailed discussion around the models of giftedness that underlie our attempts to develop the ability/talent/creativity of gifted children, Worrell et al. (2019) state, '[T]he most intelligent people are those who know and can capitalise on their strengths, while also being aware of and compensating for their weaknesses' (p. 554). As teachers, our desire is to 'value add' during the time a gifted child is in our care. Let the former statement be our guide so that by providing comprehensive and challenging learning experiences in the class we are promoting the development of self-knowledge. By allowing her to be bored intellectually the gifted child will descend into confusion, self-doubt and negative social effects.

The concept of a gifted student being at the top percentile of ability or performance in every aspect of learning is now quite archaic. All people are asynchronous to some extent and, as we will further explore, the 2e child is more asynchronous than most.

Below is a list of recent and classical research in the field of gifted education that presents the picture of how curriculum should be designed for talent development for our most intellectually able students.

Instructional strategies to develop giftedness

VanTassel Baska's (1988) seminal work includes a list of guidelines by Feldhusen for unit planning for the gifted that should become part of a teacher's toolkit:

1. Focus on *major ideas*, issues, themes, problems, concepts and principles.

2. Emphasise the need for a large knowledge base.

3. When possible, use an *interdisciplinary* approach.

4. Emphasise in-depth *research* and *independent study* with original and high-level products or presentations.

5. Teach *research skills and thinking skills* as metacognitive processes.

6. Incorporate *higher level thinking skills in content study* – in discussions, independent study, research and writing.

7. *Increase the level, complexity and pace* of the curriculum to fit the precocity of the students.

8. Teach methods for *independence, self-direction and self-evaluation* in learning. (p. 113)

The following model has much to offer teachers in schools and is consistent with the NSW Department of Education policy:

The Talent Development Megamodel (TDMM)

Sternberg and Ambrose (2021) comprehensively explored the different viewpoints in this 'porous, fragmented and contested (p. 518)' field of gifted education calling for the need to integrate gifted education studies into the wider fields of education, psychology and creative studies in order to broadly identify giftedness and find the best way to develop it when it is noted in a student. The TDMM has been developed by Subotnik, Olszewski-Kubilius & Worrell (2021) .

The TDMM…

- is focused on seeing potential in individuals rather than finding 'gifted individuals'
- involves *doing* rather than *being*
- involves *identifying* then *serving*
- suggests the inclusion of children with high motivation and achievement in talent development/gifted education programmes even if ability is somewhat lower
- recognises the opportunities provided by outside-of-school activities such as special programmes, clubs and groups
- acknowledges the importance of psychosocial skills in talent development.

Potential (intellectual ability or IQ) → competence → expertise → creative productivity in adulthood

'The goal of teachers and mentors should be to **increase the probability** of an upward talent development trajectory by preparing students with the skills, competencies, mindsets, and insider knowledge they need to transition effectively to the next higher stage of talent development' (Subotnik et al. p 438).

The following table is a visual display summarising the evolution of The Talent Development Megamodel (TDMM) from its roots in earlier models.

The TDMM integrates the following conceptions of giftedness (Table 4.5).

TABLE 4.5 The evolution of the TDMM from earlier models designed to develop giftedness

Sternberg's (2005) triarchic theory of giftedness.	Tannenbaum's (1983)	Renzulli & Reis's (2018) Three-ring model
Analytic abilities, creative production and practical intelligence including tacit knowledge ➜ domain-specific expertise via knowledge and skills	Domain-specific knowledge ➜ Creative ideas or performances including beauty, which lead to physical & psychosocial wellbeing and ultimately contribute to the world	 Based on the school-wide enrichment model→ more domain-specific opportunities for those motivated and inspired by the enrichment, and providing a chance to develop a project that brings together interests, passions, and abilities into a creative product for the most committed students.
Subotnik and Jarvin (2005)	**Jarvin & Subotnik (2010)**	**The TDMM**
developed the Scholarly Productivity/Artistry model: different talents begin, peak and end at different ages. (e.g. voice and woodwind talent develop a bit later than other musical production as they require maturity of the larynx, throat or mouth)	Developmental framework for psychosocial skills in classical music talent.	'General abilities, including intelligence, contribute to success in many domains, but to differing degrees, and domain-specific abilities are more important contributors to moving beyond competencies to expertise and beyond' (p. 428)

Over the history of the field of gifted education teachers have bemoaned the lack of a wide variety of researched and developed curricula to use with their gifted and advanced students.

Teachers trained in gifted education know that gifted students

'spend up to 80% of their time in classrooms working on the same content, knowledge and skills as all other students, resulting in a lost opportunity to learn' (Callahan et al., 2014, p. 139).

Every *modification of curriculum* we make is designed to *reduce this wastage of time and opportunity.*

Acceleration

The gifted education literature is full of evidence to support the underutilised option of accelerating students. Using Acceleration as a programme option to provide advanced curriculum to students has the strong support of research from the Belin-Blank College of Education at the University of Iowa and in gifted education research, in general. Hattie and Zierer (2019) found an Effect Size of 0.58 (anything above 0.4 is recommended) for the effects of acceleration on the academic achievement of gifted students. They found that such a simple structural change in the child's education was more likely to bring challenging lessons, higher engagement in learning and improved performance.

The four volumes, *A Nation Deceived,* Vols 1 & 2 (2004) and *A Nation Empowered,* Vols 1 & 2 (2015) from The Templeton Foundation cite the compelling research base for acceleration and give 20 ways in which the acceleration of students can be organised. Acceleration is noted as a relatively inexpensive, somewhat easily administered, programme format. But Australian schools have not traditionally embraced it for fear of social maladjustment. Siegle and colleagues (2013) found that teachers across a wide sample of geographical areas do not use acceleration because they have concerns about the social implications of accelerating students more than they do about not meeting their academic needs. There are very big resource constraints particularly in our public schools for using this option. It does require copious amounts of documentation and monitoring by the teachers assigned to care for 'diverse learning' students to ensure that accelerated students thrive outside their age cohort. Yet, acceleration in its more than twenty documented forms is an effective model and a distinct option for Australian schools.

We suggest that it is very hard to learn about these strategies, to work out how to do them and which students to include, to advocate at school then monitor it while adjusting curricula, and teaching it, when you have not been introduced to it in your Initial Teacher Education (ITE) degree. Teachers with a low sense of efficacy for meeting the needs of the gifted will not tend to choose mastery experiences for their students as they have a low view of student motivation, and this in turn tends to undermine students' cognitive development and students' judgments of their own capabilities (Pajares, 2002; Rowan & Townend, 2016). Of course, that is a matter requiring reform in our ITE degrees. We believe this is one complex reason that acceleration is an underutilised option in Australian schools.

But, do be assured that acceleration works.

Curriculum Differentiation Models aim to enhance student self-efficacy

One goal of any curriculum model for the gifted is to build individuals' self-efficacy. Bandura's seminal work (1994) showed that individuals' self-beliefs are powerful factors in academic achievement (Bandura, 2019). Growth in self-efficacy occurs through mastery experiences in which individuals prove to themselves their capabilities through success coming out of effort in a valued task. Strong self-efficacy develops through the demonstration of competence and results in the growth of confidence. It will then determine how much effort will be expended on any future activity, how long the individual perseveres with a task and how resilient she can be in the face of setbacks and adversity. By placing appropriate challenge before a student (that is within the student's capacity, with effort) a teacher has offered the possibility of enhanced self-efficacy and growing self-confidence in her academic capability.

Note, here, that there is a big difference between self-efficacy and self-concept (self-esteem) (Parker et al., 2014). Pajares (2002) defines them very clearly:

> *Self-efficacy is the context-specific assessment of competence to perform a specific task or a range of tasks in a given domain – an individual's judgment of his or her capabilities to perform given actions.* **The notion of 'I can do ... this work/ that exercise...'.**

> *Self-concept is a cognitive appraisal, integrated across various dimensions, that individuals attribute to themselves, typically accompanied by self-evaluative judgment of self-worth (self-esteem).* **The notion that 'I am... a successful student/ good at maths'.**

Our schools' emphasis on self-esteem building with external inducements of stickers, certificates and awards is no substitute for authentic success. In the words of Erik Erikson (Maree, 2022), the German psychoanalyst:

> *Children cannot be fooled by empty praise and condescending encouragement. They may have to accept artificial bolstering of their self-esteem in lieu of something better, but what I call their accruing ego identity gains real strength only from wholehearted and consistent recognition of real accomplishment, that is, achievement that has meaning in their culture.*

Curriculum compacting

Professor Miraca Gross presented the rationale behind the compacting of curriculum for gifted students: they often already know most of a subject's content before it is taught and without compacting there is little time to meet the needs of gifted students (Gross & Smith, 2021). Rogers' (2002) definition is, 'streamlining the regular curriculum to "buy time" for enrichment, accelerated content and independent study (p. 97).' Rogers (2007) found from a mega-analysis of 13 studies that the ES for curriculum compacting was 0.83, which is highly recommended. With the support of cited studies, she favours the grouping of gifted learners with intellectually like-minded peers for some or all of their time in school. Where ability grouping is not a full-time option it is important to group learners and to compact their curriculum to ensure that they are actually learning new material, always considering what will be offered to them when they prove they already know the content of planned instruction.

Curriculum Differentiation Models for gifted/high potential learners

VIGNETTE

In her first practicum as a student teacher, Marcie was given the task of teaching the mathematical operation, division, to Year 5. She dutifully did what she thought was right, teaching the steps carefully and systematically over many days. When it came time to test, she enthusiastically created a test paper based on Bloom's taxonomy (below).

The test was set on the 6 levels and she thought it was appropriately challenging for the highest achieving students. But, in her inexperience, she had not given the class enough time or exposure to the operation to be able to manage the manipulation of it and, unfortunately, most of the students failed. Interestingly, her supervising teacher, who was also the school principal, said very little but offered her a job at the school the following year!

Marcie's principal saw potential … in her valiant attempts to differentiate for higher order thinking.

One of the most useful schemes for designing curriculum is the original Bloom's Taxonomy of Educational Objectives (1956) and the revised version by Anderson & Krathwohl (2001). Both schema are developed fully in their original texts but are simplified here. The schema provide criteria to ensure that curricular objectives and test items encompass sufficient depth to address the most complex levels of thinking in order to assist gifted/high potential students to actually learn new ideas and concepts, and to thrive as learners.

A summary by Wilson (2016) can be found at https://quincycollege.edu/wp-cont ent/uploads/Anderson-and-Krathwohl_Revised-Blooms-Taxonomy.pdf

TABLE 4.6 Bloom's Taxonomy (1956) compared with Anderson & Krathwohl's Revision (2001) from the original sources

Bloom's Taxonomy (1956)	Anderson & Krathwohl's Taxonomy (2001)	
Evaluation – judge, assess, decide, appraise	Create – putting elements together to create a new product, plan or form	to 'abstract' complex thinking
Synthesis – compose, invent, propose, construct	Evaluate – judgments based on criteria standards	
Analysis – compare, survey, classify, contrast	Analyse – breaking down concepts into component parts-> charts, diagrams, details	
Application – organise, practise, operate, use	Apply – use of learned materials in products like models, dioramas, interviews	
Comprehension – restate, identify, discuss, infer	Understand – construct meaning from texts, classifying, summarising, explaining	from 'concrete' simple thinking
Knowledge – know, identify, define, recognise	Remember – recalling from memory – definitions, facts, learned information	

Anderson & Krathwohl (2001) present Question Starters (question stems) that belong to each level in their revised taxonomy. They are very useful. A summary of question stems for each level of the taxonomy was prepared and can be found at:
https://education.illinoisstate.edu/downloads/casei/5-02-Revised%20Blooms.pdf.

NB. 'create' is not about 'making' something such as a diorama, but rather about the higher order thinking of original and unique thought (for a student of that age).

Tips when using the Question Starters in your classroom:

■ Where possible, pre-prepare the questions to be used in a lesson. Consider the capacity of individuals in the class and target particular questions to suit their needs.

■ Expect all students, whatever their capacity, to respond to questions.

■ Teach students about the levels of questions and encourage them to use the variety of levels themselves, in their discussions and oral presentations.

The power of good questioning

The power of effective questions is indisputable for gifted students' capacity to prompt intended types of responses and promote learning objectives. Questions are powerful instructional tools. Higher-order questions are required to stimulate more complex cognitive responses, yet Tofade et al. (2013), and Larson and Lovelace (2013), found that lower order questions are used even by instructors when teaching under-graduate students in university lectures. In the latter research, 78.2% of the questions in an observational study were related to the remembering or understanding levels of Anderson and Krathwohl's Taxonomy. Although set in lecture-style settings there is likelihood of this finding being prevalent across all levels of education including schools. The skill of asking questions for a specific purpose needs to be explicitly taught and to be a part of every teacher's 'tool-kit'.

Recommendations by Larson & Lovelace (2013) include:

1. Generate questions that require higher-order thinking skills (and the development of this skill needs practice).

2. Make questions count – use fewer, but well-developed questions rather than many fast questions. Rapid questioning is likely to be in the lower order.

3. Allow for 'wait-time'. If a question is complex, then allow time for students to discuss it with a peer or to write down a response before answering aloud or ask a student who has high 'ego-strength' and then give him time to respond. This will require that you teach your class to tolerate silence in the whole group, a skill that develops within a classroom with purposeful training.

NB. Research also recommends, in addition to wait time for thinking, that allowing for more answers will enhance creative thinking (Kettler, Lamb & Mullet, 2021). In fact, the initial answers are usually not very creative but, in time and building on other ideas, the thinking becomes more creative. Allowing exercises, for example, 'think-pair-share' over and again can allow the creative process to unfold more effectively.

... open-ended questioning

In a mixed-ability classroom open-ended questions give scope for children of all ability levels to respond. For example, Tunnicliffe (2010) presents the following schema for open-ended questions. Included are examples drawn from a unit of work on Australian society:

- Speculate, e.g. What will Australian society be like in 20 years' time?
- Reason, e.g. Why do all students need to know how our federal government works?
- Discriminate, e.g. What makes a good citizen?
- Problem-solve, e.g. How could we improve the experience of Australian people living in poverty?

Other models with specific purposes include the seminal work of the Betts' Autonomous Learner Model, see Betts, Carey et al. (2021), Maker's Curriculum Modification model (1982), Kaplan's 'Content-Process-Product Grid' model (1986) and Williams' Cognitive-Affective Interaction model (1970) (Gross, 2015; Samawi et al., 2020) – details are in 'Go To' Resources, below.

The *Williams model* is another starting point for understanding the use of a model. It was developed on the basis that schools should teach higher-order thinking skills, including divergence and evaluation to all students but that they are essential for gifted students. Williams claimed that his three-dimensional model assists teachers to reveal creative potential in their students:

Dimension 1: is about subject matter including syllabus material
Dimension 2: contains a list of 18 teaching strategies for positive learning behaviours with the first 11 considered to be the most ignored in school curricula.
Dimension 3: contains the creative processes to uncover potential.

Williams' definitions of the teaching strategies

Use of the Williams model allows a teacher creative licence to choose from any of the strategies above and can be used within a unit of work for specific students or groups:

TABLE 4.7 The Williams model

Paradox	Situations opposed to common sense; self-contradictory statement, observation
Attribute Listing	Essential properties, identities, elements
Analogy	Unlike things or situations being compared
Discrepancy	Missing links or gaps in knowledge
Provocative Question	to prompt exploration and curiosity
Examples of Change	The way things work with changes/modifications/alterations
Example of Habit	Build sensitivity to thinking bound by habits
Organised Random Search	Finding a new way to build a case
Skills of Search	Research to study something done before; trial and error on new ways
Tolerance for Ambiguity	Posing open-ended situations, 'What if …?'
Intuitive Expression	Expressing emotion through all senses Guided imagery, role-playing, empathy
Adjustment to Development	Examine pay back of mistakes, failures
Study Creative Development	Analyse traits of creative people, creative process
Evaluate Situations	Extrapolate from ideas and actions, analyse implications, consequences
Creative Reading Skill	Generate novel ideas by reading
Creative Listening Skill	Generate novel ideas by listening
Creative Writing Skill	Generate novel ideas by writing
Visualisation	Express ideas in 3-D, non-traditional forms

Williams Model Creative Behaviours

Cognitive-Intellective Behaviours

Synthesis	Putting known ideas together into a new whole or form
Fluency	Generation of a quantity, flow of thought, number of relevant responses
Flexibility	Variety of kinds of ideas, shift in categories, directions of thought
Elaboration	Embellishment, improvement of ideas, adding details, stretching
Originality	Unusual, unique ideas and responses Production away from the obvious

Affective-Temperament Behaviours

Risk Taking	Expose self to failure, take a guess Function in unstructured conditions
Curiosity	Be inquisitive, toy with ideas Follow hunches, be open to puzzlement
Complexity	Delve into intricate problems willingly Seek alternatives, see gaps
Imagination	Visualise, build mental images, feel intuitively, reach beyond reality

TABLE 4.8 Example of Williams model activities related to the topic of Ancient Rome

Paradox	The Roman Empire established many of the structures of modern European civilisation (courts, taxes, civil authorities) yet it held many values that we cannot embrace today (slavery, inferiority of women and foreigners). Discuss.
Attribute Listing	What were the rights of a Roman citizen? Both in order of importance during the Roman Empire and then in order of importance for values in Australia.
Analogy	How was the Roman army like a bulldozer?
Discrepancy	The rights of Roman citizens were not extended to slaves. Was this a problem?
Provocative Question	Would the world have been a better place without the Ancient Roman empire?
Examples of Change	After the Roman conquest of Greece, there were Greeks in Rome who became teachers. How might this have changed the education of young, patrician boys?
Examples of Habit	How and why were Roman forts built identically in conquered lands? Give examples.
Organised Random Search	Read different accounts of the effects of the Roman Empire and its influence on us today.
Skills of Search	Begin by reading about the Roman influence on Britain at www.english-heritage.org.uk/visit/inspire-me/blog/articles/what-did-the-romans-do-for-us/. Choose three influences and explore them further, offering your insights.
Tolerance for Ambiguity	What if Mt Vesuvius had not erupted in 79AD?
Intuitive Expression	Imagine you were a wealthy farmer in the first century near Rome. Tell us about your daily life.
Adjustment to Development	Why was slavery tolerated in Roman times?
Study Creative Development	Examine the work of Pliny the Younger. How did his life give us insights into the way the imperial culture of Rome worked?
Evaluate Situations	What was the effect of Julius Caesar's famous 'crossing of the Rubicon'?
Creative Reading Skill	History is written by the winners!! Select a book about the Roman Empire and write a blurb about it from the perspective of the senator and a blurb from the perspective of the slave.
Creative Listening Skill	Listen to the excerpts from the Roman poet Virgil Aeneid (https://naxosaudiobooks.com/aeneid-the-unabridged/), or popular music of the time for different celebrations/rituals then write a poem about the importance of mythology and superstition for the people of Rome.
Creative Writing Skill	What characteristics do the people of the Roman Empire need in order to grow and survive? Create a taxonomy for growth and survival for each of these inhabitants of the Roman Empire: Senators, Equestrians, Commons, Freed People, and Slaves. Then choose two of these inhabitants and write one letter home for each of them which demonstrates their perspectives during the rise (or collapse) of the Empire.

TABLE 4.8 (Continued)

Visualisation	If the Romans had to give up one of their inventions/innovations every month over 12 months, how would the Roman Empire evolve to look different? Create a model, map, or sketch of how the Roman Empire would have looked each month as something was given up, e.g. roads or concrete or aqueducts. What would be the reach of the empire after the 12 months of modelling? What should be given up first or last to maintain maximum reach and/or the best quality of life for Roman citizens and their slaves?

e.g. *ANCIENT ROME – Year 7*
Choose six questions and present your responses.

Teachers need more than tacit encouragement from school leaders to innovate and gain mastery with differentiation principles. They need proactive support for differentiation practices and growth in school culture that promotes more individualisation of programming, with rigour, according to need. VanTassel-Baska and Stambaugh (2005) state that differentiation of curriculum for the gifted is critical in all teacher planning and suggest that the following *teacher characteristics* are necessary for successful differentiation of curriculum for the gifted:

■ advanced subject matter knowledge beyond the standard curriculum

■ strong classroom management skills so they are comfortable with students doing different activities concurrently

■ an understanding that students learn at different rates, vary widely in their interests and abilities and that they acquire knowledge through different media

■ working knowledge of curricula standards before and after the current grade and how to modify it in a variety of ways to take students into higher levels of content and thought

■ capacity to source materials and an understanding of how suitable they are, how they can be utilised and how much scaffolding or instruction students will require when using them

■ allocation of planning time in daily and weekly segments to confer with grade colleagues and those in upper grades

■ preparedness to access available training in pedagogical models and strategies

■ pre-assessment of students' knowledge with an 85% indicator that advanced curriculum will be substituted for these students

■ a flexible approach allowing student choice in process or concepts

■ an understanding that higher-level work is not more work. It may, in fact, be much less in quantity, but requires more deep thought and deliberation.

When considering if the needs of gifted/high potential students are being met, *Passow's Test of Appropriate Curriculum* asks three questions (Callahan et al., 2015; Passow, 1988):

■ Would all students want to be involved in such learning experiences?

■ Could all students participate in such learning experiences?

■ Should all students be expected to succeed in such learning experiences?

If the answers are all 'Yes' then the curriculum offerings are, at best, enrichment, but are not differentiated for the needs of gifted/high potential students.

If you wish to gain more knowledge and experience in how to differentiate for the gifted/high potential child then use the resources listed below. Also, request that the Professional Learning programme in your school should support you in the way recommended by Dixon et al (2014) that is, demonstration through workshops allowing the writing of levelled lessons together with other teachers followed by time to observe the delivery of differentiated lessons with feedback offered. Wiggins (1998) and Munro (2012) suggest that professional development on the skills and strategies required in differentiating the curriculum may help teachers. The Effect Size for professional development found by Hattie and Zierer (2019) is 0.49 (which is very good) and a highly recommended way to use school resources for improved outcomes for students while increasing the professional satisfaction of teachers.

Asynchronous development

'Asynchronous development' can occur where a gifted student's intellectual abilities develop before their emotional, physical or social aspects and the student can be frustrated by not being able to communicate or demonstrate his advanced ideas through written expression or artworks. A link to a National Association for Gifted Children (US) PDF that explains Asynchronous Development, written for parents, can be found here: http://dev.nagc.org/sites/default/files/Publication%20PHP/ NAGC%20TIP%20Sheet-Asynchronous%20Development-FINAL%20REVI SED-OCTOBER%202017(1).pdf

Underachievement

Underachievement is noted amongst the gifted population. The Centre for Education Statistics and Evaluation (CESE) summarises some findings about underachievement:

> 'Students whose underachievement may be attributed to inadequate provision of opportunity at school have been referred to as "involuntary underachievers" (Siegle & McCoach 2002). Lack of challenge at school can be a major factor in underachievement and can contribute to boredom and disengagement (Sisk 1988). Unchallenged gifted students may also become "selective consumers" choosing to disengage from school if they feel that their learning needs are not met, and instead seek stimulation and achievement elsewhere (Figg et al. 2012). In studies of exemplary teachers who supported high achieving students, it was found that:

> ■ *expert content knowledge*
> ■ *feedback*
> ■ *supportive learning environments and*
> ■ *teacher enthusiasm*

were key to gifted student motivation, learning and engagement' (Ayres, Sawyer & Dinham 2004; Gentry et al. 2011, p. 8).

Blaas (2014) notes the research-evidenced correlation between underachievement (gaining academic results lower than a student's assessed potential) and a low sense of social-emotional well-being, but the direction of causation is not established. In a meta-analysis of 14 studies Steenbergen-Hu et al. (2020) found there was no evidence that underachievement interventions significantly improved the academic performance of gifted underachievers. They did find, though, that these students benefited from attempts to support them with increased motivation for learning and better psychosocial outcomes.

Jackson and Jung (2022) note that the various measures used to calculate underachievement in the gifted population are not equivalent, making results noncomparable. Among their conclusions is the suggestion that there may be more advantage in measuring the educational 'health' of schools and teacher effectiveness rather than the differences between individuals' assessed intelligence and performance results which are subject to socio-economic and other individualised factors.

Of course, before seeking to support underachieving gifted students it is imperative that their learning profiles and needs have been fully explored and the possibility of underlying learning or processing difficulties carefully examined.

'Go to' resources

Australian

- ACER administration of the Cognitive Abilities Test (CogAT)
  https://shop.acer.org/cogat-online-administration.html
- Hawker Brownlow Education
  www.hb-digital.com.au
  HBE were specific publishers for gifted education but now specialise more in differentiated instruction.
  The CARS and STARS Comprehension Strategies series with 8 levels A–H (approximately Year 1 to 8) are recommended. Students can work on advanced levels of the same strategies within a class programme.
- MindQuest
  High-quality holiday courses for gifted children
  www.mindquest.net.au
  Shelagh Poray–Director
  NSW Talent Centre Pty Ltd
  P.O. Box 577
  Toronto NSW 2283
  Ph: 02 9748 1084.
- Reading Australia for literature units
  www.readingaustralia.com.au

- UNSW ICAS School Competitions in literacy (English, Writing and Spelling Bee) and STEM (Mathematics, Science and Digital Technologies) www.icasassessments.com
  If your school has not participated in these competitions, you will find that your brightest students will enjoy them for their complex, interesting questions in their domains of strength. Good, quantitative results data is generated for you, too!

- UNSW Student Programmes held twice a year for gifted students and are open to all students regardless of geographical location.
  www.unsw.edu.au/arts-design-architecture/our-schools/education/professio nal-learning/gerric-gifted-education/gifted-students-parents

- GATEWAYS Programmes for students across Australia: www.gateways.edu.au/

USA

- Carbaugh, E.M. & Doubet, K.J. (2015). *The differentiated flipped classroom: A practical guide to digital learning.* Corwin Press.

- Betts, G. T., Carey, R. J., & Kapushion, B. M. (2021). *Autonomous learner model resource book.* Routledge.
  www.taylorfrancis.com/books/mono/10.4324/9781003233183/autonomous-learner-model-resource-book-george-betts-robin-carey-blanche-kapushion
  Chapter abstracts are available assisting you to decide if the activities will work well with your students.
  Betts Autonomous Learner Model
  https://presentlygifted.weebly.com/autonomous-learner-model.html
  This website contains an explanation of the Autonomous Learner Model and has a very useful page on 'Helpful Websites'.

- College of William and Mary, Virginia, USA
  https://education.wm.edu/centers/cfge/
  School of Education
  Center for Gifted Education
  Online Enrichment Resources
  Contact details are here for *NASA, American Museum of Natural History 'Ology'* site and *Renzulli Learning*

- Davidson Institute www.davidsongifted.org/resource-library/gifted-resources-guides/

- Education Perfect for enrichment, extension and differentiation of content and purposes www.educationperfect.com

- Iowa State University
  Center for Excellence in Learning and Teaching
  A Model of Learning Objectives: A Revision of Bloom's Taxonomy of Educational Objectives.

Download the Revised Bloom's Taxonomy (PDF): www.celt.iastate.edu/wp-content/uploads/2015/09/RevisedBloomsHandout-1.pdf

■ Johns Hopkins University Center for Talented Youth, Baltimore, USA. Online Programs for Grades 2–12 across a full range of topics. https://cty.jhu.edu/programs/online

■ Kaplan, S.N. (1986). The grid: A model to construct differentiated curriculum for the gifted. In J.S. Renzulli (Ed.), *Systems and models for developing programs for the gifted and talented* (pp. 180–193). Mansfield Centre, CT: Creative Learning Press.

■ Maker, C.J. (1982). *Curriculum development for the gifted*. Austin, TX: PRO-ED.

■ National Association for Gifted Children (USA) www.nagc.org NAGC PDF on Asynchronous Development for parents http://dev.nagc.org/resources-publications/resources-parents/social-emotional-issues/asynchronous-development

■ Peer nomination forms Kaya, F. (2013) The role of peer nomination forms in the identification of lower elementary gifted and talented students. *Educational Research & Reviews 8*(24): 2260–2269 DOI:10.5897/ERR2013.1674 www.researchgate.net/publication/283461895_The_role_of_peer_nomination_forms_in_the_identification_of_lower_elementary_gifted_and_talented_students

■ Renzulli Scales www.routledge.com/go/scales-for-rating-the-behavioral-characteristics-of-superior-students (2013) Prufrock Press Inc.

■ The Iowa Acceleration Scale www.accelerationinstitute.org/tools/ias.aspx

The Connie Belin & Jacqueline N. Blank International Center for Gifted Education and Talent Development, College of Education, University of Iowa

■ Tomlinson, C (2017) How to Differentiate Instruction in the Academically Diverse Classroom, ASCD, Virginia, USA.

■ Wiggins, G., & McTighe, J. (2011). *The Understanding by Design guide to creating high-quality units*. Alexandria, VA: ASCD.

(Association for Supervision and Curriculum Development (ASCD) is a not-for-profit educational organisation based in Virginia, USA. www.ascd.org)

■ Williams, F.E. (1993). The cognitive-affective interaction model for enriching gifted programs. In J.S. Renzulli, (Ed.), *Systems and models for developing programs for the gifted and talented* (pp. 461–484). Highett, Vic.: Hawker Brownlow.

Bibliography

Anderson, L. W., & Krathwohl, D. R. (2001). *A taxonomy for learning, teaching and assessing: A revision of bloom's taxonomy of educational objectives* (Complete Edition). New York: Longman.

Assouline, S. G., Colangelo, N., VanTassel-Baska, J., & Lupkowski-Shoplik, A. (Eds). (2015). *A nation empowered, volume 2: Evidence trumps the excuses holding back America's brightest students.* University of Iowa Press.

Ayres, P., Sawyer, W., & Dinham, S. (2004). Effective teaching in the context of a Grade 12 high-stakes external examination in New South Wales, Australia. *British Educational Research Journal, 30*(1), 141–165. Cited in Centre for Education Statistics and Evaluation (2019), Revisiting Gifted Education, NSW Department of Education, www.cese.nsw. gov.au/publications-filter/revisiting-gifted-education

Bandura, A. (1994). Self-efficacy. In V. S. Ramachaudran (Ed.), *Encyclopedia of human behavior* (Vol. 4, pp. 71–81). New York: Academic Press. (Reprinted in H. Friedman (Ed.), Encyclopedia of mental health. San Diego, CA: Academic Press, 1998)

Bandura, A. (2019). Applying theory for human betterment. *Perspectives on Psychological Science, 14*(1), 12–15. https://doi.org/10.1177/1745691618815165

Blaas, S. (2014). The relationship between social-emotional difficulties and underachievement of gifted students. *Australian Journal of Guidance and Counselling, 24*(2), 243–255, published by Cambridge University Press on behalf of Australian Academic Press Pty Ltd 2014 | doi 10.1017/jgc.2014.1. www.cambridge.org/core/terms. https://doi.org/10.1017/jgc.2014.1

Brulles, D., & Winebrenner, S. (2011). The schoolwide cluster grouping model: Restructuring gifted education services for the 21st century. *Gifted Child Today Magazine, 34*(4), 35–46. https://doi.org/10.1177/1076217511415381

Callahan, C. M., Moon, T. R., Oh, S., Azano, A. P., & Hailey, E. P. (2015). What works in gifted education: documenting the effects of an integrated curricular/instructional model for gifted students. *American Educational Research Journal, 52*(1), 137–167. https://doi.org/10.3102/0002831214549448

Centre for Education Statistics and Evaluation. (2019). *Revisiting gifted education.* NSW Department of Education, www.cese.nsw.gov.au/publications-filter/revisiting-gifted-education

Clark, B. (2013). *Growing up gifted* (8th edn). Upper Saddle River, NJ: Pearson Prentice Hall.

Colangelo, N., Assouline, S., & Gross, M. (2004). *A nation deceived: How schools hold back America's brightest students. The Templeton National Report on acceleration. Volume 1.* Connie Belin & Jacqueline N. Blank International Center for Gifted Education and Talent Development, University of Iowa.

Dai, D. Y. (2020). Rethinking human potential from a talent development perspective. *Journal for the Education of the Gifted, 43*(1), 19–37.

Delisle, J. (2021). *Understanding your gifted child from the inside out: A guide to the social and emotional lives of gifted kids.* Abingdon: Taylor & Francis.

Dixon, F. A., Yssel, N., McConnell, J., & Hardin, T. (2014). Differentiated instruction, professional development and teacher efficacy. *Journal for the Education of the Gifted, 37*(2), 111–127. https://doi.org/10.1177/0162353214529042

Erikson, E. (1902–1994). *Exploring your mind.* Retrieved on 12 July 2022, from https://exploringyourmind.com/seven-famous-erik-erikson-quotes/

Gagné, F. (2010). Motivation within the DMGT 2.0 framework. *High Ability Studies. 21*, 81–99. https://doi.org/10.1080/13598139.2010.525341

Gentry, M., Steenbergen-Hu, S., & Choi, B. (2011). Student-identified exemplary teachers: insights from talented teachers. *The Gifted Child Quarterly, 55*(2), 111–125. https://doi.org/10.1177/0016986210397830

Gifted NSW. *The state association for gifted and talented children.* www.giftednsw.org.au

Gross, M. U. (2001). Musings: serving gifted students in schools—bland protestations or practical action? *Understanding Our Gifted, 13*(2), 16–18. https://eric.ed.gov

Gross, M. U. (2015). Characteristics of able gifted highly gifted exceptionally gifted and profoundly gifted learners. In *Applied practice for educators of gifted and able learners* (pp. 3–23). Rotterdam: SensePublishers. https://doi.org/10.1007/978-94-6300-004-8_1

Gross, M. U., Smith, S. R., & Garces-Bacsal, R. M. (2021). Put them together and see how they learn! ability grouping and acceleration effects on the self-esteem of academically gifted high school students. In *Handbook of giftedness and talent development in the Asia-Pacific* (pp. 377–403). Singapore: Springer Singapore. https://doi.org/10.1007/978-981-13-3041-4_17

Hattie, J., & Zierer, K. (2019). *Visible learning insights*. Abingdon: Routledge.

Jackson, R. L., & Jung, J. Y. (2022). The identification of gifted underachievement: Validity evidence for the commonly used methods. *British Journal of Educational Psychology, 92*(3), 1133–1159. https://doi.org/10.1111/bjep.12492

Kettler, T., Mullet, D. R. & Lamb, K. N. (2021). *Developing creativity in the classroom: Learning and innovation for 21st-century schools* (1st edn). Abingdon: Routledge. https://doi.org/10.4324/9781003234104

Krathwohl, D. R. (2002). A revision of bloom's taxonomy: An overview. *Theory into Practice, 41*(4), 212–218. https://doi.org/10.1207/s15430421tip4104_2

Maree, J. G. (2022). The psychosocial development theory of Erik Erikson: Critical overview. In R. Evans, & O.N.. Saracho (Eds). *Gifted young in science. The influence of theorists and pioneers on early childhood education* London & New York: Routledge (pp. 119–133). https://doi.org/10.4324/9781003120216

Munro, J. (2012). *Effective strategies for implementing differentiated instruction* [Paper presentation]. 2012 – School Improvement: What does research tell us about effective strategies? https://research.acer.edu.au/research_conference/RC2012/27august/14

Munro, J. (2014). *Gifted knowing & thinking: Research tells us what it looks like*. The Melbourne Graduate School of Education's 2014 Deans Lecture Series Presented by Associate Professor John Munro, MGSE https://youtu.be/6yRjHOA3T3A

Neihart, M. (2016). *The social and emotional development of gifted children: What do we know?* (M. Neihart, S.M. Reis, N.M. Robinson, & S.M. Moon. (Eds) (2nd edn). Abingdon: Routledge. https://doi.org/10.4324/9781003238928

NSW Department of Education. *High potential and gifted education policy*. https://education.nsw.gov.au/policy-library/policies/pd-2004-0051

Olszewski-Kubilius, P., Subotnik, R. F., & Worrell, F. C. (Eds). (2018). *Talent development as a framework for gifted education: Implications for best practices and applications in schools* (1st edn). Abingdon: Routledge. https://doi.org/10.4324/9781003238454.

Pajares, F. (2002). *Self-efficacy beliefs in academic contexts: An outline*. Retrieved on 12 July 2022, from http://emory.edu.EDUCATION/mfp/efftalk.html.

Parker, P. D., Marsh, H. W., Ciarrochi, J., Marshall, S., & Abduljabbar, A. S. (2014). Juxtaposing math self-efficacy and self-concept as predictors of long-term achievement outcomes. *Educational Psychology, 34*(1), 29–48. https://doi.org/10.1080/01443410.2013.797339

Passow, A. H. (1988). The education and schooling of the community artisans in science. In P. F. Brandwein and A. H. Passow (Eds). *Gifted young in science: Potential through performance* (pp. 27–38). Washington, DC: National Teachers Association.

Reis, S. M., Renzulli, S. J., & Renzulli, J. S. (2021). Enrichment and gifted education pedagogy to develop talents, gifts, and creative productivity. *Education Sciences, 11*(10), 615. https://doi.org/10.3390/educsci11100615

Renzulli, J. S. & Reis, S. M. (2018). *The schoolwide enrichment model: A how-to guide for talent development* (3rd edn). Waco, TX: Prufrock Press.

Renzulli, J. S. & Reis, S. M. (2018). The three-ring conception of giftedness: A developmental approach for promoting creative productivity in young people. In S. I. Pfeiffer,

E. Shaunessy-Dedrick & M. Foley-Nicpon (Eds). APA handbook of giftedness and talent (pp. 185–199). Washington, DC: American Psychological Association.

Rogers, K. B. (2002). *Re-forming gifted education: Matching the program to the child.* Tuscon, AZ: Great Potential Press, Inc.

Rogers, K. B. (2007). Lessons learned about educating the gifted and talented: A synthesis of the research on educational practice. *Gifted Child Quarterly, 51*(4), 382–396. https://doi.org/10.1177/0016986207306324

Rowan, L., & Townend, G. (2016). Early career teachers' beliefs about their preparedness to teach: Implications for the professional development of teachers working with gifted and twice-exceptional students. *Cogent Education, 3*(1), 1242458. https://doi.org/10.1080/2331186X.2016.1242458

Samawi, F. S., Alshoubaki, N. H. H., & Shaheen, H. R. A. (2020). The effectiveness of a training program based on Frank Williams' model in developing the divergent creative feeling among students in Jordan. *International Journal of Learning, Teaching and Educational Research, 19*(1), 74–94. https://doi.org/10.26803/ijlter.19.1.5

Shaughnessy, M. (2019). A reflective conversation with Joe Renzulli: What hath the last 20–30 years wrought in terms of gifted education? *Gifted Education International, 35*(3), 275–281 https://doi.org/10.1177/026142941986

Siegle, D., Wilson, H., & Little, C. (2013). A sample of gifted and talented educators' attitudes about acceleration. *Journal of Advanced Academics, 24*(1), 27–51. https://doi.org/10.1177/1932202X12472491

Steenbergen-Hu, S., Olszewski-Kubilius, P., & Calvert, E. (2020). The effectiveness of current interventions to reverse the underachievement of gifted students: Findings of a meta-analysis and systematic review. *Gifted Child Quarterly, 64*(2), 132–165. https://doi.org/10.1177/0016986220908601

Sternberg, R. J., & Ambrose, D. (Eds). (2021). *Conceptions of giftedness and talent.* London: Palgrave Macmillan. http://dx.doi.org/10.1007/978-3-030-56869-6

Subotnik, R. F., Olszewski-Kubilius, P., & Worrell, F. C. (Eds). (2019). High performance: The central psychological mechanism for talent development. In R. F. Subotnik, P. Olszewski-Kubilius, & F. C. Worrell (Eds). *The psychology of high performance: Developing human potential into domain-specific talent* (pp. 7–20). Washington DC: American Psychological Association. https://doi.org/10.1037/0000120-002

Subotnik, R. F., Olszewski-Kubilius, P., & Worrell, F. C. (2021). The talent development megamodel: A domain-specific conceptual framework based on the psychology of high performance. In R. J. Sternberg & D. Ambrose (Eds), *Conceptions of giftedness and talent* (pp. 425–442). Cham: Palgrave Macmillan/Springer Nature. https://doi.org/10.1007/978-3-030-56869-6_24

Swanson, J. D., Brock, L., Van Sickle, M., Gutshall, C. A., Russell, L., & Anderson, L. (2020). A basis for talent development: The integrated curriculum model and evidence-based strategies. *Roeper Review, 42*(3), 165–178. https://doi.org/10.1080/02783193.2020.1765920

Tannenbaum, A. J. (1983). *Gifted children: psychological and educational perspectives.* New York: Macmillan.

Tofade, T., Elsner, J., & Haines, S. T. (2013). Best practice strategies for effective use of questions as a teaching tool. *American Journal of Pharmaceutical Education, 77*(7), 155. https://doi.org/10.5688/ajpe777155

Tomlinson, C. A., & Imbeau, M. B. (2010). *Leading and managing a differentiated classroom.* (1st edn). Alexandria, VA: ASCD.

Tomlinson, C. A., & McTighe, J. (2010). *Conversations: Integrating differentiated instruction and understanding by design.* Alexandria, VA: Association for Supervision and Curriculum Development. Retrieved at USYD Library, July 23, 2021.

Tomlinson, C. A., & Strickland, C. A. (2005). *Differentiation in practice: A resource guide for differentiating curriculum, grades 9–12*. Alexandria, VA: ASCD.

Tunnicliffe, C. (2010). Teaching able, gifted and talented children: Strategies, activities and resources. In C. Tunliffe (2010) *Teaching able, gifted and talented children: Strategies, activities and resources* (1st edn). London: SAGE. https://doi.org/10.4135/9781446251157

VanTassel-Baska, J. (1988). *Comprehensive curriculum for gifted learners*. Boston MA: Allyn and Bacon.

VanTassel-Baska, J. (2021). Curriculum in gifted education: The core of the enterprise. *Gifted Child Today Magazine, 44*(1), 44–47. https://doi.org/10.1177/1076217520940747

VanTassel-Baska, J., & Stambaugh, T. (2005). Challenges and possibilities for serving gifted learners in the regular classroom. *Theory into Practice, 44*(3), 211–217. www.jstor.org/stable/3497000

Westman, L. D. (2018). *Student-driven differentiation: 8 steps to harmonize learning in the classroom.* Los Angeles CA: SAGE Publications, ProQuest Central. Retrieved on 23 July 2021, from http://ebookcentral.proquest.com/lib/usyd/detail.action?docID=6261968. Visit the companion website at http://resources.corwin.com/studentdrivendifferentiation\\

White, S. L. J., Graham, L. J., & Blaas, S. (2018). Why do we know so little about the factors associated with gifted underachievement? A systematic literature review. *Educational Research Review*, 24 (June 2018), 55–66. https://doi.org/10.1016/j.edurev.2018.03.001

Wiggins, G. P. (1998). *Educative assessment: Designing assessments to inform and improve student performance* (1st edn). San Francisco, CA: Jossey-Bass.

Wilson, L. O. (2016). *Anderson and Krathwohl Bloom's Taxonomy Revised Understanding the New Version of Bloom's Taxonomy* https://quincycollege.edu/wp-content/uploads/Anderson-and-Krathwohl_Revised-Blooms-Taxonomy.pdf

Winebrenner, S. (2018). *Teaching gifted kids in today's classroom: Strategies and techniques every teacher can use* (4th edn). Minneapolis, MN: Free Spirit Publishing Inc.

World Council for Gifted and Talented Children. (2021). *Global principles for professional learning in gifted education.* https://world-gifted.org/professional-learning-global-principles.pdf

Worrell, F. C., Subotnik, R. F., Olszewski-Kubilius, P., & Dixson, D. D. (2019). Gifted students *Annual Review of Psychology, 70*, 551–76 https://doi.org/10.1146/annurev-psych-010418-102846

Wu, E. H. (2013). The path leading to differentiation: An interview with Carol Tomlinson. *Journal of Advanced Academics, 24*(2), 125–133. https://doi.org/10.1177/1932202X13483472

Specific Learning Difficulties and Disabilities (SLD)

Rhonda Filmer

VIGNETTE

'How's it going, Johnny?' asked Jeannie, his Year 4 teacher, as light-heartedly as possible. She looked at his scrap paper where words were scribbled out with increasing force as she looked down the page.

'I just can't decide how to spell athlete/athleet/athleat and I need to know!'

Literacy lessons had been revolutionised since the school began to teach using a systematic synthetic phonics programme in Years K-4 and Johnny had benefited from it since Year 2. He had been taught well in a small group support setting but his problems with spelling and handwriting persisted.

Jeannie began to think how to adjust his programme for this term.

Is it time to give him IT support for writing tasks?

What it is

While 15 to 20% of a school population will experience learning *difficulties* for a variety of reasons including absenteeism from school, an educational setting that does not suit their needs, English is their second language, visual or auditory acuity weaknesses or behavioural, emotional or psychological problems, 3 to 5% of students will have *learning disabilities (disorders)* in specific aspects of their academic performance. Interestingly, the DSM-5-TR estimates the prevalence rates of SLDs (including all types) to fall between 5 and 15% of school-age children.

DOI: 10.4324/9781003404972-7

A diagnosis of a Specific Learning Disorder (SLD) requires the presence of academic and learning symptoms that persist for at least six months despite the provision of interventions that target those difficulties (DSM-5-TR). The symptoms are caused by underlying neurodevelopmental factors of genetic origin. To qualify for a diagnosis, an individual must have affected academic skills that are below those expected for their chronological age and are causing 'significant interference with academic or occupational performance, or with activities of daily living, as confirmed by individually administered standardised achievement measures and comprehensive clinical assessment (p.36).'

Specific Learning Disorders (SLD) are:

Dyslexia – SLD in *reading*
Dysgraphia – SLD in *written expression and/or handwriting*
Dyscalculia – SLD in *mathematics*.

A child may have an SLD in one, two or all three of these areas.

This definition for dyslexia was adopted by the International Dyslexia Association (IDA) and is endorsed by AUSPELD and therefore, all the SPELD state associations in Australia:

> *Dyslexia is a specific learning disability that is neurological in origin. It is characterized by difficulties with accurate and/or fluent word recognition and by poor spelling and decoding abilities. These difficulties typically result from a deficit in the phonological component of language that is often unexpected in relation to other cognitive abilities and the provision of effective classroom instruction. Secondary consequences may include problems in reading comprehension and reduced reading experience that can impede the growth of vocabulary and background knowledge.*

Why it is relevant to twice-exceptionality

Learning difficulties/disabilities that directly impact the acquisition of reading, spelling, writing, the comprehension of written text and/or the retention of mathematical facts and processes can have a profoundly negative affect on learning in a gifted/high potential student prohibiting him from acquiring knowledge through independent reading and often excluding him from enrichment and extension programmes. Without accurate diagnosis accompanied by evidence-based and explicit intervention the twice-exceptional student is at great risk of not thriving at school or in life outcomes.

What you will see in the classroom

The symptoms of SLD with impairment in reading (dyslexia)

A learner's oral reading accuracy and fluency progress slowly as compared with the rest of the class. If the child can read accurately, her oral reading may have poor phrasing, be full of self-correction and actually never really flow.

- The child does not retain the sounds in a stable way, often confusing the vowels, particularly *e* and *i,* despite specific and targeted teaching.
- The effortful reading takes enormous energy and creates such 'cognitive load' that the child loses track of a text's meaning, missing details of sequence, relationships between characters and the opportunity to understand inferential meaning.
- Behaviourally, a child may simply avoid reading aloud by making excuses or by refusing to read aloud. Or, he may choose to sit at the back of the room or exhibit anxiety that looks like a rebellious attitude, as a defence mechanism.

The symptoms of SLD with impairment in written expression (dysgraphia)

- Dysgraphia may or may not occur along with dyslexia.
- A child's spelling is weaker than expected e.g. he may add, omit or substitute vowels or consonants.
- A child may make multiple grammatical errors or punctuation errors within sentences; employs poor paragraph organisation; written expression lacks clarity.
- In a bright or gifted student, I see a big difference between his multiple ideas expressed orally and what actually makes it into the written text.
- Sometimes, handwriting difficulties called motor dysgraphia, accompany these problems, where letter-formation can be illegible and slow. A child may find it so laborious that she starts to avoid written tasks altogether.

The symptoms of SLD with impairment in mathematics (dyscalculia)

'Dyscalculia is an innate difficulty in learning or comprehending mathematics. Students with dyscalculia have trouble understanding numbers, learning how to manipulate numbers, learning mathematical facts and a number of other related difficulties.' AUSPELD Understanding Learning Difficulties Guide, p. 9.

The DSM 5-TR defines it as 'Difficulties mastering number sense, number facts, or calculation (e.g. has poor understanding of numbers, their magnitude and relationships; counts on fingers to add single-digit numbers instead of recalling the math fact as peers do; gets lost in the midst of arithmetic computation and may switch procedures)' and/or 'Difficulties with mathematical reasoning (e.g. has severe difficulty applying mathematical concepts, facts or procedures to solve quantitative problems)' p. 36.

- Dyscalculia can occur along with the other SLDs or with ADHD (hyperactive or inattentive) or it may occur singly.
- In a young student you may notice he has:
  - trouble understanding the one-to-one correspondence between objects and numbers
  - trouble connecting a numerical symbol (8) with its word (eight)
  - difficulty recognising and creating a sequence of symbols or numbers
  - a need to count on his fingers. Cannot easily *subitise*, e.g. say how many dots are on a page without actually counting.
  - an unmistakable need to use concrete materials to assist with counting
  - trouble telling time

- In an older child, she may have:
  - difficulty with estimation and approximation
  - slowness in mental calculation and often less accurate than his apparent general ability
  - poor long-term memory for mathematical processes particularly algorithms

In 45 years of teaching I have only met two children with diagnosed dyscalculia. One child had co-morbid ADHD which meant that his memory for mathematics was limited at the verbal and working memory levels. He could not remember how to start an algorithm. The other child also had dyslexia. Although her applied maths reasoning was well-developed, she struggled with attainment in number and algebra. In every other case of low mathematical achievement, I found it was a matter of missed learning opportunity. A specifically targeted Tier 2 or individualised programme provided improvement; given sufficient planning, intention, concentration and time. I write this merely as a caution against discounting, too early, a child's capacity to learn mathematics. It can often be a case of inattention, lost lessons or even poor teaching at an early stage in a child's mathematical development.

SLDs can be diagnosed at the *Mild*, *Moderate* or *Severe* levels. (DSM-5-TR)

Even a *Mild* presentation requires *intervention*.

What do I do about it?

The quintessential free resources for this topic are:

1. AUSPELD's *Understanding Learning Difficulties A practical guide* (2014)for parents www.uldforparents.com. The teacher's guide is available to download on www.scootle.com.

2. The PDF document from the IDA–Dyslexia in the Classroom: What Every Teacher Needs to Know www.interdys.org/ewebeditpro5/upload/DyslexiaInTheClassroom.pdf

I recommend that you obtain them immediately. There is no point in my rewriting or over-quoting their contents when these seminal resources do it so well.

What should I actually do when I see an articulate, bright child who cannot read/spell at age level?

Use a screener

1. *School Age Dyslexia Screener* – the Colorado Learning Disabilities Questionnaire – Reading Subscale (CLDQ-R) is recommended by IDA and is printed in the IDA resource I have recommended (Dyslexia in the Classroom). Though it is a screener and not a diagnostic tool it is reliable, validated by Willicutt et al. (2011) and gives you all the information you need to start an intervention programme.

2. *Motif* On the Macquarie University website at www.motif.org.au is a battery of 15 free, accessible, highly reputable screening tests to help you gain knowledge about your student's reading difficulties with immediately available results and norms. You need to create an account and log-in to download a PDF of it.

   The tests include:

■   The Castles and Coltheart 2 (CC2) which tests different processes in single-word reading.

■   The Test of Everyday Reading Comprehension

■   Specific spelling tests and Letter-Sound tests.

This is an excellent resource.

3. *DIBELS (Dynamic Indicators of Basic Early Literacy Skills)* from the University of Oregon, USA. The 8th edition of this assessment battery has been updated and validated for use in screening for dyslexia-related deficits in order to identify students who need additional instructional support. It is free and downloadable from the website with training opportunities offered. www.dibels.uoregon.edu.

Use norm referenced tests

More information about the perceived problems may be required so it may be appropriate to test beyond the scope of a screener.

   The following tests are available from PsychCorp and can be purchased and administered by teachers who have *special education* experience. Although the use of these tests is not standard practice in primary schools in NSW, there is valuable information to be found from their use. They are expensive to buy initially so it is a matter requiring a whole school approach to this issue.

1. Comprehensive Test of Phonological Processing (CTOPP-2) is a comprehensive instrument designed to assess phonological awareness, phonological memory and rapid naming which are the essential skills required to learn to read.

2. Wechsler Individual Achievement Test (WIAT, 3rd Edition) Australian and NZ norms.
There are four Indices: Oral Language, Reading, Written Language and Mathematics. Just the required subtests within each index can be used. The results are comprehensive, reliable and informative yielding percentile rankings with age and grade equivalent levels. This information helps with the diagnostic procedure of where to start a remedial programme.

3. Dyslexia Toolkit by Pearson Clinical (released in late 2021). Their website states: 'The Pearson Dyslexia Toolkit is specially developed for teachers and special educators to proactively screen and assess for literacy difficulties, to support struggling learners by identifying relevant evidence-based interventions and monitoring progress.' I note it is expensive, but it contains parts of the WIAT III, the WRMT III and the Raven's 2. This looks like a product worth investigating for your school.

4. The Woodcock Johnson Fourth Edition–Australasian Adaptation (WJ–IV) has two tests, the WJ IV Tests of Achievement and the WJ IV Tests of Oral Language that can be bought and administered by *special education* teachers. There is a Cognitive Abilities battery in this suite of tests that can only be administered by experienced registered psychologists. The WJ IV can be bought from PAA Psychological Assessments Australia Pty Ltd.

The Phonics Check is an important tool in Year 1 and regular screening for growth in literacy should occur in the K–2 years with a wide brush of inclusion into support services applied for all students who may be 'at risk'. To identify students as 'at risk' only to find that they thrived a little later is better than to have missed them entirely.

It should be assumed that 20–25% of students in K–2 will be slower to start, low progress or less confident readers or writers and we need to plan for that proportion in the allocation of support services. It is a 'no-brainer' to ensure that an appropriate level of resourcing is allocated to these students, so they reach appropriate benchmarks before Year 2. There is more opportunity for a child to be given time to catch up in this window of opportunity, long before the Primary years when the curriculum assumes a higher level of competence. By Year 3, readiness to 'read to learn' is assumed and programmes contain a far more crowded curriculum. The little child who needs more time to thrive is not so obvious within the K–2 setting because interventions at this point are less obtrusive or threatening to his self-esteem.

'When we consider the extraordinary amount of time it takes to improve reading performance in the later grades, estimates suggest that if intervention is not initiated until fourth grade, it takes four times as much instruction as it would have in first grade (Lyon & Fletcher, 2001) to see similar rates of improvement; early intervention in both word level reading and listening comprehension is essential' (Solaria, Grimma, McIntyrea & Denton, 2018, p. 204).

Start remediation/intervention immediately

For Dyslexia teach:

1. Phonemic awareness – the ability to identify and manipulate the sounds within words is the essential base line and the most highly predictive skill of later reading and spelling success (Castles and Coltheart, 2004).

2. Phonics – Scientific research has demonstrated that initial phonics instruction is the single most effective word-decoding approach for students. All children benefit to some extent from such instruction but children at risk of reading failure and those who are making progress, but slowly, achieve greater success under a phonics regime.

3. The term Systematic Synthetic Phonics (SSP) means that a programme is designed with an incremental order for the learning of the sound-letter relationships. SSP schemes recommended by AUSPELD include:

   - Sounds-Write
   - Phonics Books UK
   - MultiLit Reading Tutor Programme, MacqLit, Word Attack Skills Programme, MiniLit Early Intervention Programme, PreLit Literacy Preparation and InitiaLit-Foundation
   - Letters and Sounds
   - Teaching Reading in the Early Years developed by SPELD NSW. There are many others. Refer to the AUSPELD ULD Guides.

4. Fluency is obtained by guided oral reading with explicit instruction rather than by independent silent reading (National Reading Panel, 2000).

5. Vocabulary is the most powerful predictor of reading comprehension. A randomised controlled trial by Clarke, Snowling, Truelove, and Hulme (2010), reported that enhancing children's vocabulary development using explicit instruction methods was more effective at improving reading comprehension than the teaching of comprehension strategies. It is clear that the knowledge of word meanings is essential if a reader is to understand what has been decoded in a text.

   This is an area where we expect verbal precocity in gifted children in their spoken language. 'Unless children develop strong vocabularies early in life and continue to deepen and broaden their vocabulary knowledge throughout the schooling years, they will predictably face difficulty in understanding what they read, will not use advanced and mature words in their writing, will have problems with academic subjects, will perform poorly on national achievement tests and will fall steadily behind their more vocabulary-proficient peers.' (See www.fivefromfive.com.au Vocabulary page.)

   Explicit instruction with carefully aligned outcomes and content is essential e.g. English work sheets, class games and competitions, use of the thesaurus etc. We know that reading is a huge source of new vocabulary, especially in the classical works, where children's authors did not attempt to appeal to a lower common denominator of interest or reading capacity. Exposure to a library of rich English literature deeply nourishes the lives of competent readers. Thompson (2001) gives a compelling case for developing vocabulary through classic literature. Verbally gifted children need exposure to complex words as a vehicle for developing thought and ideas. Class lessons should contain explicit exposure to passages of literature and discussion on word meanings involving the morphology of words: root words, prefixes and suffixes, the Greek and Latin word origins that assist with meaning.

6. Comprehension skill is dependent on the proficiency of a child's reading fluency. Automaticity releases the processes of the brain to pay full attention to the meaning in a passage. This is cognitive load theory and the whole reason why early intervention for students with reading difficulties/SLDs is recommended … in order that the child is not prohibited from progressing in all these aspects of reading skills. There is widespread evidence to support the use of teaching strategies for finding Main Idea as the essential first step in understanding the more complex structures in a passage of English text.

In a study of over 400,000 students from Year One to Three, in Australia, it was revealed that among students whose decoding and vocabulary were developing normally, fewer than 1% displayed reading comprehension problems (Spencer, Quinn and Wagner, 2014, cited in Hempenstall, 2016, p. 25).

We must continue to model the reading of a wide range of books –paper or e-books for pleasure. Children who are readers are higher achievers because of their exposure to advanced vocabulary, ideas, knowledge, syntax and plot complexities. It is as simple as that! For students whose reading skills are still poor it is essential to expose them to audiobooks of high quality and complexity in order to avoid their programme being 'dumbed down' to meet their reading or motivational level.

Nation (2019) notes the importance of shared book reading for the healthy development of language in young children. Book language is information dense, more morphologically complex, abstract and more meaning-bearing than child-directed speech. More emotion language is contained in picture books allowing children to develop the use of emotion words in their writing. Studies are suggesting that exposure to book language is associated with mental health. She recommends Cecile Ferreira's site Book Share 9 (see www.booksh aretime.com) for its huge array of picture books that encourage speech and language development in young children.

For Dysgraphia

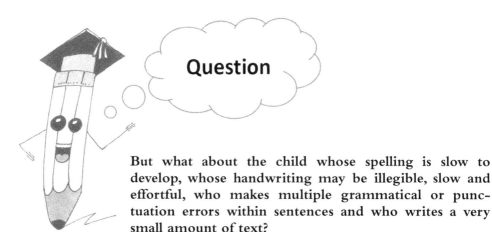

Question

But what about the child whose spelling is slow to develop, whose handwriting may be illegible, slow and effortful, who makes multiple grammatical or punctuation errors within sentences and who writes a very small amount of text?

This child is at risk of developing dysgraphia which is a problem involving multiple processes, with the writing of words. McBride (2019) states that dysgraphia remains under-researched despite an estimated prevalence of 7% to 15% of children having some form of writing difficulty. The problem with researching it, according to McCloskey and Rapp (2017) is that students vary enormously in the manifestation of symptoms and only individualised qualitative studies will reveal that variety of difficulties. Group research assumes homogeneity in the subjects chosen.

We do know that dysgraphia is nearly always about illegible handwriting, but it can be <u>primarily</u> about:

- a motor problem i.e. about the mechanics of forming letters, moving the arm and hand and sustained physical application to the task of writing.

    OR

- a visual-spatial problem of using space on the paper to create legible letters involving the spacing, size and shape of them. The child does not notice omitted or substituted letters.

If a child in your class appears to have the above problems at a moderate to severe level and his parents are keen and able to assist, then I recommend that an Occupational Therapist's assessment be obtained privately.

It can also be a reading-related problem involving spelling and the development of orthographic skills:

- the patterns of letters we use in English e.g. *st* but not *sf*; our words do not end in *v, j or u*.
- knowing which alternate spelling to use eg /ae/ can be spelled *ay, ai, a–e, a, ea*
- the rules of English spelling e.g. adding prefixes and suffixes to particular root words.

Teach brainstorming and planning skills for writing

The 2e child with dysgraphia who has many complex ideas, is impeded by the recording of them. Regardless of the text type being prepared it is essential that those ideas are recorded simply, messily if need be, but clearly enough for later retrieval using the following steps below. Despite the childish nature of the pro forma (below), I use it with all ages of students with some amusement.

"WRITING IS THE PAINTING OF THE VOICE!"

VOLTAIRE

When you are writing texts …

- *BRAINSTORM*

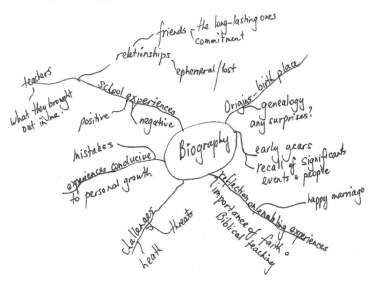

FIGURE 5.1 Brainstorm.

- *NUMBER THE ORDER* to 'sequence' your ideas in red pen

  1
  2
  3

- *WRITE YOUR DRAFT*: one idea to a paragraph
- *EDIT*

  Does each sentence say what I want it to say?

  Are there more examples/description I can include to make the idea clearer?

  Is my language too informal for the purpose?

- *PROOFREAD*

  Check for:
  - Verb–noun agreement
  - Sentence structure
  - Variety of sentence length and beginnings
  - Spelling
  - Is there a better verb?
  - Can I use one word for a phrase?

NOW, Read Aloud every word and follow with your finger to see that it is correct!

Rhonda Filmer Twice Exceptional Educational Consultancy 2019

- The Brainstorm stage has to be taught.
- An initial brainstorm map will characteristically contain a minimum of ideas if a creative or narrative text is being prepared.
- I simply wait … and wait … and encourage and question, until the brainstorm sheet is filled with ideas.

For a child with dysgraphia the writing of a text overloads her cognitive processes and can bring back memories of past attempts that were less than successful. Putting new processes in place allows for a 'fresh start' with a new approach. Remember that time taken to teach, encourage and succeed at each point in the process below is an investment in the child's future. The writing of texts has become the single most important skill for school success at the upper stages of secondary education. For those who are particularly impaired, the use of word processing has revolutionised their text writing but, in NSW, we still have handwritten final exams for the Higher School Certificate and very few students are granted the use of a computer, though scribes are used for those who can prove their need of one.

It is not possible for students to avoid writing. Not only is it an educational skill but it is also required as a life skill: applying for jobs, filling out bank and tax forms and surveys, writing notes and emails. Fortunately, handwriting for adults has been largely replaced by spell and grammar check aided word processing and voice-to-text software.

Modify a writing task in the following ways

- give advanced notice of the topic so a brainstorm can be completed at home
- make the completion of a detailed brainstorm the only requirement in the 'new skills' phase
- break the task into 4 or 5 pieces and complete one each day over a week
- make the 'messy brainstorm maps' a part of a collection with pride at their ever-increasing complexity and capacity to map thought
- use other graphic organisers for the 'sequencing' or planning stage after the original brainstorm map has been completed (see www.educationoasis.com)
- set an assignment to be the presentation of a researched project using multimedia

- grade the idea generation and general logic of a written piece as a separate, highly valued category

- grade the four categories of spelling, grammar, creativity of the story and vocabulary used with 25% for each part thus giving the dysgraphic student a chance to excel in his areas of strength (McBride, 2019, p. 63)

- avoid asking the child to copy from a whiteboard or presentation. It is laborious and frustrating and does not result in learning. Prepared notes can be given to an older child or an agreement with a 'buddy' might result in the sharing of notes by photocopying or taking a screenshot.

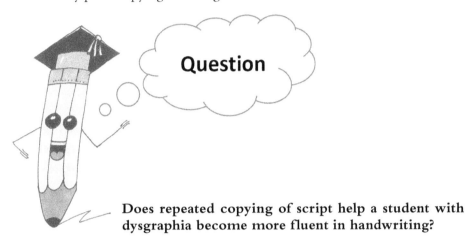

Question

Does repeated copying of script help a student with dysgraphia become more fluent in handwriting?

Children in every culture are taught to write by copying script. As with every skill in life, more practice approximates higher skill acquisition so it would be reasonable to assume that teaching a defined way to form letters e.g. for the letter b 'the bat before the ball' (l + o = b) enables a child to utilise muscle memory with greater control of the formed letters and, over time, control of the pencil. Logically, such rehearsal must assist students and especially those who, because of their weaknesses, need more practice. As for the child with dysgraphia the early learning of skills toward automatisation or mastery has enormous benefits.

Yet, schools have been burdened by overcrowded curricula and a pervasive culture of not requiring children to do repetitive tasks. To spend half an hour a day working hard on handwriting 'flies in the face' of our cultural context somewhat, yet we have no problem with this approach in sporting or music tuition contexts. Writing lessons can be a brief but quiet reprieve from high energy activity in classrooms and all children can make progress, particularly if the tasks are suitably modified where required. But, where there is a child in the class with dysgraphia, it must be a time of reaching for his 'personal best' and not a time when he is open to criticism or derision by his classmates. Another advantage of intensive practice in the K–2 years is that younger children are able to encourage and support each other as they all learn, from the beginning, together.

With Dehaene's research we can have no doubts about the importance of handwriting in the early stages of literacy acquisition and much more so for the child with dysgraphia (see in the Going Deeper section below).

Often, teachers ask students to complete a text writing task to its end in one sitting. This is impossible for a student with dysgraphia and would be particularly difficult if he has ADHD as well. An opportunity to look at the text again the next day will allow for better correction of errors in the editing and proofreading stages. This is true for all students but so much more for the child with dysgraphia.

Taking a long-term view, it is important that while you have the child in your care for that one calendar year that he learns new skills in order to BUILD his sense of control over the writing process and his confidence in his capacity to carry out written tasks that actually represent his intellectual ability.

For Dyscalculia

Numeracy screening tests

- Dr Nadia Nosworthy and Dr Daniel Ansari of Brain and Mind Institute at Western University, USA, have developed a numeracy screener available free at www.numeracyscreeener.org . Short tests for each year, K–3, can be printed, administered and the scores submitted for norming (Canadian norms). Performance on the Numeracy Screener can explain individual differences in children's arithmetic skills.
- Butterworth (2003) developed a Dyscalculia Screener but it is not free.

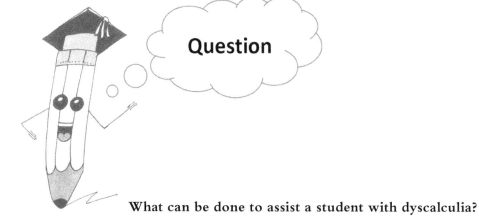

What can be done to assist a student with dyscalculia?

Students who demonstrate the symptoms of dyscalculia need:

- to master the number facts. It is worth pursuing this goal as every fact learned is a support structure for the 'big picture' and development of essential concepts. ABC Number Blocks (ABC for Kids) is a wonderful animated programme featuring number patterns and music
- to use graph paper to keep handwritten examples in columns
- to use pencil for mathematics so it can be rubbed out
- their knowledge 'gaps' identified. I draw *My Wall of Maths* on a whiteboard and explain to the child that bricks missing from the lowest level will cause the rows above to 'collapse' (see Figure 5.2).

- Some children know they missed earlier work and love the opportunity to have it explained to them explicitly and systematically.

FIGURE 5.2 My Wall of Maths

- to have access to concrete materials/manipulatives as needed:
  - a ruler, to be used as a portable number line
  - a bag of counters
  - dice, all sizes and shapes, particularly 12-sided, are invaluable when learning number facts. Two dice randomly thrown create a 'hands-on' activity for addition and multiplication fact learning
  - maths games using flash cards, puzzles, quizzes and board games
  - NB Dienes' Base 10 materials were designed to show how place value works and can be further used by the slow progress child until he can visualise large numbers without the blocks being present
  - Cuisenaire rods can assist with the connections between multiplication and division eg 3 x 4 = 12 from which 12 ÷3 = 4 and 12÷4 = 3 can be discovered. They are excellent for teaching fractions and the essential understanding that ¾ means '3 of the 4 parts', that is, a regular shape is cut into 4 parts and we have 3 of them.
  - plastic rings and counters to use as 'set notation' to represent the pushing together of sets as addition etc. (see Figure 5.3).

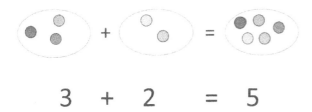

FIGURE 5.3 Use of counters to represent numbers and the physical action of addition.

- digital clocks. Analog clocks can be problematic to 'read'. We have almost come to the time in history where a child can manage without reading an analogue clock!

- short, sharp lessons on one concept →memorisation techniques including 'silly statements' … Be creative! Use dialogue to instruct with a story to aid working memory and engage with humour appropriate for that student, for example:

FIGURE 5.4 Sample dialogue and action to aid memory for algorithm processes.

Sample dialogue:

3 take away 9 -> can't do
Hey Mr Tens gimme one of yours!
Cross out the 6 and make it 5
13 take away 9 is 4
Write down 4
5 take away 2 is 3
The answer is 34.

- very specific goals for each lesson with multi-sensory elements in each one including verbalising aloud the sequence of steps when doing an algorithm type.
  - a minimum of examples to complete, but sufficient in quantity to enable learning
  - the use of a calculator to aid the successful completion of an example type.
- appropriate use of apps for practice e.g. Prodigy, Khan Academy for Kids
- an attitude from teachers that he can learn the work, with support, enabling the child to believe in himself. Openly acknowledge the SLD with the child along with the potential that he may worry about it. Realistic expectations

of success accompanied by opportunities to demonstrate high level reasoning, where applicable, are important

■ daily sessions are optimal; three sessions a week is minimal

■ negotiated amount of homework; (little or none in primary school other than learning maths facts!)

Going deeper

Multi-sensory structured language teaching

The IDA advocates the use of visual, auditory and kinaesthetic-tactile pathways in learning to read and spell. This is so much fun for K–2 children and will benefit everyone, not just the children who are at risk of SLDs.

VIGNETTE

I recall my own year in kindergarten, learning the initial code of single letter-sounds. Low blackboards were mounted around the classroom at child height. Every child would draw a new letter in a huge size as we made the sound. Then we would draw it in the air, then with a finger on another child's back and we would dance using coloured scarves while saying the sound and making the shape of the letter-sound in the air.

Letter–sound correspondence was built into the structured play activities of our happy, active days.

I am old enough to have been taught by phonological methods prior to the supremacy of the 'whole language' movement, a philosophy of teaching reading involving the use of the whole word to be learned without breaking it down into its component parts. Teaching by 'whole language' was a very costly experiment which was initiated in the 1980's in NSW and persists to this day in some of our schools.

As a result of many years of advocacy from academics and community organisations, NSW now has an English K–2 Syllabus, mandated for 2023, which has the science of reading at its base and includes teaching advice.

Research validates that reading is based on the alphabetic principle, the understanding that spoken words are made up of sounds that can be recognised in print. We have the important work of Stanislas Dehaene (2019) that has shown us how this works in the human brain. With highly sophisticated MRI machines it is possible to map the brains of children. Their brain circuits of speech light up (even in children as young as two months of age) showing that speech is normally effortlessly learned when a child lives in a verbal household and that speech is the essential first step in the development of literacy.

Speech Development

Phonology, hearing words spoken, leads to the development of a

↓

Lexicon, which is an understanding of language as a system including its formal rules, structures and limitations, leads to the development of

↓

Syntax, which is a set of rules that govern how words are combined to form phrases and sentences, leads to the development of

↓

Semantics, which is concentration on the meaning of language.

Dehaene (2019)

The general understanding we have of speech development has been validated in science and it is interesting to note that *Reading Development* fits into the same brain system.

At pre-school, these circuits are already in place and a new interface into these circuits comes from the stimulus of written language.

Seeing words written (Vision) leads to → the recognition of Letter strings leads to → Phonology – the sounds that make up the words linking back into the speech circuit!

Application of Neuroscience to Teaching (Dehaene, 2019) adds evidence for 'the science of reading':

1. We must capitalise on children's pre-existing phonological and linguistic abilities. They come to school with varying levels of speech development. Classrooms need to be verbal places where topics are discussed in a targeted fashion.

2. Focus on the grapheme-phoneme correspondence.

3. Children effortfully analyse words, converting each grapheme into a phoneme, then they listen and understand.

4. Reading must be explicitly taught because it is difficult. The 'space' of the visual word is converted into the 'time' of the spoken word.

5. Reading becomes increasingly automatised year after year, all the time developing a more direct unconscious route. Teachers must focus on this initial route as the direct route develops spontaneously with experience.

   Author note: Reading is not 'global' or 'whole word' until a child reaches a high level of competency. When the school system threw out phonics as the primary methodology for young readers in the 1980's, it was because of the misconception that the human brain reads whole words. Competent older readers do read the whole word once experience has taught them to automatically recognise it, but young readers cannot learn this way. We are sure of that now.

The fundamental mistake was to extrapolate the observed reading behaviour of adults to the classroom, as a model for teaching young children. Teaching by the 'whole word' is inefficient, with no opportunity for automaticity, as every word is a new word. Taught that way, the child does not learn a code for reading.

6. Language comprehension is taught first orally, then in writing.

7. Many variables are required to learn to read:
   - Attention.
   - Automatization. This is crucial as it liberates the brain to attend to meaning.
   - Decoding. This becomes automatic, rapid and unconscious in the second and third year.
   - The ability to learn longer words – this is dome more quickly as experience with texts increases.

8. Writing: Our brains comprise a specialized circuit for recognising writing gestures. Learning to read improves when children are simultaneously taught how to write and to explore the characters by touch – this leads to memorisation.

   We should continue to teach handwriting to young children in K–2. We can teach touch-typing later on, once writing is established.

Acquiring strong literacy

For a comprehensive article on the science of acquiring excellent literacy, read Castles, Rastle and Nation (2018). There was once a rather silly debate on the relative importance of phonics and 'whole language', but the jury is now in. The Rowe Report (2005) commissioned for the Australian Minister for Education, Brendan Nelson, acknowledged current research studies when it stated that, 'all students learn best when teachers adopt an integrated approach to reading that explicitly teaches phonemic awareness, phonics, fluency, vocabulary knowledge and comprehension' (p. 11) but there was no action to follow this up in mandated curricula.

Teaching phonological awareness as the foundation of reading along with sound-letter (phoneme-grapheme) correspondence will assist all children to reach their potential and provide a strong foundation of instruction for those with a predisposition for reading difficulties and SLDs.

Phonics must form the basis of all reading and writing acquisition in beginning learners and we know how to build upon that foundation with excellent, research-evidenced practice for children to become expert readers. I want all teachers in NSW to be fully taught and supported in the use of these methods for their professional satisfaction and for the benefit of all our children.

It is patently clear from science that by ensuring that all students have access to a quality education and are as literate as we can make them then employment, productivity, mental health, self-esteem and well-being are all positively impacted. Our students with learning difficulties and disabilities need maximum resourcing at the K–2 level, not later in their schooling where they risk never gaining maximal competency.

According to data from the International Assessment of Adult Competencies reported on the Australian Bureau of Statistics (ABS) website, *44% of Australian adults lack the literacy skills required to cope with the complex demands of modern life.* They are, in fact, functionally illiterate for many of the reading and writing tasks required to maintain ordinary life. Most people would suggest this cannot be true, but it is. The ABS found that illiteracy was masked among people who are not in the workforce or who hold down jobs that do not require high levels of literacy. In order to work and maintain life, these people have had to choose jobs where their inability to read is not constantly exposed to scrutiny. The causes of reading dysfunction are varied, as mentioned earlier, but some would have undiagnosed and untreated SLDs. Some would be gifted in one or more domains.

Our approach to education in NSW does not do enough to assist not only native English speakers but also the vast range of non-English speakers to gain high levels of competence in English literacy. Our staffing levels should be equitable in schools based on literacy needs, not rigidly on numbers of children, as staffing allocation policy.

At the time of writing, I am Board Chair of the Specific Learning Difficulties Association of NSW (SPELD NSW), an honorary role with this not-for-profit, charitable organization, that has as its mission offering support, assistance and advice to children and adults with specific learning difficulties, their families, tutors, teachers and schools.

On the website www.speldnsw.org.au you will read:

SPELD NSW's vision 'is that individuals in New South Wales with specific learning difficulties will have every opportunity to achieve their full potential in life'.

Full potential will be achieved when individuals with specific learning difficulties receive:

■ *'early identification and intervention* during the critical early years of education
■ *instruction with evidence-based methods* in key literacy and numeracy skills
■ *specialist teaching* and appropriate adjustments during their school years
■ *support and adjustments* in further education and the workplace'

See SPELD NSW website www.speldnsw.org.au 'About Us'.

Identification of students with SLD

Siegel (2012) calls the current reliance on IQ tests for the diagnosis of SLD 'a circus'. It has become 'unnecessarily complicated and bureaucratic' involving a great deal of waiting for the school counsellor to have time to see each underachieving child. Inevitably, scarce resources only go to the children who are the lowest achievers, leaving the 2e child with dyslexia without remediation until after that optimal K–2 period. Waiting for the school counsellor to test using a WISC 5 and a WIAT 3 may involve a wait of two years.

Since the DSM-5-TR definition requires that the child is given instruction with an evidence-based reading scheme for six months, why not start the instruction as soon as the reading problem is detected? Why wait for the child to fall further behind? The recommended remediation is the same, whatever the eventual diagnostic decision. IQ is an unnecessary and distracting component of the ways in which we think about learning disability according to Lyon and Fletcher (2001).

Another problem with the identification of bright children with SLDs is that, typically, 2e children cannot meet the outdated but still commonly used, Ability-Achievement Discrepancy Criterion, for a diagnosis of SLD because of the complexity of the child's profile and achievement. Depending on the child's 'profile' of underlying weaknesses, a gifted child may not be able to demonstrate intellectual giftedness and will be deemed at an Average level along with the performance on reading, therefore, despite quite debilitating weaknesses in phonological processing, a child may not qualify for support services because the 'discrepancy' has been measured as not significant.

I will explain …

Often in my practice I was presented with a school psychologist's report which concluded there was 'no evidence' of an SLD because the child's IQ was not significantly higher than the scores on the achievement tests. Every level assessed on IQ and achievement was 'Average', a category that encompasses a very wide band of scores. In every case, after working with the child on a targeted programme, I found that the child was anything but Average. The typical 'saw-tooth' range of results had been averaged to a mean by the scoring procedures. I would find areas of academic or creative thinking that were exceptional and evidence of a learning difficulty/disability in the child's performance on reading or writing activities, often accompanied by no records of intervention.

I would recommend that you do not take such psychometric reports on face value. If you are reading this book, you have a deep interest in being a highly knowledgeable teacher aware of individual differences in your students. Observe the child and consider the child's thinking as it is expressed orally. Especially in primary and K–2 classes you have opportunities to explore a child's profile through his responses in multiple settings and lesson types. If there is a big difference between the complexity of his thinking and what is expressed in written form that is enough to assume there is, at least, a learning difficulty or disability and/or perhaps an attention disorder (ADHD). Surprisingly, they are not always noticed by qualified psychologists.

Figure 5.5 shows the pattern of WIAT 3 results in a child who is underachieving at school. The acronyms on the horizontal axis refer to the subtests and the vertical axis shows the Standard Scores. This child gained high results in Reading Comprehension yet lacks precision in phonic decoding indicating poor underlying skills in phonemic awareness and in phoneme-grapheme correspondence. She is an avid reader, but she prefers audio books because her lack of oral reading fluency (ORF) is frustrating her. This is a typical pattern for a child with SLD dyslexia and possibly dysgraphia. As noted previously, a diagnosis cannot be given until the child has been taught by research-evidenced methods in a programme lasting at least six months. Her school was not using phonic methodology so her word reading (WR), pseudoword decoding (PD) and spelling (SP) were below average. Note that the mathematics scores are low also but her school programme had not taught her to be fluent with number facts as indicated in Maths Fluency Addition (MFA), Maths

Fluency Subtraction (MFS) and Maths Fluency Multiplication (MFM). Yet, she was gaining average scores on Number Operations/algorithms (NO). Immediate remediation is required for this child across all subjects and revision within six months to seek a possible diagnosis of SLD. Her oral language, vocabulary and love of words and stories is strong. This is probably the profile of a 2e child.

It is rare in NSW that a young gifted or very bright student with dyslexia will receive individualised attention for learning skill weaknesses because the oral precocity and comprehension ability of the gifted student will mask the reading difficulties which will not be identified until later in their schooling, leaving the possibility of appropriate early intervention unlikely.

It must be understood that gifted children are very clever – definitionally! They can predict, assume, surmise, envisage or logically deduce responses to questions and they often have high levels of spoken vocabulary. They can score in the top percentiles in reading comprehension while masking very weak and unstable phoneme-grapheme correspondence. Dyslexic people are contextual readers in that, once they catch the theme of a passage of text from the first paragraph, they will go into full flight of deduction to read and interpret it. There are some educators who consider precision of reading as unimportant, but every experienced primary teacher knows the importance of effortless reading if a child is to continue to grow and thrive to a high level of competence in the English language. So much theory

A 'Saw–Tooth' Achievement Profile of a child with SLD

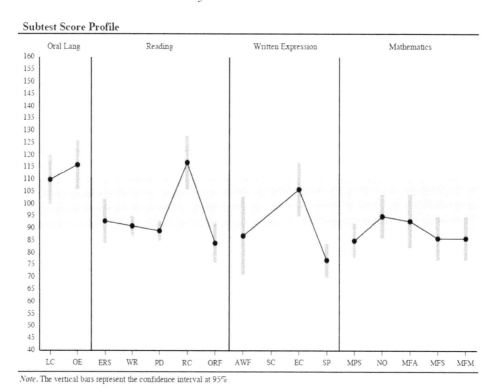

Subtest Score Profile

Note. The vertical bars represent the confidence interval at 95%

FIGURE 5.5 Example of WIAT 3 scores from a student report showing the 'saw-tooth' profile of learning strengths and weaknesses.

and research support the need to be a competent, mechanical reader who can break down new words into their component parts in order to correctly say them and interpret their meaning. Reading is the use of a code. Decoding incompetence, even in the brightest most creative person, is an impediment. A student may thrive during the early grades by compensation but once texts become more demanding in complexity, length and syntax, a child's capacity to cope will be stretched and the possibility of failure becomes more likely.

I have seen gifted students perform well up to Year 7 in secondary school only to find that the increased workload and the student's own high expectations have uncovered an SLD. The student has been able to compensate for it, performing at least an average level, until there was too much to do in the time available. Fatigue can be an indicator of masked problems in students with undiagnosed SLDs.

Recent research findings and potential future directions

… for teaching children with dyscalculia

Many studies have reported that maths difficulties may co-occur with ADHD, autism and speech and communication difficulties. Morsanyi et al. (2018) found that children with SLD in mathematics were 16 times more likely to have a diagnosis of another developmental condition than children without the diagnosis. They found that this group is heterogenous, showing a wide range of particular weaknesses in mathematics and that gender made no difference with prevalence rates, at around 6% of boys and girls in a large sample. Soares and Patel (2015) state there is no single presentation of dyscalculia, that symptoms may be manifest at any age and are often mediated by the degree and nature of instruction and presence of comorbid learning and other developmental–behavioural conditions. If a child has had strong, effective teaching in the K–2 years then dyscalculia may be masked for a time until the curriculum overtaxes the child's capacity.

A search on a university library database brought up 11,362 references for dyscalculia but 119, 964 for dyslexia. It has received much less attention than the other SLDs.

Of all the SLDs, this one is the hardest to discern between a difficulty where a child is an 'instructional casualty' and a disability, a deeply rooted neurobiological issue. Schools can have entrenched practices of too little time allocation or insufficient attention to strong, consistent, explicit instruction in mathematics so that some pupils leave primary school having never 'mastered' any topic. There was a trend in primary schools to spend two weeks on a mathematics topic, to test and move on to the next topic. Sometimes, a topic may not be revisited for a whole term in which time students' recall of it had diminished. Any child with an inherent difficulty in mathematics may find that no knowledge has been retained.

Chinn (2015) summarises several points about dyscalculia from the chapters of his book in the Overview:

1. The field is in its infancy.

2. About 20% of adults are functionally innumerate.

3. Students who have dyscalculia are a heterogeneous group.

4. Several researchers (Gowramma and Ho, Wong & Chan) point to the idea that a poor understanding of place value can be a cause of computational errors.

5. McGrath (p. 370) advocates the use of storytelling with props and mathematical content with young children, to enhance the language of mathematics and encourage metacognition, visualisation and engagement with creativity.

6. Weak working memory is often a problem so adjustment of lesson formats to accommodate this will be helpful for students. This would assume the use of visual prompts in the classroom.

7. The importance of metacognition cannot be underestimated. 'What do I need to think about?' Students with LDs need strategies for retrieval of information and application.

8. Donlan (p. 12) emphasises that the concepts of 'more' and 'less' can be predictors of success with basic calculations along with the role of words such as 'all, few and some' in developing mathematical understanding. Questions such as 'Will the answer be bigger or smaller?' can encourage prediction and appraisal of answers.

9. Students with difficulties in spatial organisation or a poor understanding of place value will have problems learning division and fractions.

10. Students expect that Algebra will be difficult because of its reputation so it can be a source of concern even before it is taught.

11. Harskamp in Chapter 29, found that 'IT effects are stronger for students with low mathematics ability.... .probably due to IT providing well-structured programmes with individual learning pathways and scaffolded intervention' (p. 16).

Sharma (in Chinn, 2015, Chap 20) points out that in early literacy phonemic awareness is the basic skill while in numeracy it is 'numbersense and numberness'. To read, a child must focus on phonemes, while in maths she must visualise small clusters of objects and their integration into larger clusters. Failure to progress with groups of objects leads to habitual one-to-one counting which is an essential conceptualisation of one-to-one correspondence but, in order to progress, the child needs to learn *arithmetic facts at an automatised level. Visual perceptual integration* and estimation by observation 'is essential to the development of numberness' (p. 309).

Desoete (in Chinn, 2015, Chap 5) concluded from cited research that the chief predictors of dyscalculia in kindergarten were *seriation* (arranging objects in order by size, location or position) and *classification*, as logical thinking skills, and conceptual counting knowledge. She demonstrated the importance of a child's use of language in kindergarten as a predictor for success in mathematics. Number representation abilities in kindergarten could add to the prediction of dyscalculia and serve as powerful early screeners in the detection of children at risk (Stock & Desoete, 2009 cited in Chinn, 2015). Tasks such as being asked to represent 25 on a 0–100 number line, to estimate the number of dots in a pattern or to estimate the number of squares (in a black-and-white pattern) on a screen were all found to have a significant relationship with mathematical abilities in kindergarten. The working memory was limited in most children found to have dyscalculia. Interestingly, it was reported that 87.50% of children at risk for dyscalculia could be detected in kindergarten. Bugden & Ansari (in Chinn, 2015, p.32) concluded from a literature review of the field that the causal factors for dyscalculia are unknown and it is impossible to describe the condition in generalities. They found that children with dyscalculia often have *working memory impairments.*

There appears to be consensus on the idea that adjusting lessons for weak working memory is effective; visual aids with procedural prompts for sequence displayed on the classroom walls and/or short videos 'at call' on the class interactive whiteboard may be effective for individual students along with lesson requirements that do not overtax working memory.

Ho, Wong and Chan (in Chinn, 2015, Chap 12) commented on the learning of mathematics and the difficulties that children experience in Hong Kong. Some interesting general contrasts between the teaching of mathematics in western and Asian cultures were drawn. They emphasise the amount of effort that teachers and parents put into the learning of mathematics as it is considered a very important academic skill area. Children in Hong Kong start formal education in mathematics from the age of three with a majority of kindergartens teaching two-digit addition in kindergarten, some teaching it with the carrying of tens. The Chinese culture puts great emphasis not only on early numeracy but on the language to be used in the Chinese number system.

(*Author note*: I suggest that this amount of time devoted to formal and informal mathematics in a young child's life may be in stark contrast to that in western cultures and would account in part for the general differences between the mathematical achievement of children in western and Asian cultures. This comment is anecdotal only.)

Ho, Wong and Chan (in Chinn, 2015, p.196) explain that two factors have been shown to be essential to mathematical understanding: number sense and place value. Chan and Ho (2010) tested elementary school children on elements of number sense involving comparison of number magnitudes, number sequencing, estimation and number sense application in practical situations. The scores on these tests correlated highly with their scores on a standardised mathematics achievement test (r=.50). They found that the other absolutely essential skill to the learning of mathematics is place-value, particularly because of our Hindu-Arabic number system which uses base ten. Of course, the value of a numeral is dictated by its place in a number (its 'power of ten'). It appears that children evolve developmentally in their understanding of place-value and that it underlies mathematical achievement.

(*Author note*: It could be concluded that children may reach an understanding of place-value at very different times within a cohort so that opportunity to revisit it and to answer questions may need to occur periodically throughout a school year and even in subsequent years.)

Through the findings of many cited studies they concluded that persistent low performance in number sense and place-value are indicators of specific learning disability in mathematics (dyscalculia).

Multiple components make up arithmetic ability so that 'no one size fits all' for intervention strategies and that (targeted) remediation strategies can be highly effective (Dowker & Morris in Chinn, 2015, p. 9). Landerl (in Chinn, 2015, Chap 7) states that when preparing intervention, 'the profile of risk and protective factors of the individual child' should be taken into account (p.121).

Judy Hornigold (in Chinn, 2015, Chapter 23) uses the case study of Frederick Bird Primary School in Coventry, UK, where 88% of children in the school progressed two levels to above national targets in mathematics through the introduction of an innovative programme. It was a school with 'challenging demographics'. The school collaboratively drew upon many elements that were known to work, from research into mathematics teaching and from general education sources. In effect, they designed the programme that their school needed after examining their school assessment data. (Time taken to apply for an innovative grant would ensure that staff had the time for this purpose.)

Key points in this innovative programme for all students were:

■ Staff were trained in metacognition and problem solving using Bloom's taxonomy.

■ Constructive feedback was given to students verbally and in written form each lesson.

■ Children were taught to talk about thinking and to be aware of their own strengths in problem solving. This approach, which de-emphasises 'getting everything right', draws the child with dyscalculia into the collaborative problem-solving class efforts. The child's capacity to reason means he can see his value within his contribution to the class team.

■ Children are encouraged to teach what they know to others as a way of con-solidating their understanding.

■ Flexible planning occurred daily (in contrast to the term's maths work being pre-programmed and inflexible at the start of term; a school trend that I have never viewed as wise).

■ Mathematical processes were taught with direct instruction, but the emphasis was then organic, moving away from maths schemes and worksheets into group problem solving, to build motivation and enjoyment in mathematics within the school. Children became comfortable with learning from their mistakes rather than being pressured to come up with 'The Right Answer' as the only criterion for success.

The website www.dyscalculia.org/home contains resources to assist with screening, remediation and intervention. This is a not-for-profit group in the USA with the support of an international group of mathematics researchers including Steven Chinn, Daniel Ansari and Stanislas Dehaene.

Use of computer technology programs with low achieving students

In a mega-analysis of 16 studies (involving 2,599 students and 34 schools) seeking the effects of mathematics computer programs in primary schools, Harskamp (in Chinn, 2015) found a medium positive effect for computer tutorials as a teaching programme (Effect Size 0.48) and that students with low mathematical ability gained especially when compared to whole-class teaching. This was true for programs that are of a tutorial type rather than exploratory in their goals and for programs in Number Sense, Number Operations, Geometry/Measurement and Word Problems. Slavin and Lake (2008, p. 391) found that computer programs were effective if used regularly, for more than 30 minutes during a longer maths period and if they were integrated into the classroom instruction.

Australian tutorial programs are:

- Maths Online www.mathsonline.com.au (K–12)
  Students can call up visual presentations to explain concepts, on demand.
- Mathletics www.mathletics.com
  NSW curriculum Stages 1–5 (Years 1 to 10).
- Maths Pathway www.mathspathway.com (K–12)
  The Early Insights Assessment Tool looks very interesting and is worth investigating.

Online resources that may be of assistance are:

- Number Sense http://number-sense.co.uk
  Provides two systematic and structured programs giving teachers resources for daily lessons in number sense in the early years. Involves staff development and clear guidance for use.
- The Number Catcher www.thenumbercatcher.com
  Computer games that teach basic concepts of number and arithmetic.
- Oxford Owl on Youtube: www.oxfordowl.co.uk contains short videos that explain elements of mathematical understanding.
- Khan Academy for Kids App–for very young children to gain a sense of number through play.

A course suggestion:

> A course run by Jillian Zocher and Liz Dunoon is offered through Get into Neurodiversity www.getintodiversity.com . 'Teaching Strategies to Overcome Maths Learning Difficulties & Dyscalculia: Identification, Diagnosis and Intervention' by Prof Steve Chinn offers 9.5 hours of online learning. Details of its content can be found on their website.

Lu, Ma, Chen & Zhou (2021) suggest that students who did an *abacus course* demonstrated better performance in arithmetic computation and spatial short-term memory. This is a whole new way of approaching a child's number sense. Anecdotally, I believe there is distinct possibility in this approach because it is linear, multi-sensory and it assists with visualisation using a computational aid. In addition, groups of beads may be coloured as an aid to subitising (estimating the number in a group).

As with all SLDs, start intensive remediation as soon as a child's progress is noted as below expectations and do not wait for a diagnosis. There is no one way to do Tier 2 interventions for dyscalculia. Ashlock (in Chinn, 2015, p. 234) suggests doing 'error analysis' to find out why a student learned a concept or procedure erroneously and the errors will reveal how that particular student with dyscalculia is thinking about mathematics. Tier 2 interventions are more intensive, mastery focused periods of instruction in small groups.

Currently, there is a need for much more research in this area.

Summarising

Managing the Child with Dyscalculia in the Classroom

TABLE 5.1   A summary of intervention responses to use with a child with dyscalculia

Observed Problem/Issue	Response
Repeated failure at gaining arithmetic concepts	Use a screening test Do not wait for a diagnosis or full clarity–start remediation immediately!
	Adjust the child's programme.
	Consider WM and EF deficits by giving visual displays to show the sequence of activity where possible. Even stick-figures on a whiteboard would help.
	Differentiate using available resources utilising: ■ the time of available learning support teachers ■ Tier 2 small group setting ■ appropriate apps ■ computer programs such as Mathletics ■ peer buddies (occasionally, in K–2) ■ games, 'repeated silly statements' and multi-sensory materials.

Note on using a Response to Intervention (RtI) approach

'With RtI, schools use data to identify students at risk for poor learning outcomes, monitor student progress, provide evidence-based interventions, adjust the intensity and nature of those interventions depending on a student's responsiveness, and identify students with learning disabilities or other disabilities' (National Center on Response to Intervention, 2010, p. 2 cited in Hempenstall, 2012, p. 4). RtI began in the US in the early 2000s. It assumes that all students can learn and that the quality of their instruction will be high and evidence-based, both at the classroom level and at the intervention levels for those students who do not attain expected goals.

In principle, the use of the RtI approach means that all students will receive excellent literacy instruction at the whole class, Tier 1 level, and approximately 80% of students will have acquired strong early reading and writing skills within the grade-level classes.

Students who are not in the 80% will be given small group instruction that modifies the teaching of reading for pace, intensity and/or duration. Research has found that 15% of the year cohort tend to respond to Tier 2 instruction in this small group, explicit instruction setting.

For the 5% of students who do not respond adequately, then an individualised, 1:1 staff to student ratio setting is required. NSW public schools do not routinely allocate this level of resourcing and there is little in the research to indicate exactly how to teach students at this level. A student might receive intensive reading support from a learning assistant four times per week with close monitoring of her progress. Despite decades of research on special education and remedial instruction there are still major gaps in knowledge on how to teach these students. Sometimes there are undiagnosed perceptual or cognitive process weaknesses or students need a perceptive professional to design a programme that will address their needs in a highly targeted way.

A wonderful group called *read3* has developed a Tier 3 programme https:// read3.com.au/pages/read3-in-schools. On their website you can download a free *Check How I Process Screener* (CHIPS) which will probe how to help readers who are struggling at this stage. It screens for four cognitive processing skills that can predict a child's ability to learn to read:

- Phonological Awareness (PA)
- Letter-Sound Knowledge (LSK)
- Phonological Working Memory (PM)
- Rapid Automatic Naming (RAN)

It has been found that children who 'fail to start' or 'fail to respond' are weak in these underlying areas. CHIPS is not normed but gives diagnostic information.

TABLE 5.2 Response to intervention – general conception

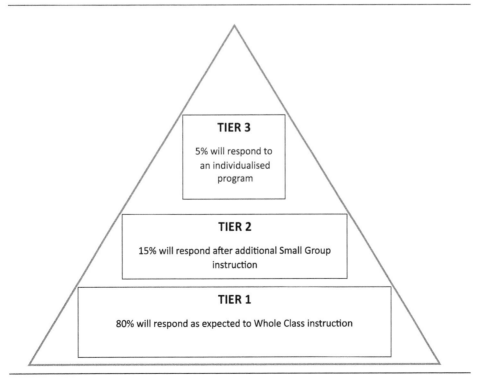

If the RtI approach was adopted it would mean that all students would be included simply based on their learning needs in the K–2 years. Madeleine and Wheldall (2019) in the Nomanis Notes claim that this approach 'makes very good conceptual sense' but, so far, we have few research studies that confirm its use, definitively.

Sarah Asome's webinar (2021) on reform at her school in Victoria is an interesting and affirming use of the RtI model and worth a viewing.

The Colorado Department of Education (CDE) has a definition that is inclusive of all students. It defines RtI as 'a framework that promotes a well-integrated system connecting general, compensatory, gifted, and special education in providing high quality, standards based instruction and intervention that is matched to students' academic, social-emotional, and behavioural needs' (CDE, 2008, p. 3).

Foley-Nicpon et al. (2013) in discussing the potential use of RtI methods for 2e students, warn that it is important to ascertain how the method would address student strengths as well as disability. Reisman & Severino (2020) emphasise the importance of mobilising students' creative strengths while teaching in a student's area of need. I have had enormous success through joke books, quizzes, games and puzzles with young students who are working with me on remediation for their learning difficulties. Short, sharp, highly targeted sessions of work with revision to mastery followed by card (or other) games can be a source of fun, growth in self-efficacy and creativity. For some 2e students a time of collaboration with a chosen peer can follow, to balance the setting and stimulate creative thought. It is all a matter of knowing the student's profile of interests and strengths and how to engage her in pleasurable and creative activity.

In my observation, RtI techniques are used more frequently in independent schools in NSW than in public schools and I suspect that is because staff are more likely to be offered training and there are staff to assist class teachers to manage, analyse and interpret data collected from classroom programmes and interventions. The tight allocation of staff in NSW public schools makes these data collection tasks and the follow-up, whole-school decisions, more difficult to achieve. But they are certainly achievable if there is a whole-school approach to training and implementation and if the important role of School Learning Support Officers (SLSO) is enacted fully. After 9–12 months of tertiary education and 100 hours of work placement in schools these staff members can be allocated to implement RtI programmes at Tier 2 or 3. Trained in the legislation and the science of literacy, behaviour and disabilities, they can be valuable assets as observational and operational support for class teachers. A skilled and knowledgeable SLSO role can make a huge difference by assisting a class teacher to identify additional needs, to deliver appropriate strategies to support students and can directly contribute to successful student outcomes both academic and social-emotional.

Case study of a 2e student with Specific Learning Disabilities (SLD)

Eleanor

When I met Eleanor in November of her Year 6, she was 12 years and 3 months old and had above-average oral language abilities, expressing herself fluently and proficiently using a rich vocabulary. Yet, she had not thrived particularly well at primary school and her parents were seeking a clear picture of what to do for her.

I tested Eleanor using the WIAT 3 and found she was very inefficient in her reading, making a variety of errors in her decoding and her spelling was below average. Yet, she could comprehend age-level text at the 66th percentile level of her age cohort. Her Essay Composition result was at the 79th percentile.

Eleanor is a natural writer with a well-developed, innate sense of storytelling and an understanding that demonstrated she had been taught about texts and their structures. She had a simple but effective style of characterisation. It was obvious that this was where her strengths lay. She professed a great love of horses, horse-riding and had a huge factual knowledge of everything to do with horses. Eleanor looked very much like a student of 'high intellectual potential' who was underachieving.

There was no specific history of dyslexia or attention disorders in the family but there was some history of 'later than expected' development in English, after some intervention. There were no records of specific details.

Looking at the chart below, Eleanor's *Word Reading* result was in the 9th percentile, meaning that she is better at reading a list of graded words than only 9% of her age cohort. This level is equivalent to that of an eight-year-old child. She faltered on multi-syllable words and made repeated errors on word endings.

In *Pseudoword Decoding* Eleanor gained a result in the 27th percentile at an age equivalent of 9 years, 8 months. The Pseudoword Decoding test checks for understanding of the sounds of English and their representations in letters. It is an excellent indicator of phonic decoding skills because the words have no meaning, ('pseudo-words') and the child cannot use the word's context to assist her to correctly read the words. Eleanor's knowledge of digraphs (letter combinations eg *ur, or, oa, aw*) was strong with simpler digraphs but she faltered on *dge, que, ion*. She used a strategy of guessing from the initial sounds in many words and she faltered when the words were multi-syllabic. Eleanor demonstrated a tendency to jumble the letters in words, eg she read *sany* for snay and *dory* for droy. I believed that Eleanor had not been taught how to decode phonically but that she could learn the skills, with targeted teaching, regardless of whether she had an SLD of dyslexia, or not.

Unsurprisingly, Eleanor 's *Oral Reading Fluency* was slow for her age, in the 13th percentile.

Interestingly, and despite her poor mechanical reading skills, Eleanor gained a result in the 66th percentile in *Reading Comprehension*. In the more difficult passages she told me she 'finds it easier to read it in my head' which may have been a way of avoiding reading aloud exposing many mistakes in pronunciation.

Eleanor's WIAT 3 results

Eleanor needed a clear understanding of the context of a passage and was then able to comprehend written text at a level far above her mechanical skills. But she would need to improve those skills in order to thrive in the secondary school environment where there would be fewer visual images and more complexity in texts. This was achievable if she was prepared to work and if given research-evidenced tuition.

TABLE 5.3 WIAT 3 initial testing at 12 years, 3 months and retest at 13 years, 10 months

SUBTEST	WIAT 3 TEST Chronological Age: 12 years, 3 months November in Year 6			WIAT 3 RETEST Chronological Age: 13 years, 10 months June in Year 8		
	Percentile Rank	Age Equivalent	Qualitative Description	Percentile Rank	Age Equivalent	Qualitative Description
Listening Comprehension	68	13:00	Average	Not retested		
Reading Comprehension	66	16:00	Average	Not retested		
Word Reading	9	8:00	**Low Average**	70	16:00	**Average**
Pseudoword Decoding	27	9:8	**Low Average**	47	12:4	**Average**
Spelling	18	9:4	Average	39	12:8	**Average**
Essay Composition	79	18:00	Average	Not retested		
Mathematics - Problem Solving	37	11:8	Average	Not retested		
Maths Fluency	13	9:00	**Low Average**	Not retested		

(See Table 5.5 for improvement in centile points and years.)

Her reading weakness had been masked by her ability to comprehend and possibly predict the outcomes of narratives. This particular capacity is prevalent amongst students who are at least above average in their intellectual ability and are underachieving because of an undetected learning difficulty.

Spelling is a relative weakness for Eleanor. Her result was in the 18th percentile. She gained credit for the first 22 words but then demonstrated that she did not understand quite basic rules and conventions of English spelling. This is directly related to her decoding weakness and I made the (correct) assumption that she had not been taught the necessary patterns and rules in a way that she could retain.

Eleanor gained a result in the 68th percentile in the Theme Development and Text Organisation mark but her Word Count of 153 words took the *Essay Composition* subtest rank to the 79th percentile. Her essay response was well expressed but she lost credit for not using the language of cause and effect overtly and for not setting out the Introduction and the Conclusion with clear structure. It is a creditable result. With consistent teaching through secondary school in how to plan and execute a written text, with far more detail in the initial plan, I believed that Eleanor could excel in all aspects of written expression.

Eleanor was at least an 'instructional casualty' and I needed to give her six months of research-evidenced reading instruction before I could determine if she had a Specific Learning Disability. Using the Sounds-Write programme, Eleanor applied herself fully and learned the entire 49 units of the programme during

TABLE 5.4 Semester 2 school report and teacher comments

Subjects	Overall Achievement
English	**Sound**
	Teacher comment suggests she has been fully engaged in complex texts but still needs work in inferential comprehension, spelling and advanced vocabulary. She was working on a programme called WordFlyers to address these skills.
	It was noted that 'she has difficulty responding to short answer and analysis questions.'
Science, Technology, Visual Arts	**High**
History, Music	**Outstanding**

her Year 7. She was remarkable in her application with rarely a spelling mistake in her weekly reviews. I took the approach with her that I do with most older students: attention to the 'recoding' process of the multiple ways to spell each of the 44 sounds of English is an aid to the correct reading of each sound.

Eleanor's tutoring programme with me for 1 hour per week throughout Year 7 prioritised the Sounds–Write program. But she also worked on Maths facts, decimals and division. Her secondary school placed her in a Learning Support programme for Mathematics called *Maths Pathway* where she made very good progress on an individualised programme. The biggest weakness I could see in that programme was insufficient support teachers to answer the students' questions without time loss. Eleanor brought questions to my tutoring sessions after school where they were answered and instruction given.

Eleanor's progress was remarkable over one year demonstrating the 'saw tooth' pattern of achievement of the 2e child especially considering that she was already 12 years of age when targeted intervention began.

Throughout her report it was noted by her teachers that Eleanor's work ethic was mature and consistent, her personal organisational skills very strong and that her work demonstrated high levels of creativity.

Once she was in Year 8, I briefly retested her using the following subtests of the WIAT 3 as shown in Table 5.5, in June, 2019, and found the following *improvement* after 19 months.

TABLE 5.5 Eleanor's improvement in centile points and years after 19 months of instruction

Word Reading	61 centile points	8 years
Pseudoword Decoding	20 centile points	2:8 years
Spelling	21 centile points	3:4 years

In July 2019, Eleanor received a diagnosis from an educational psychologist of Specific Learning Disorder with impairment in reading (reading rate and fluency) and with impairment in mathematics (number sense, memorisation or arithmetic facts, accurate or fluent calculation) as indicated by her persistent relative weakness with decoding, some aspects of reading comprehension, and in processing numerical information. Her SLD conditions of dyslexia and dyscalculia were considered to be of mild severity, meaning that she can maintain a high level of academic achievement in a supported learning environment.

Eleanor's parents were concerned about her organisation and concentration but, interestingly, when the Conners 3 Scale was administered, she was found to have elevated levels of inattention and hyperactivity but at insufficient levels to recommend a diagnosis of ADHD.

Eleanor's family moved to another city that year, in mid-Year 8, and she was able to join an educational stream within her new comprehensive school called *The Broad Plan Pathway*. It is a student-led, project-based programme which carefully selects students for inclusion based on personality and character along with ability and the individual's academic profile. The advantage in this programme was that she did not have to sit for timed exams either at this level or in the final year of school but, rather, continual assessment by portfolio was the recognised route to university. This pathway allows a student of high intellectual potential and SLD to work within their interest area, to go deeply into research, to work at a pace that is achievable and to choose the style of their output products. I understand that students in this programme are mentored and challenged to investigate beyond their current 'comfort zones'. I believe that Eleanor, as a student of high intellectual potential and motivation, will excel in this carefully designed, mentored environment.

While removing time-pressured tasks this programme potentially abolishes the sequential structure of traditional curriculum. As in the implementation of innovative programmes everywhere, success for individual students is dependent upon the wisdom and capacity of their supervising teachers. Eleanor's work in mathematics throughout secondary school has been modified as she has chosen a career path for which mathematics is not a high-level requirement.

'Go to' resources

These are embedded within this chapter to enable explanation regarding their use and their reference details are listed below.

Bibliography

American Psychiatric Association: Desk Reference to the Diagnostic Criteria From DSM-5-TR. Washington, DC: American Psychiatric Association, 2022, pp. 34–36

Asome, S. (2021) Webinar: Response to Intervention – Getting it Right for All, Right from the Start, Learning Difficulties Australia website. www.ldaustralia.org/information-resources/response-to-intervention/

Australian Bureau of Statistics (ABS) www.abs.gov.au *Program for the International Assessment of Adult Competencies*, Australia 2011–2012, released 9/10/2013.

★Explanation: 620,000 adult Australians fell below level 1 (out of 5 levels) in literacy skills, that is, below the expectation that a participant could locate a single piece of information in a very short text that contained exactly the same information as in a question or directive.

44% of participants in the survey fell at or below level 2 which required the above task to be achieved with some paraphrasing or low-level inferences. This low level of literacy in the Australian population is, indeed, a hidden problem that masks a whole range of incompetencies with multi-generational effects.

Australian Federation of The Specific Learning Difficulties Association (AUSPELD). (2014). *Understanding learning difficulties: A practical guide.*

Barnes, M. A., Clemens, N. H., Fall, A-M., Roberts, G., Klein, A., Starkey, P., McCandliss, B. Zucker, T. & Flynn, K. (2020). Cognitive predictors of difficulties in math and reading in pre-kindergarten children at high risk for learning disabilities. *Journal of Educational Psychology, 112*(4), 685–700. https://doi.org/10.1037/edu0000404

Burns, M. K., & Gibbons, K. (2012). *Implementing response-to-intervention in elementary and secondary schools: Procedures to assure scientific-based practices* (2nd edn). London: Routledge. https://doi.org/10.4324/9780203133903

Butterworth, B. (2018). *Dyscalculia: From science to education* (1st edn) Abingdon. Routledge. https://doi.org/10.4324/9781315538112

Castles, A., & Coltheart, M. (2004). Is there a causal link from phonological awareness to success in learning to read? *Cognition, 91*(1), 77–111.

Castles, A., Rastle, K., & Nation, K. (2018). Ending the reading wars: Reading acquisition from novice to expert. *Psychological Science in the Public Interest, 19*(1), 5–51. https://doi.org/10.1177/1529100618772271

Clarke, P. J., Snowling, M. J., Truelove, E., & Hulme, C. (2010). Ameliorating children's reading-comprehension difficulties: A randomized controlled trial. *Psychological Science, 21*(8), 1106–1116. https://doi.org/10.1177/0956797610375449

Colorado Department of Education (2008). *Response to intervention: A practitioner's guide to implementation.* Denver, Colorado. www.cde.state.co.us/sites/default/files/documents/rti/downloads/pdf/rtiguide.pdf

Costa, L.-J. C., Edwards, C. N., & Hooper, S. R. (2016). Writing disabilities and reading disabilities in elementary school students: Rates of co-occurrence and cognitive burden. *Learning Disability Quarterly, 39*(1), 17–30. https://doi.org/10.1177/0731948714565461

Dehaene, S. (26 Oct 2013) *How the brain learns to read.* www.youtube.com/watch?v=25GI3-kiLdo

Dehaene, S. (2019, April) *Reading in the Brain.* Paper presented at the Dyslexia–SPELD Foundation Conference Language, Literacy & Learning, Perth: Australia.

Dehaene, S. (2021). *How we learn: The new science of education and the brain.* UK: Penguin Books.

Desoete, A. (2015). Predictive indicators for mathematical learning disabilities/dyscalculia in kindergarten children. In S. Chinn (Ed.) *The Routledge International Handbook of Dyscalculia and Mathematical Learning Difficulties.* (pp. 90–100). London: Routledge. https://doi.org/10.4324/9781315740713

DIBELS tests at www.dibels.uoregon.edu

Döhla, D., Willmes, K., & Heim, S. (2018). Cognitive profiles of developmental Dysgraphia. *Frontiers in Psychology, 9*, 2006–2006. https://doi.org/10.3389/fpsyg.2018.02006

Donlan, C. (2015). Linguistic factors in the development of basic calculation. In S. Chinn (Ed.) *The Routledge International Handbook of Dyscalculia and Mathematical Learning Difficulties.* (pp. 346–356). London & New York: Routledge. https://doi.org/10.4324/9781315740713

Dowker, A., & Morris, P. (2014). Targeted interventions for children with difficulties in learning mathematics. In S. Chinn (Ed.) *The Routledge International Handbook of Dyscalculia*

and Mathematical Learning Difficulties. (pp. 256–264). London: Routledge. https://doi.
org/10.4324/9781315740713

Eloranta, A., Närhi, V. M., Eklund, K. M., Ahonen, T. P., & Aro, T. I. (2019). Resolving
reading disability — Childhood predictors and adult-age outcomes. *Dyslexia (Chichester,
England)*, 25(1), 20–37. https://doi.org/10.1002/dys.1605

Ervin R.A. Considering Tier 3 Within a Response-to Intervention Model RTI Action Network
www.rtinetwork.org/essential/tieredinstruction/tier3/consideringtier3
An excellent website for learning all about RtI and how to start implementing it.

Ferreira, C. *Website book share time*. www.booksharetime.com Retrieved 4 August, 2023.

Five from Five website. Vocabulary page. www.fivefromfive.com.au

Foley-Nicpon, M., Assouline, S. G., & Colangelo, N. (2013). Twice-exceptional
learners: Who needs to know what? *The Gifted Child Quarterly*, 57(3), 169–180. https://
doi.org/10.1177/0016986213490021

Gierczyk, M., & Hornby, G. (2021). Twice-exceptional students: Review of implications for
special and inclusive education. *Education Sciences*, 11(2), 85–95. https://doi.org/10.3390/
educsci11020085

Gough, P. B., & Tunmer, W. E. (1986). Decoding, reading, and reading disability. *Remedial and
Special Education*, 7(1), 6–10.

Harskamp, E. (2015) The effects of computer technology on primary school students' mathematics achievement: a meta-analysis. In S. Chinn (Ed.) *The Routledge International Handbook
of Dyscalculia and Mathematical Learning Difficulties*. (pp 383–392). London & New York:
Routledge. https://doi.org/10.4324/9781315740713 https://doi.org/10.1177/0741932
58600700104

Hempenstall, K. (2012). Response to intervention: Accountability in action. *Australian Journal of
Learning Difficulties*, 17(2), 101–131. https://doi.org/10.1080/19404158.2012.704879

Hempenstall, K. (2016). *Read about it: Scientific evidence for effective teaching of reading*. CIS Research
report, 11, Australia.

Hornigold, J. (2014). Teacher training: Solving the problem. In S. Chinn (Ed.) *The Routledge
International Handbook of Dyscalculia and Mathematical Learning Difficulties*. (pp. 315–325).
London: Routledge. https://doi.org/10.4324/9781315740713

Insight program on SBS TV, *Reading between the lines*, Season 2016, Episode 29 (with Jenny
Brockie as compère).

Landerl, K. (2015). How specific is the specific disorder of arithmetic skills? In S. Chinn (Ed.)
The Routledge International Handbook of Dyscalculia and Mathematical Learning Difficulties.
(pp. 115–124). London: Routledge. https://doi.org/10.4324/9781315740713

LD OnLine WETA Public Television ldonline@weta.org

Lewis, K. E., & Lynn, D. M. (2018). An insider's view of a mathematics learning disability: Compensating to gain access to fractions. *Investigations in Mathematics Learning*,
10(3), 159–172. https://doi.org/10.1080/19477503.2018.1444927

Livingston, E. M., Siegel, L. S., & Ribary, U. (2018). Developmental dyslexia: emotional
impact and consequences. *Australian Journal of Learning Difficulties*, 23(2), 107–135. https://
doi.org/10.1080/19404158.2018.1479975

Lu, Y., Ma, M., Chen, G., & Zhou, X. (2021). Can abacus course eradicate developmental dyscalculia. *Psychology in the Schools*, 58(2), 235–251. https://doi.org/10.1002/
pits.22441

Lyon, G. R., & Fletcher, J. M. (2001, Summer). Early warning system: How to prevent reading
disabilities. *Education Next*, 1(2), 22–29. www.educationnext.org

McBride, C. (2019). *Coping with dyslexia, dysgraphia and ADHD: A global perspective*.
Abingdon: Routledge. Chapters 3 & 8. https://doi.org/10.4324/9781315115566

McCloskey, M., & Rapp, B. (2017). Developmental dysgraphia: An overview and framework
for research. *Cognitive Neuropsychology*, 34(3–4), 65–82. https://doi.org/10.1080/02643
294.2017.1369016

Maki, K. E., & Adams, S. R. (2020). Specific learning disabilities identification: Do the identification methods and data matter? *Learning Disability Quarterly*, *43*(2), 63–74. https://doi.
org/10.1177/0731948719826296

Montgomery, D. (2017). *Dyslexia-friendly strategies for reading, spelling and handwriting: A toolkit
for teachers* (1st edn, Vol. 1). Chapter 4, pp. 96–129. Abingdon: Routledge. https://doi.
org/10.4324/9781315405582

Morsanyi, K., Bers, B. M. C., McCormack, T., & McGourty, J. (2018). The prevalence of
specific learning disorder in mathematics and comorbidity with other developmental
disorders in primary school-age children. *British Journal of Psychology*, *109*(4), 917–940.
https://doi.org/10.1111/bjop.12322

Motif tests. See www.motif.org.au.

Nunn, G. (2022, 3 January) What it's like to live with dyscalculia, the little-known
'mathematical dyslexia' that often goes undiagnosed. *ABC News online*. Retrieved
from:www.abc.net.au/news/2022-01-03/dyscalculia-the-mathematical-disability-youve-
never-heard-of/100729798

Nation, K. (2019). *Book Language–Implications on Children's Language and Literacy Development*.
Address at SPELD NSW Literacy Summit. The Reading Research to Practice
Continuum. 3 August 2023.

Nomanis Notes: Madelaine, A., & Wheldall, K. (2019). What is Response to Intervention? Issue
11. https://57ebb165-ef00-4738-9d6e-3933f283bdb1.filesusr.com/ugd/81f204_24640
8f75a2644eabf071320cbc472d9.pdf

Pandey, S., & Agarwal, S. (2014). Dyscalculia: A specific learning disability among children.
International Journal of Advanced Scientific and Technical Research, *4*(2), 912–916.

Reisman, F., & Severino, L. (2020). *Using Creativity to address dyslexia, dysgraphia, and dyscalculia: Assessments and techniques* (1st edn). United Kingdom: Routledge. https://doi.
org/10.4324/9781003038313

Rosselli, M., Matute, E., Pinto, N., & Ardila, A. (2006). Memory abilities in children with
subtypes of dyscalculia. *Developmental Neuropsychology*, *30*(3), 801–818. https://doi.
org/10.1207/s15326942dn3003_3

Rowe, K. (Chairman) (2005). *Teaching reading report and recommendations: National inquiry into
the teaching of literacy*. Canberra: Australia Commonwealth of Australia. Retrieved from
http://research.acer.edu.au/tll_misc/5/

Rubinsten, O., & Tannock, R. (2010). Mathematics anxiety in children with developmental dyscalculia. *Behavioral and Brain Functions*, *6*(1), 1–13. https://doi.org/
10.1186/1744-9081-6-46

Siegel, L. S. (2012). Confessions and reflections of the black sheep of the learning disabilities
field. *Australian Journal of Learning Difficulties*, *17*(2), 63–77. https://doi.org/10.1080/19404
158.2012.722115

Sternberg, R. (1999). *Perspectives on learning disabilities: Biological, cognitive, contextual* (1st edn).
Abingdon: Routledge. https://doi.org/10.4324/9780429498381-ebook published
in 2019.

Soares, N., & Patel, D. R. (2015). Dyscalculia. *International Journal of Child and Adolescent Health*,
8(1), 15–26. Retrieved from: http://ezproxy.library.usyd.edu.au/login?url=https://
www-proquest-com.ezproxy.library.sydney.edu.au/scholarly-journals/dyscalculia/docv
iew/1705546083/se-2?accountid=14757

Solaria, E. J., Grimma, R. P., McIntyrea, N. S., & Denton, C. A. (2018). Reading comprehension development in at-risk vs. not at-risk first grade readers: The differential roles of
listening comprehension, decoding, and fluency. *Learning and Individual Differences*, *65*,
195–206. https://doi.org/10.1016/j.lindif.2018.06.005

Thompson, M. C. (2001). Vocabulary and grammar: Critical content for critical thinking.
Journal of Advanced Academics, *13*(2), 60–66. https://doi.org/10.4219/jsge-2002-367

Thompson, M. C. (1996). Mentors on paper: How classics develop verbal ability. In Van Tassel-Baska, J., Johnson, D. T., Boyce, L. N. (Eds), *Developing Verbal Talent: Ideas and Strategies for Teachers of Elementary and Middle School Students* (pp. 56–74). Boston: Allyn and Bacon.

Westwood, P. (2017). *Learning disorders: A response-to-intervention perspective* (1st edn). London: Routledge. https://doi.org/10.4324/9781315174228

Attention Deficit Hyperactivity Disorder (ADHD)

Rhonda Filmer

VIGNETTE

Remember 'Tom', the child I described in the Author's story?

The vicinity of his desk suggested mayhem. By the third week of first term the storage compartment was crammed with crumpled pieces of paper and unfinished work. At any point in the day the partial contents of his pencil case, his homework folder, his geometry kit and his backpack could be found languishing on the floor. As his desk was the one next to mine, I had designated a line beyond which his possessions must not encroach. He was a good-natured, witty young man liked by everyone in the class, but he was an organisational disaster zone.

Tom has ADHD, combined type, at a moderate to severe level.

What it is

Attention Deficit Hyperactivity Disorder (ADHD) is one of the most pervasive and obtrusive conditions that can inhibit the progress of early learning. As a cause of underachievement, it is often missed because it can manifest in a wide variety of ways that I will describe in this chapter and in the case studies that follow. There are two types of ADHD:

- hyperactivity/impulsivity
- inattentive (predominantly inattentive presentation or PIP).

OR a diagnosis of combined type can be made.

DOI: 10.4324/9781003404972-8

Diagnosis of ADHD

ADHD is not a learning disability but a neurodevelopmental condition as it potentially reduces the life chances of a sufferer if not diagnosed early and treated. Diagnosis of ADHD is done according to the Diagnostic and Statistical Manual (DSM-5-TR), the instructional manual of the American Psychiatric Association, which is used for the diagnosis of disorders in Australia.

In both types of ADHD a child has to demonstrate six or more of a list of symptoms, for at least six months, that are inconsistent with the child's developmental level and negatively impact directly on social and academic activities.

Why it is relevant to twice-exceptionality

ADHD can mask giftedness very effectively because its symptoms can profoundly inhibit the expression of high intellectual ability. The presence of ADHD causes enormous academic, social and mental health challenges for students resulting in low self-esteem and self-concept and an understanding of its potential effects on the twice-exceptional student is important.

What you will see in the classroom

A diagnosis can be for:

1. The *hyperactivity/impulsivity type* where the symptoms are:
    - fidgeting, squirming, tapping feet or hands
    - leaves the seat when being seated is expected
    - runs about or climbs when it is inappropriate
    - unable to engage in leisure activities quietly
    - talks excessively
    - blurts out answers before a question is completed
    - expresses raw emotion before considering it
    - has difficulty waiting in turn
    - interrupts or intrudes on others.

2. The *inattentive type (predominantly inattentive presentation or PIP)* where the symptoms are:
    - makes careless errors or overlooks details in work
    - difficulty in sustaining attention to tasks, conversations or sustained reading
    - seems distracted
    - does not follow through with instructions, finishing tasks or schoolwork; easily 'side-tracked'
    - disorganised, not sequential, poor time management, belongings are messy
    - reluctant to engage in tasks that require mental effort
    - loses items necessary for tasks

- distracted by 'extraneous stimuli'
- forgetful in daily activities.

3. The *combined type* where symptoms of the two above types can be observed.

(Desk Reference to the Diagnostic Criteria From DSM-5-TR
    Washington, DC, American Psychiatric Association, 2022 pp 31–34+).

A DIAGNOSIS OF ADHD CAN BE FOR:

Hyperactive Type OR Inattentive (PIP) Type OR BOTH

- Several symptoms need to have been present before the age of 12 years, in *two or more settings*, for example, home and school or sport or anywhere else
- The symptoms need to be intrusive in the normal daily functioning of the child
- ADHD is a 'spectrum disorder' meaning that students can have a *mild* to *severe* form of the condition
- It can occur across the full range of IQ levels, *from gifted to intellectually impaired*.

Selikowitz (2021) states that ADHD is characterised by impairments in brain function in the areas of executive function, frontal lobe underactivity and neuro-transmitter depletion (insufficient quantities of dopamine, noradrenaline and other chemical messengers in the child's brain). Gene defects of familial origin are present. The combination of these characteristics causes a person to be unable to sift out what is important in the stimuli of the environment and what is not. For example, an adult's voice competes, in the child's perception, with the sound of the traffic outside, a bird scratching at the window or even the sound of another child playing nearby. It is not hard to see how such distraction leads to poor listening skills, little awareness of expectations and, at school, a tendency toward poor academic achievement or underachievement over time.

Hyperfocus … is about absorption in a task …

Ashinoff & Abu-Akel (2019) define it as being comprised of four criteria:

'(1)   To engage in hyperfocus, the task has to be engaging (i.e. fun, interesting, important etc.).
(2)   Hyperfocus is characterised by an intense state of sustained or selective attention.
(3)   When engaged in hyperfocus, there is a diminished perception of non-task relevant stimuli.
(4)   During a hyperfocus state, task performance improves.' (p. 14)

Hyperfocus is often cited as a reason why a child cannot possibly have ADHD … because she can focus when she chooses to … .

> It can actually be *a symptom of ADHD* because it is usually during an activity of great personal interest that brings pleasure and not on an imposed or required activity that offers no instant gratification.

What do I do about it?

As educational professionals we are not entitled to suggest medical diagnoses, but we can describe symptoms and draw attention to patterns of behaviour.

If you suspect that a student has ADHD …

1. Record the symptoms that you are actually seeing from the lists above.

2. Read thoroughly through the student's school records.

3. Check her previous teachers' comments in past school reports and records.

4. Suggest to the Head of Learning Support that you suspect the student has ADHD.

    Do not make that suggestion to the student's parents until you have checked your school's policy on these matters.

5. Begin immediately to give classroom support for poor attention and Executive Function (EF) weaknesses (see Section 3, Chapters 10 & 11).

6. Accept that at least some aspects of the child's behaviour are currently beyond his control. Beware of adopting an attitude of 'blame the victim' while you do not yet fully understand how the symptoms are impacting on this child's school performance.

7. Prepare to assign support teacher time, and your time, to curriculum adjustments and possibly to planning and implementing remediation in areas of weakness.

8. Enlist the support of the child's parents, seeking to develop a good working relationship with them which will be mutually beneficial for the child's development and harmony.

9. Be a 'squeaky wheel' with your school counsellor in seeking further understanding of how this child learns. School counsellor time is very limited, but someone has to be granted it! Seek advice on appropriate strategies and modification to curriculum.

10. Sit the child near you at the front of the room, within the body of the class seating arrangements, not under a fan or air conditioner that may hum or buzz.

11. Keep the classroom uncluttered striking a 'balance' between 'somewhat unadorned' and 'overstimulating'.

12. Gain rapport with the child so she grows to trust and admire you. Demonstrate that you respect her needs by being patient in everything from the simplest of instructions to full explanations of a work task. Give one instruction at a time.

Particularly in secondary school, where a student has multiple teachers, the 'Learning Support Team' model of holding meetings with all stakeholders for the purpose of putting systematic adjustments and supports in place will serve the student well. These meetings can be held initially with a wide-sweeping group of teachers and support personnel with a designated review period. Records of interventions and 'what works' for the student should be recorded carefully and passed on to the child's successive groups of teachers annually, in face-to-face meetings.

Going deeper

Prevalence of ADHD in the Australian population

The Australian Government Institute of Health and Welfare's website, last updated on 25 February 2022, found that ADHD was the most common disorder for children (8.2%) and also the most common disorder among boys (11%).

Goodsell et al. (2017) in their analysis of the educational outcomes from the *Young Minds Matter Survey* noted that this figure included 4.3% of females and that is a large disparity between the genders that is not supported elsewhere in the research.

Diagnosis

The Australian ADHD Practitioners Association released a guideline for diagnosing and treating the condition in 2022. It includes 132 recommendations that cover the whole of a patient's life from childhood to adulthood. It is fully evidence-based and endorsed by the National Health and Medical Research Council (NHMRC). Acknowledgement of the current under-diagnosis in women and girls is prominent in the recommendations which are clear, comprehensive and a 'break-through' for Australian medical practice regarding ADHD. A reading of the recommendations brings an understanding of all the known factors in the identification, diagnosis, treatment and support, non-pharmacological interventions, pharmacological interventions and considerations regarding sub-groups in the population with ADHD. See https://adhdguideline.aadpa.com.au/about/recommendations-summ ary/#recommendations

The medical diagnosis of ADHD is done very differently in Australia than in the USA where a family GP can make a diagnosis from a set of behaviour scales administered by the parents and by the class teacher. That is merely a part of the diagnostic procedure here. In Australia, a parent or any other person in the child's life, a teacher, a psychologist or an educational consultant can notice a set of symptoms either by observation or in a clinical testing situation. The symptoms would be noted and the family is sent to the local GP who would then refer to a developmental paediatrician. No-one other than that paediatrician can diagnose and initiate a medication trial. The medication supply is strictly controlled through governmental regulatory authorities. We are well served here in Australia by these controls. By proceeding through several levels of authority including the specialist paediatrics field there are 'checks and balances' applied which mitigate against overdiagnosis of ADHD.

Teachers are underprepared

The national charity *ADHD Australia* surveyed, in 2021, 1024 primary, secondary and tertiary educators in all Australian states and territories to identify their knowledge, training and experience to support students with ADHD. The findings suggest that Australian education institutions are not adequately preparing educators to support these students.

Findings were:

- 33% of respondents had received professional learning, coaching or mentoring from their school on supporting students with ADHD;
- 87% of educators said they had not received adequate professional learning on how to recognise the symptoms of ADHD;
- 45% believe they have the knowledge and understanding to support students with ADHD;
- 87% reported that they have formally diagnosed students with ADHD in their classrooms.

Yet, 93% reported they would like more professional learning and resources to help them teach students with ADHD.

ADHD (PIP), the Inattentive Type

Most commonly, it is ADHD (PIP) or the Combined Type which tends to occur in the 2e child. Clinical experience has suggested this is still being missed in schools, in bright and gifted students and most particularly in gifted girls, although no statistics can prove it as identification rates are low. The hyperactive boy in the classroom will attract attention, particularly if he is behaving poorly out of frustration, but the ADHD (PIP) child can be dreamy, unable to recall instructions and unable to sustain effort on a task that has no immediate gratification, and in fact, looks disengaged or unthinking. We sometimes excuse this dreamy behaviour in a young child whom we assume is 'lost' in imaginative worlds and play but, in the context of school learning, opportunities will be lost. It is worth exploring one aspect of ADHD (PIP), the matter of processing speed which is variably understood.

Slow processing speed, as defined by Jones (2021), 'means that he takes a bit longer than other kids his age to make sense of the information he takes in. He might have trouble assimilating written or spoken information, or take longer to answer questions or finish tests' (p. 1).Thorsen, Meza, Hinshaw & Lundervold (2018) found that children with ADHD (PIP) show slower processing speed compared to individuals with other presentations of ADHD. All children with ADHD do not have impaired speed overall, but Kibby, Vadnais, & Jagger-Rickels (2019) found in their research that as task demands increase the ADHD group demonstrated less efficient processing speed than those in the control group. For children with ADHD (PIP) slower processing speed may contribute to less efficient performance and worse attention to detail on tasks with a higher perceptual and/or psycho-motor load. Their results suggest that processing speed deficits are primarily linked to the inattention dimension of ADHD but not exclusively. Findings also suggest processing speed is not a singular process but rather a multifaceted system that is differentially impacted in ADHD.

Interestingly, Jacobson, Ryan, Martin, Ewen, Mostofsky, Denckla, & Mahone (2011) found that processing speed and working memory may play an important role in deficits in reading fluency in ADHD. Findings from a longitudinal study by Thorsen et al. (2018) reveal that dimensions of ADHD (PIP), including processing speed, are important factors in predicting peer problems in preadolescence and could be linked to later peer problems three to four years later.

Rommelse, Luman & Kievit (2020), however, conclude that the precise nature of processing speed, and how and why it relates to poor functional outcomes, remains unclear in the research.

Whatever the precise processes underlying ADHD (PIP) it most often goes without detection especially in a very bright or gifted child who can perform 'soundly' but is actually underachieving, way below intellectual potential. Such children may be 'functionally present' for only a small percentage of the day.

In the K-2 years the ADHD (PIP) child is at risk of not attaining foundational understanding or skills in literacy and numeracy. Please note that research tells us that the early mechanics of reading acquisition are unrelated to intelligence.

Observing the 2e child with ADHD (PIP)

When I observe such children during an engaging activity in the relatively quiet, clinical setting of my office I notice from their facial expressions and eye movements that they shift apparently seamlessly from one focus of attention to another and back again. I can only imagine how much learning opportunity is being lost in the classroom setting. The undiagnosed child with ADHD (PIP), in a classroom of vibrant personalities, can simply drift in and out of a dream world and sadly, teachers can miss it.

There are patterns of behaviour amongst students with ADHD but *every child with ADHD is one child with ADHD.* Because of the enormous diversity of genetic, cognitive, emotional, environmental and every possible combination of factors in one child, no two students will manifest the same set of symptoms and impairments.

ADHD is poorly understood or not managed well in most Australian schools because there is no mandated training for teachers and inadequate resourcing within schools to manage it well in our students.

Co-morbidities in this population

ADHD is 'extremely co-morbid' (Masi & Gignac, 2015, p. 1) with many other conditions. Co-morbid conditions of behaviour are sometimes associated with ADHD making it hard to manage in the classroom. Ghanizadeh (2011) found that two-thirds of children with ADHD in their clinical samples have one or more co-morbid psychiatric disorders which are more often oppositional defiant and anxiety disorders. ADHD has a strong psychological impact on students' self-esteem, but the presence of a co-morbid disorder may lead to considerably worse outcomes academically and socially.

After ADHD, which is the most common childhood mental health disorder, anxiety disorders rated at 6.9% of the population aged 4–17 years, major depressive disorder was at 2.8% and conduct disorder 2.1%. Almost one-third of children and adolescents with a disorder had experienced two or more disorders in the previous 12 months according to the *Young Minds Matter Survey* of the Australian Government Department of Health.

Anxiety

The Calm Kids Study at Murdoch Children's Research Institute states that 25%–50% of children with ADHD also experience anxiety. Rodríguez et al. (2014) concur with a figure of 25% while Sciberras et al. (2018) found that in children with ADHD, 26% had one anxiety disorder and 39% had two or more. Selikowitz (2021) states that anxiety disorder is five times more common in children with ADHD. It can manifest as 'bodily symptoms such as cold and clammy hands, a feeling of a lump in the throat, a racing heart, abdominal discomfort or diarrhoea … may be constant or episodic. Sometimes acute episodes of extreme anxiety are experienced (*panic attacks*)' (p. 83). Masi & Gignac (2015) found anxiety in one-third of children with ADHD.

Anxiety can present in the form of generalised worry about anything that may happen and this may be expressed through perfectionism. Selikowitz (2021) states that children with ADHD and strong symptoms of anxiety will be insecure and constantly require reinforcement yet 'no amount of reassurance or positive experience dispels her fearfulness' (p. 83). He recommends that treatment with cognitive behaviour therapy (CBT) and relaxation techniques has been shown to be effective.

An undiagnosed 2e student who does not understand why she is not finding clarity in an explanation or why she reacts in undesirable ways to stimuli or why she feels like she does, is vulnerable to the development of anxiety. Anxiety is a response to uncertainty if there is a genetic predisposition. Thorp (2021, cited in Taylor, 2022) found 611 genes linked to the development of anxiety and there must be an environmental trigger in order to develop it. In the same article Nithianantharajah reported that the brain of an anxious person shows 'changes in connectivity' which lead to impaired behaviours. The brain that is anxious is prone to 'shut down' which is often explained as 'fight or flight mode' under perceived threat.

Much is being written of the higher incidence of anxiety and depression in our school students since the lockdowns for COVID-19. For some people, isolation with no information about when it would end, was indeed a trigger. Headspace, an Australian government-funded foundation has produced the factsheet *Understanding Anxiety* found at https://headspace.org.au/assets/Factsheets/headspace_understanding-anxiety_Fact-Sheet_FA01_DIGI.pdf.

In the school setting, a *panic attack* may be triggered when an anxious 2e student's learning weaknesses are exposed in the presence of peers. The student needs to remove himself from the situation and to have a pre-arranged place to go to settle. A good working relationship with the school counsellor is important:

- as the conduit between his mental health therapist and school
- for setting up safe 'time-out' arrangements
- feeding back to stakeholder staff about the student's triggers, responses and the process to follow.

Oppositional Defiant Disorder (ODD)

This condition is found in 20% of children with ADHD (Selikowitz, 2021) but estimates can be as high as 60% (Noordermeer et al., 2017). The latter study found that the precise diagnosis and treatment of both conditions with early intervention leads to less functional impairments and better lifetime outcomes than for those with ODD and inadequate intervention.

The DSM-5-TR defines ODD as evidence of at least four symptoms from any of the categories exhibited during interaction with at least one individual who is not a sibling.

The categories are:

- Angry/Irritable Mood – loses temper, often touchy or easily annoyed, angry and resentful.
- Argumentative/Defiant Behaviour – argues with authority figures, actively defies or refuses to comply with requests or rules, deliberately annoys others, blames others for mistakes or misbehaviour.
- Vindictiveness – spiteful or vindictive at least twice in the last six months.

Three levels of severity are listed:

- Mild – when symptoms are confined to one setting only (eg at home, at school, with peers). It is possible that a child with a mild level of presentation can mask his symptoms at school but be very difficult at home which impacts the completion of homework and the general level of well-being in the household. His parents will be under considerable stress.
- Moderate – some symptoms are present in at least two settings.
- Severe – symptoms are present in three or more settings (pp 219–220).

Conduct disorder (CD)

This occurs in about 3% of school-aged children, it most often co-occurs with ADHD and is more frequent in males than females according to Fairchild et al. (2019) in their 'primer' article giving a global overview of what is known about this disorder.

The DSM 5-TR classification requires the presence of at least 3 of the 15 listed criteria in the last 12 months with at least one criterion present in the past six months:

- aggression to people and animals, destruction of property; and
- deceitfulness or theft, serious violations of rules.

Age of onset is significant for diagnosis as is the child's attitude toward his behaviour.

Three levels of severity are diagnosed according to the frequency and degree of harm shown to others (pp 221–224).

Tic disorders

Neurodevelopmental disorders with motor and vocal tics affect about 3% of children in either a transient or ongoing presentation. Tourette's Syndrome (TS) is a subset condition which may affect 1% of children of whom two-thirds will have ADHD (Ganos et al., 2017). There is a wide variety of reported prevalence in co-morbid conditions of ADHD and TS depending on the nature of the studies and the definitions of the syndrome. Many children grow out of their tics at puberty.

Autism Spectrum Disorder (ASD)

Cremone-Caira et al. (2021) give the range of 30% to 80% of children with ASD who also have symptoms of ADHD. There are genetic, clinical and neuropsychological overlaps between these two disorders with the possibility that as many as 85% of children on the autism spectrum will have symptoms of ADHD (Masi & Gignac, 2015, p 4).

Developmental Co-ordination Disorder (DCD)

Students with DCD have ongoing physical and sensory challenges that can affect all areas of their lives. Masi & Gignac (2015) estimate the prevalence of DCD at 2–5% of the population and the co-morbidity with ADHD as high as 50% of those with DCD. Multiple sources cited in Chapter 8 claim up to 6% of children present with DCD.

Management of children with ADHD and any of these co-morbidities in schools requires the assistance of medical advice and a whole-school, team approach, involving parents.

- Pro-active approaches avoid the need for constant punitive measures and school suspensions in this population: planning for contingencies and expecting the behaviour you are observing while being prepared with a clear and, if appropriate, negotiated set of consequences for unacceptable behaviour.
- You cannot be expected to manage a child with these symptoms without support from school leadership, your school counsellor and the allocation of classroom assistance.

What the research says

Educational intervention

Both types of ADHD are associated with academic risk and reduced life outcomes, but it is generally agreed that it is the inattentive behaviour of ADHD that is the hardest to monitor in the teaching situation. It is not difficult to see how an inattentive kindergarten child will have lower grade outcomes in Year 1 than an attentive child.

The cumulative effect of poor attention and inadequate mastery of learning over the primary school years is significant with far-reaching consequences of poor academic achievement. Inattentive behaviour, poor working memory and poor academic achievement are interrelated and constitute a 'risk triad' (Tannock & Martinussen, 2007). Lawrence et al. (2021) drawing data from the *Young Minds Matter Survey* and an eight-year longitudinal collection of NAPLAN data found that in Year 3, students with ADHD were, on average, 1 year behind students with no mental disorder in reading and numeracy, and 9 months behind in writing. In Year 9, the gaps were much larger with students with ADHD on average 2.5 years behind in reading, 3 years behind in numeracy, and 4.5 years behind in writing. They conclude that children and adolescents with ADHD need substantial support to manage inattention, impulsivity, and hyperactivity. Skilled remediation in literacy and numeracy should be available throughout all school years.

Treatment

The main approach used to improve inattention and hyperactivity is medical treatment: paediatric medications such as ritalin, dexamphetamine and others. These paediatric medications have been researched and refined since the 1930's. They act directly on the levels of neurotransmitters in the frontal part of the brain to 'normalise' brain function and are, by far, the most effective aspect of treatment. Mark Selikowitz (2021) says that every child with ADHD should be considered for these medications. They have the potential to improve academic outcomes because, for the period that they are at work in the child's body, they allow the retention of information and fewer long-term behavioural and emotional complications than would otherwise occur in a child with ADHD. Paediatric medication for ADHD is not addictive. Yet, the medications remain highly controversial in the public perception. Not only do families become confused but they refuse to countenance the use of these stimulants. Many families have read such frightening, unsupported claims on the internet about these paediatric medications that they will not consider using them for their child's ADHD and the child suffers from loss of opportunity at school.

Simply expressed, the medication makes the child's brain more 'teachable'.

Paediatricians advise that you may have to tweak the type or dosage of medications in search of the desired treatment support. It is well known that the medications, however, do not work for all children. For about 20% of children, the effects are not optimal and for some in that category they do not work at all. However, in many children the change in their behaviour and capacity to learn is truly remarkable.

It is clear from the research that the **optimal treatment** for ADHD is:		
stimulant medication +	remediation and academic intervention for work that was not fully mastered including the use of technological support +	coaching for executive function deficits relaxation techniques and/or CBT for anxiety

The developmental paediatrician should take a very comprehensive clinical interview with the child's parents taking in factors about home, family and school, particularly regarding the family history of ADHD, anxiety, social problems and the underachievement of close family, when seeking a diagnosis. Also included should be the child's early history regarding language development, the acquisition of early developmental milestones and the foundational skills of early literacy and numeracy.

The place of neuropsychological tests in the diagnosis of ADHD is questioned by Brown (2021). In support of his hesitancy, I have read plenty of private psychologists' reports on individual children using a variety of standardised, norm-referenced tests, where ADHD was missed entirely.

Russell Barkley (2019), a 'guru' in the field of ADHD, says that there are many problems with the detection of the deficits associated with ADHD through standardised testing. He favours the rating scales that are commonly used to detect ADHD symptoms and their severity from a series of questions. The scales, filled out by more than one person, e.g. a parent and a teacher, will assist a doctor toward an official diagnosis. Incidentally, the Conners' scales can identify behaviour difficulties in the whole spectrum of childhood disorders.

Common Rating Scales are:

■   Conners' Comprehensive Behaviour Rating Scales (Conners CBRS) for children 6 to 18 years. There are forms for parents and teachers and a self-report form.

■   Swanson, Nolan, and Pelham-IV Questionnaire (SNAP-IV), which is for children aged 6 to 18.

■   National Institute for Children's Health Quality (NICHQ) Vanderbilt Assessment Scale, for children aged 6 to 12.

Executive functions impaired in ADHD

Stanislas Dehaene, in his book *How We Learn,* published in 2020, helpfully applied his scientific findings about the brain's development in learning, to the field of education. He concludes that, 'Only by getting to know ourselves better can we make the most of the powerful algorithms with which our brains are equipped.'

All children would probably benefit from knowing about the four pillars of learning:

attention, active engagement, error feedback and consolidation.
Four slogans effectively summarise them:
'fully concentrate'
'participate in class'

'learn from your mistakes'
'practise every day, take advantage of every night' (p. 243)

Dehaene tells us of the new, sophisticated, non-intrusive MRI methods that have shown the brain's learning circuits at work and we now have evidence for 'what works'. We can now discard ideas that clearly have no neurological research backing and we have our proof of the way that children learn to read, spell, do maths, memorise and grow in their knowledge and skills.

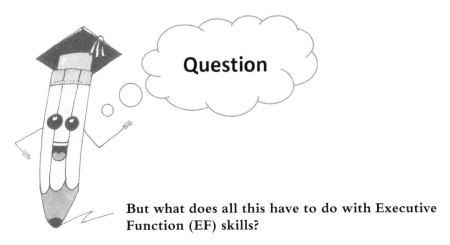

But what does all this have to do with Executive Function (EF) skills?

It is important that we define these skills, understand exactly what we mean by them and their importance in all our children's learning throughout their school years.

Barkley (2021) suggests there is no definitional consensus for EF in the field and he prefers the definition, 'those neuropsychological processes needed to sustain problem-solving toward a goal' (p. 2) emphasising ...

Self-regulation is the primary deficit in ADHD.

Barkley redefines all the EF deficits in this way:

Inhibition -> self-restraint
Self-awareness-> self-directed attention
Verbal working memory-> self-speech (or self-talk internally)
Non-verbal working memory-> using visual imagery to recall
Problem-solving -> self-directed play with ideas
Self-control in emotions
Self-motivation (p. 2)

Poor EF skills, particularly Working Memory, have been found to have a huge impact on academic success. All children, but particularly high-potential and gifted children, can underachieve enormously because their EF skills cannot support their high intelligence sufficiently for them to demonstrate what they know.

As teachers, we want to know how to help children improve their EF skills so they can access curriculum and especially advanced curriculum and to show what they know when performing academic and creative activities and test papers.

The Executive Function Skills are:

1. *Working memory*: a cognitive system with a limited capacity that can hold information temporarily. Working memory (WM) is the part of short-term memory that allows for the manipulation of stored information. Working memory is important for reasoning and the guidance of decision-making and behaviour. A weakness in WM shows in the classroom in so many ways:
   - A student who cannot calculate a maths question mentally, who may actually count on her fingers.
   - The little child who is standing on the mat looking bewildered when everyone else has gone to their tables with your instructions in their heads.
   - The child who gets to the next room and can't remember why he walked there.
   - The adolescent who cannot remember deadlines and can't even remember to write the homework task into his diary.

2. *Cognitive flexibility (also called flexible thinking)*

   The website www.understood.org suggests:
   - Flexible thinking allows children to switch gears and look at things differently.
   - It includes the ability to 'unlearn' old ways of doing things eg when a new method is taught for tying shoe laces ... Instead of using two loops ... being able to move on to one loop and the tie going around.
   - Flexible thinking plays a key role in all types of learning. You can see how that would work in mathematics as new language is introduced for the same concept and mental division moves on to long division, but it involves the same language and the same process albeit more complex.
   - An example of inflexible thinking is the child who is expecting to be going to the park, but Grandma arrives and she can't manage to walk there so everyone stays at home. The child whinges and complains, unable to adjust to the new arrangements.

3. *Inhibitory control (which includes self-control)*
   - the ability to resist calling out in class or expressing opinions that might be inappropriate in that setting or to feel like melting down but being able to stop himself through reasoned 'self-talk'. Obviously, the cumulative effect of getting into trouble in class and going into Time Out is that a child loses valuable learning time and reduces his chances of school success.

For an explanation of Executive Function skills, watch this video from Harvard University's Center on the Developing Child: https://developingchild.harvard.edu/science/key-concepts/executive-function.

ADHD is associated with deficits in Executive Function. The pre-frontal cortex is the last part of the brain to develop (the brain develops from the back to the front) and a child with ADHD will be up to 30% delayed in executive function skill relative to his neuro-typically developing peer.

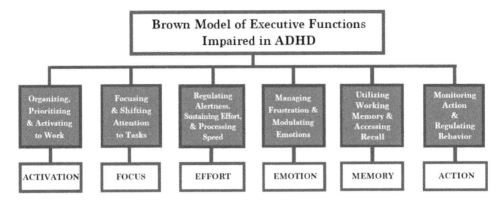

FIGURE 6.1 The Brown Model of Executive Functions Impaired in ADHD. Used with permission from the Brown Clinic.

This model from the website of Dr Thomas E Brown www.brownadhdcli nic.com/the-brown-model-of-add-adhd is useful. Listen to the video *ADHD in 28 Minutes with Thomas E. Brown, PhD* who explains these elements of impaired executive functions. We all have trouble with these actions sometimes, but people with ADHD have a greater level of impairment which significantly reduces their chances of academic and life success.

Children will demonstrate some but not all of these categories of symptoms and sometimes they might not manifest fully until high school when there is more demand on children's organisational skills.

I actually use Figure 6.1 as a 'map' to record from observation where a child's EF deficits are particularly impaired and to discuss specific elements of the child's symptoms with parents. On www.understood.com in the article by Alloway *How Parents Can Take N.O.T.E. of Signs of Learning and Thinking Differences to Help Students Thrive at School* is a tool function called *N.O.T.E.* to assist with the observation of children's (executive function) behaviour over time, something that is of immense value to a paediatrician in the subsequent diagnostic phase.

> All students with ADHD have
> **reduced capacity to self-monitor**
> and
> **poor sense of time**
> until they are coached and taught new effective strategies.

Building the EF skills of the child with ADHD

Future success in the life of a child with ADHD is dependent on the quality of the relationships he has with the adults in his life. A strong relationship should be fostered through trust, authenticity, integrity and consistency. It cannot be built if misdemeanours attract only punitive measures. Prior negotiation can result in a memorandum of understanding between teacher and child with previously decided consequences for non-compliance. Barkley (2008) suggests that learning is enhanced where a child plays an active part in a negotiated contract.

Goodrich (2017), who stresses that parents can gain a great deal from undergoing parent coaching to assist their child, makes the following suggestions to teachers and coaches:

> ADHD is a problem of *showing what you know*.
> It is a performance disorder.

The bright child with ADHD knows information and may have many ideas but what actually is expressed on paper or screen is only a small proportion of what is known/thought/imagined. WM weaknesses or lack of clarity in a line of sequential thinking may cause delays, a loss of motivation and a reduction in output.

New strategies need to be taught through the use of mind maps, the framing of a series of steps to organise a task, motivational timers and apps.

- Such a child is *a dependent learner*, relying on teachers to further scaffold the work beyond what is being provided for the class. Independence cannot be the immediate goal for interventions because the child does not have the skills to work out how to execute a task until those underlying 'micro' skills have been learned. Independence comes only after many skills are acquired.
- Always aim for *attention regulation* as the starting point in every lesson or activity. Gain attention and create motivation through *connection* by eye contact, discreet verbal or non-verbal communication and by creating a sense of safety for the child in the classroom.
- Recognise the emotional element in the work environment at school. The ADHD child will have *low self-efficacy and self-esteem* and may be close to frustration at times during the school day.

Teaching the child with ADHD

- Aim for predictable routines in the classroom wherever possible.
- Through authentic and specific praise (more often than reprimands) a child can develop 'self-talk', a form of planning for tasks. Most students have an internal mechanism for sequentially rehearsing a task they are about to begin, using

'self-talk' to aid and anticipate the steps ahead. A child with ADHD needs to be explicitly and gently taught this skill.

■ Parents and teachers can focus on the *process* of executing work practices rather than the *product* of the completed work, breaking down tasks into small component parts and rewarding for the successful execution of each part, over time. An example of this would be to teach the planning process that involves brainstorming, recording detail on a mind map and a very clear Thesis Statement as an introduction to an essay as the initial step long before expecting a full essay. That way, the student has harnessed the thinking and planning and has identified a multi-step, achievable process long before being required to write a full, final product. Taking time to modify curriculum in this way does not 'dumb down' the outcomes but gives the student an opportunity to gain the requisite skills. Investment in the child's skill set in this way is highly beneficial.

■ Give the student the benefit of the doubt and stand by him until he teaches you to discern when he CANNOT do a step of a process (as opposed to 'won't'!). Find a moment to stop and teach it. Walk him through it. Record the sequence of steps.

■ Give clear, short, verbal instructions giving choices where appropriate.

■ Once your understanding of a child's skill and knowledge level has built and a rapport has been established with the child, then very specific individual goals can be jointly negotiated and set. The concept of attaining a 'personal best' on a specific skill or criterion can be developed in cohort with a trusted teacher. The giving of specific feedback has an effect size (ES) of 0.70 according to Hattie & Zierer (2019) and is one of the most powerful teacher tools we have in our 'tool-kits'. The valuing of teacher feedback will have a powerful effect on a student improving his skills of *self-regulation*.

VIGNETTE

Ruling lines in exercise books is vastly becoming an archaic activity but yet we still need to assist children to neatly record their work. I realised that one particular student with ADHD was writing neatly but ruling chaotic lines that spoiled his work and he was not happy about it.

> 'Do you know that you have to put the ruler right on the edge of the feint blue line and then run your pen along the edge of the ruler so that the feint blue line disappears?'

> 'No-one has ever told me that!'

He has perfect, neatly ruled lines in all of his exercise books now.

> This is a child of nine years of age, with a high IQ, who can discuss with adults such scientific concepts as the transfer of energy in electrical vehicles but he had never known how to do this simple task.

When organising adjustments for a child with ADHD in the classroom ask yourself the following question:

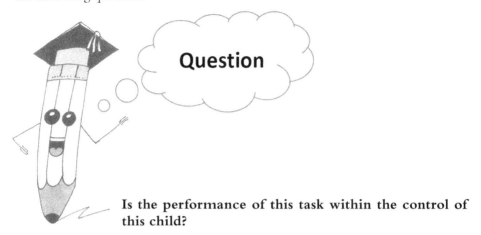

Is the performance of this task within the control of this child?

A good working relationship with her parents will reveal the truth of the situation at home. Parents should be called upon to give feedback on the type and quantity of homework tasks. Experience has taught me that teachers can rarely see how much work or heartache goes into the completion of activities if a child with ADHD lacks the skills to do the work and/or to communicate where she needs more help.

If a task is too difficult or complex then it is a risky choice on your part because it may highlight the child's lack of EF, allow stress and anxiety to develop and potentially ruin the connection you have with the child.

Problems arise when a child has poor motivation, activation and sustained effort. This is not well understood because it looks to be disobedient and disrespectful.

Our task as teachers is to discern:

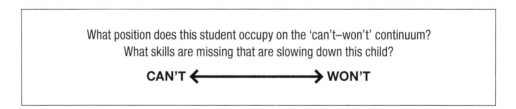

ADHD may manifest differently in women and girls

Girls exhibit compensatory strategies that may mask the underlying symptoms of ADHD according to Nadeau, Littman and Quinn (2015) who suggest:

■   *hyperactivity* in girls may be manifested more through *hyper-verbalisation and emotional excitability/reactivity* which are more difficult to measure and quantify than motoric hyperactivity particularly when they may occur at home but rarely at school. Clinical experience indicates that girls with ADHD often acculturate to *social norms and expectations* despite their symptoms.

■ McCabe (2016) concludes that girls are more mature, with *internalised*, and *largely invisible symptoms* so they are simply not diagnosed.

■ Behavioural problems for many girls with ADHD begin after puberty, accompanied by an increase in emotional over-reactivity, mood swings and impulsivity. This is a critical finding because many of these girls do not meet the DSM-5-TR requirement that evidence of ADHD problems must exist prior to 12 years of age in order to receive an ADHD diagnosis. Lynn (2019) found in her fourteen case studies of women with ADHD that they experience *intense shame* automatically triggering responsive *negative thoughts* while their functional impairments place an enormous burden on them.

As teachers, an awareness of these negative inner experiences in our female students with ADHD will assist us to support their well-being and mental health. Their mothers may be the genetic line for the condition and be struggling with the role of providing structure and stability in the domestic and family lives of their children.

Interestingly, women report a *sense of low self-esteem and self-blame* more often than men so it would appear that strong *cultural factors* are at play. Women often expect that they can run a household, maintain a relationship with husband/partner, rear children and work outside the home. It is clearly noted throughout the literature that women with ADHD will have trouble holding all these expectations together. They may demonstrate problems with sleep, a tendency toward alcohol or overeating, irritability or even stress-induced diseases such as fibromyalgia.

Understanding low self-esteem in students with ADHD

The inherent problem in raising motivation and performance is that poor self-esteem accompanies this learning profile and can be manifest in a variety of ways including apparent arrogance and negative attention seeking. Seeing these behaviours for what they are will assist adults to establish firm expectations and an attitude of understanding.

Some 'tips' on developing co-operation and positive learning experiences:

■ When giving instructions it may be necessary to stand in front of the child and to touch him or the desk near him lightly to gain attention. Sometimes a child with poor self-esteem may momentarily find it difficult to maintain eye contact, which is not an act of defiance but one of embarrassment or discomfort. Are there non-verbal ways of gaining attention? Rapport between student and teacher can be built and maintained through non-verbal signalling such as a secret code, coloured cards or eye contact cues. Such means of communication can be employed to signal distracted or elevating behaviour and to avoid disturbing the rest of the class.

■ Teach the child to reward himself with positive self-talk. Selikowitz (2021) calls this 'cognitive re-structuring' which encourages the child to be positive about himself. Statements such as, 'You must feel good about completing that work so well,' can be made by the teacher.

- Closely and unobtrusively monitor the child.
- Rules and instructions provided to these children must be clear, brief, and often delivered through more visible and external modes of presentation than is normally required (Barkley 2008).
- Consequences must be delivered more frequently, not just more immediately, in view of possible motivational deficits (Barkley 2008), allowing for frequent feedback or consequences for rule adherence and long-term tracking.
- Encourage active listening, even note-taking, as a vehicle for mental activation, particularly in successive years through secondary school.
- Students with short-term and working memory problems find it difficult to retain a two-or three-part instruction. Break instructions and class activities down into manageable pieces so that completion can be reasonably expected.
- Establish a quiet private place for formal time-outs where a student can be sent or choose to go to regain emotional control.

Unsurprisingly it appears that self-imposed expectations may be more often met than imposed goals!

Early identification and intervention

It is understood that early identification and intervention for ADHD reduces the severity and emergence of other coexisting conditions. But there are mixed responses on how best to achieve early intervention. Richardson et al. (2015) found that the effectiveness of intervention programmes depended upon teacher attitude, the decisions teachers made about treatment, the self-perceptions pupils developed about themselves, the role of the classroom environment and stigma in aggravating ADHD symptoms and the common presence of conflict in relationships among stakeholders.

Interventions include

- increased structure and support at home and school
- the teaching of specific skills such as metacognition and understanding how the brain learns, including Executive Function Skills training (see Chapter 10 for detail)
- parent training for positive and effective parenting approaches
- an understanding that all children are developing executive functions throughout childhood as a natural part of growing up to adulthood but the chemical instability in the brain of the child with ADHD makes it harder for this normal development to occur. The child needs specific instruction and patience on the part of significant adults if he is to develop the skills in time to support his school programmes.

The good news is that, given effective support and training, children do gain the requisite skills in their own time. Executive function skills continue to develop under conducive environmental conditions.

Whole of life challenges and the need for parents to care for themselves

Students with ADHD can have a very draining, and sometimes frustrating, effect upon the adults in their lives. It is important that regular contact is made between home and school so that positive feedback can be shared. Remember that marriages and family life are strained by the presence of a child with ADHD so that any encouragement that teaching and allied health personnel can offer will be well received. Also, note that ADHD has a familial genetic line, so it is highly possible, but not guaranteed, that one of the child's parents will have the condition.

Case study of a 2e Child, creatively gifted with ADHD

Liam

Liam came to me for tutoring support when he was in Year 6 and he had already been identified as a 2e child. His mother, Beverley, was a health professional and was proactive in support of her son. At this stage, he was highly misunderstood at school, was constantly in trouble and there were high stress levels in the family.

When Liam was tested on the WISC 4 his General Abilities Index (IQ) of 153, was in the 99.9th percentile of children in his age group. Liam is a visual and kinaesthetic learner who demonstrates gifts in 3-D construction, drawing and animation. He is a very creative student with an inventive gift to synthesise and express new and fresh ideas in a spontaneous way.

However, in some areas of written expression he found it hard to sustain the expression of ideas beyond the very basic and to express even a small number of the ideas he had in his head. But he worked hard to overcome these difficulties obtaining significant improvements in a 12-month period. He gained Band 6 in his NAPLAN Writing assessment in Year 7 which was a 'personal best' achievement with consistent results in Band 7 for all other subjects.

He had considerable challenges in expressing his knowledge. He has Attention Deficit Hyperactivity Disorder, combination type manifesting as variable attention, some limitations in Working Memory and problems with planning and executing complex tasks. When he was frustrated or fatigued, he could appear uncooperative but there was always a reason for this, not always easily interpreted by adults in his life. Some flexibility in modes of delivery, timing and the order of completion of tasks helped him. Like all students with ADHD he needed explicit instructions on how to plan and execute a complex task particularly regarding the sequence in which to undertake the component parts.

At the time, I wrote a letter summary of his learning needs to his school:

Liam needed in his class programme:

- stimulus for his giftedness which is masked by his tendency to only minimally express himself, that is, placement in the Gifted and Talented stream to enable the challenge provided by a gifted cohort of classmates.
- a teacher mentor, year advisor or aide; someone who will seek to build a relationship with Liam and to whom he can go for assistance as well as to set up strategies which will assist him to be organised to bring home his homework,

assessments and assignments e.g. a diary, special folder, electronic organiser or to email assignments home.

- assistance to execute and produce assignments
- allowance for a change/short break in the delivery mode of a lesson after a period of 20 minutes of concentrated effort, if required
- allowance of extra time for planning and writing and rest breaks if necessary in class and assessment activities
- teachers to be aware, sympathetic and helpful with Liam's lack of organisation as it is a learning difficulty and he cannot change it. He is not a lazy student.
- to be given notes and schoolwork in printed form rather than being required to copy them from a board
- very clear homework/assignment direction e.g. how many words required
- homework to be broken up into chunks with staggered due dates to prevent his feeling overwhelmed
- use of graphic organisers, mind mapping and story structures as class strategies so he will undertake to use these
- to use his laptop computer with voice-activated software to compose text drafts

Both Liam and his mother, Beverley, have reflected on his time at school and you will find their stories in Chapter 12: Longitudinal Case Studies.

'Go to' resources

ADDitude Magazine.
See www.additudemag.com
On the Scientific Advisory Board of this online magazine are members of high standing in the field: Dr Russell Barkley, Dr Thomas E. Brown and Dr Stephen Hinshaw among others. These medical and scientific researchers have made life-long contributions to the field of ADHD making this resource highly creditable.

ADDults with ADHD
See www.adultadhd.org.au/index.php/about-us/266-addults-with-adhd-20-years-young

ADHD Support Australia
See www.adhdsupportaustralia.com.au/

Calm Kids Study at Murdoch Children's Research Institute is calling for more families to join this research project on children with ADHD and the anxiety they experience. See www.mcri.edu.au/the-calm-kids-study

Goodrich, C. (2017). Executive function, ADHD and stress in the classroom. Eau Claire, WI: PESI Inc. VIDEO

Helpguide: See www.helpguide.org/home-pages/add-adhd.htm

How to ADHD: the YouTube channel of Jessica McCabe. See www.youtube.com/playlist?list=PLvq9Tp5JZ8oAV-GAZmvEoYj9ntBaabKMj

Oakley, B. A., Sejnowski, T. J., McConville, A. (2018). *Learning how to learn: how to succeed in school without spending all your time studying; a guide for kids and teens.* United States: Penguin Publishing Group.

Pamphlet ADHD Awareness Week (2012) The many faces of ADHD. Women's National Resource Centre on ADHD a program of CHADD

Pamphlet *ADHD – Stimulant medication.* Developed by the RCH Centre for Community Child.

Health and RCH Pharmacy, Royal Melbourne Children's Hospital. First published 2006. Updated November 2010.
Understood website. See www.understood.org/
a not-for-profit website, free to all, research evidence based.

Webmed. See www.webmd.com/add-adhd/childhood-adhd/adhd-inattentive-type

Bibliography

American psychiatric association: Desk reference to the diagnostic criteria from DSM-5-TR. Washington, DC, American Psychiatric Association, 2022, pp. 31–34.
ADHD Australia. Lucid (2021, 28 September). *Building brighter.* Pathways: ADHD.
Australia Education Survey [Preliminary report]. www.adhdaustralia.org.au/wp-conent/uplo ads/2021/10/Building-Brighter-Pathways-ADHD-Australia-Education-Survey-Prel iminary-Report.pdf
Ashinoff, B. K., & Abu-Akel, A. (2019). Hyperfocus: The forgotten frontier of attention. *Psychological Research, 85*(1), 1–19. https://doi.org/10.1007/s00426-019-01245-8
Australian Institute of Health and Welfare 2020. *Australia's children. Cat. no. CWS 69.* Canberra: AIHW.
Australian Government, Department of Health website *Young Minds Matter* http://youngmind smatter.org.au/survey-results/prevalence-of-mental-disorders
Azevedo, R. (2020). Reflections on the field of metacognition: Issues, challenges and opportunities. *Metacognition and Learning, 15*(2), 91–98. https://doi.org/10.1007/s11 409-020-09231-x
Barkley, R. A. (2008). Classroom accommodations for children with ADHD. *ADHD Report, 16*(4), 7–10. https://doi.org/10.1521/adhd.2008.16.4.7
Barkley, R. (2015). *ADHD, Self-regulation and executive functioning,* YouTube video. Slides found at https://drive.google.com/file/d/0B885LHMHOu5BT2QtbjdtXzhsdjQ/view
Barkley, R. A. (2019). Neuropsychological testing not useful in the diagnosis of ADHD: Stop It (or Prove It)! *ADHD Report, 27*(2) 1–8. https://doi.org/10.1521/adhd.2019.27.2.1
Barkley, R. A. (2021). Research findings deficient emotional self-regulation is associated with important clinical features in adults with ADHD. *ADHD Report, 29*(1), 8. https://doi. org/10.1521/adhd.2021.29.1.8
Barkley, R. A. (2021). The important role of executive functioning and self–regulation in ADHD (PDF). www.russellbarkley.org/factsheets/ADHD_EF_and_SR.pdf Retrieved 26 June 2023.
Barkley, R. A., Cook, E. H., Diamond, A., Zametkin, A., Thapar, A., Teeter, A. … Pelham, W. (2002). International consensus statement on ADHD January 2002. *Clinical Child and Family Psychology Review, 5*(2), 89–111.
Biederman, J., Wilens, T., Mick, E., Spencer, T., Faraone S.V. (1999). Pharmacotherapy of attention-deficit/hyperactivity disorder reduces risk for substance use disorder. *Pediatrics, 104*, e20. https://doi.org/10.1542/peds.104.2.e20.

Brookman-Byrne, A. (2018, June 22). *What is metacognition and how can it help students learn?* https://bold.expert/thinking-about-thinking/blog

Brown, T. E. (2021). The Brown clinic for attention and related disorders. The Brown model of executive function impairments in ADHD used by permission. www.brownadhdclinic.com/the-brown-model-of-add-adhd

Cooper-Kahn, J., & Foster, M. (2013). *Boosting executive skills in the classroom: A practical guide for educators.* San Francisco: Jossey-Bass.

Cremone-Caira, A., Trier, K., Sanchez, V., Kohn, B., Gilbert, R., & Faja, S. (2021). Inhibition in developmental disorders: A comparison of inhibition profiles between children with autism spectrum disorder, attention-deficit/hyperactivity disorder, and comorbid symptom presentation. *Autism, 25*(1), 227–243. https://doi.org/10.1177/136236132 0955107

Dawson, P., & Guare, R. (2018). *Executive skills in children and adolescents: A practical guide to assessment and intervention.* (3rd ed.). New York: Guilford.

DuPaul, G. J, Weyandt, L., & Janusis, G. (2011). ADHD in the classroom: Effective intervention strategies. *Theory into Practice, 50*(1), 35–42. https://doi.org/10.1080/00405 841.2011.534935

Fairchild, G., Hawes, D. J., Frick, P. J., Copeland, W. E., Odgers, C. L., Franke, B., Freitag, C.M., & De Brito, S. A. (2019). Conduct disorder. *Nature Reviews Disease Primers, 5*(1), 43.

Foley-Nicpon, M., Rickels, H., Assouline, S., & Richards, A. (2012). Self-esteem and self-concept examination among gifted students with ADHD. *Journal for the Education of the Gifted, 35*(3), 220–240. https://doi.org/10.1177/0162353212451735

Ganos, C., Martino, D., & Pringsheim, T. (2017). Tics in the pediatric population: pragmatic management. *Movement Disorders Clinical Practice, 4*(2), 160–172. https://doi.org/10.1002/mdc3.12428

Ghanizadeh, A. (2011). Sensory processing problems in children with ADHD, a systematic review. *Psychiatry Investigation, 8*(2), 89–94. doi: 10.4306/pi.2011.8.2.89

Goodsell, B., Lawrence, D., Ainley, J., Sawyer, M., Zubrick, S. R., & Maratos, J. (2017). Child and adolescent mental health and educational outcomes. An analysis of educational outcomes from Young Minds Matter: The second Australian Child and Adolescent Survey of Mental Health and Wellbeing. Perth: Graduate School of Education, The University of Western Australia. https://youngmindsmatter.telethonkids.org.au/siteassets/media-docs-young-minds-matter/childandadolescentmentalhealthandeducatio naloutcomesdec2017.pdf

Harstad, E., & Levy, S. (2014). Clinical report attention-deficit/hyperactivity disorder and substance abuse. *Pediatrics.* https://doi.org/10.1542/peds.2014-0992

Hattie, J., & Zierer, K. (2019). *Visible learning insights* (1st edn). United Kingdom: Routledge. https://doi.org/10.4324/9781351002226

Jacobson, L. A., Ryan, M., Martin, R. B., Ewen, J., Mostofsky, S. H., Denckla, M. B., & Mahone, E. M. (2011). Working memory influences processing speed and reading fluency in ADHD. *Child Neuropsychology, 17*(3), 209–224. https://doi.org/10.1080/09297 049.2010.532204

Jones, C. (2021, May 10). What is a 'Slow Processing Speed?' [newsletter entry]. Retrieved from www.additudemag.com/what-is-a-slow-processing-speed/

Kaskamanidis, Zoe. (May 2022). 'Infographic: Supporting students with ADHD', *Teacher Infographic.* Retrieved from: www.teachermagazine.com/au_en/articles/infographic-sup porting-students-with-adhd.

Kibby, M. Y., Vadnais, S. A., & Jagger-Rickels, A. C. (2019). Which components of processing speed are affected in ADHD subtypes? *Child Neuropsychology, 25*(7), 964–979. https://doi.org/10.1080/09297049.2018.1556625

Kooij, J. J. S., Bijlenga, D., Salerno, L., Jaeschke, R., Bitter, I., Balázs, J., Thome, J., Dom, G., Kasper, S., Nunes Filipe, C., Stes, S., Mohr, P., Leppämäki, S., Casas, M., Bobes, J., Mccarthy, J. M., Richarte, V., Kjems Philipsen, A., Pehlivanidis, A., Niemela, A., & Asherson, P. (2019). Updated European consensus statement on diagnosis and treatment of adult ADHD. *European Psychiatry: The Journal of the Association of European Psychiatrists*, *56*, 14–34. https://doi.org/10.1016/j.eurpsy.2018.11.001

Lawrence, D., Houghton, S., Dawson, V., Sawyer, M., & Carroll, A. (2021). Trajectories of academic achievement for students with attention-deficit/hyperactivity disorder. *British Journal of Educational Psychology*, *91*(2), 755–774. https://doi.org/10.1111/bjep.12392

Lynn, N. M. (2019). Women & ADHD functional impairments: Beyond the obvious master's thesis. 933. https://scholarworks.gvsu.edu/theses/933

McCabe, J. (2016). ADHD in Girls: How to recognize the symptoms. How to ADHD YouTube channel. Retrieved 23 August 2021.

Masi, L., & Gignac, M. (2015). ADHD and comorbid disorders in childhood psychiatric problems, medical problems, learning disorders and developmental coordination. *Clinical Psychiatry*, *1*(1), 1–9. www.primescholars.com/articles/adhd-and-comorbid-disorders-inc hildhoodpsychiatric-problems-medicalproblems-learning-disordersand-developmental-coordina-104677.html Retrieved 5 November 2023.

Nadeau, K., Littman, E., & Quinn, P. (2015). *Understanding girls with ADHD: How they feel and why they do what they do* (2nd edn). Silver Springs, MD: Advantage Books.

Neihart, M. (2003). *Gifted children with attention deficit hyperactivity disorder (ADHD)*. ERIC Digest ED482344 ERIC Clearinghouse on Disabilities and Gifted Education, 1110N. Retrieved 5 November 2023.

Noordermeer, S. D., Luman, M., Weeda, W. D., Buitelaar, J. K., Richards, J. S., Hartman, C. A., Hoekstra, P.J., Franke, B. Heslenfeld, D.J. & Oosterlaan, J. (2017). Risk factors for comorbid oppositional defiant disorder in attention-deficit/hyperactivity disorder. *European Child & Adolescent Psychiatry*, *26*, 1155–1164. https://doi.org/10.1007/s00 787-017-0972-4

Owens, E. B., Zalecki, C., Gillette, P., & Hinshaw, S. P. (2017). Girls with childhood ADHD as adults: Cross-domain outcomes by diagnostic persistence. *Journal of Consulting and Clinical Psychology*, *85*(7), 723–736. https://doi.org/10.1037/ccp0000217

Perold, M., Louw, C., & Kleynhans, S. (2010). Primary school teachers' knowledge and misperceptions of attention deficit hyperactivity disorder (ADHD). *South African Journal of Education*, *30*(3), 457–473. https://doi.org/10.15700/saje.v30n3a364

Richardson, M., Moore, D. A., Gwernan-Jones, R., Thompson-Coon, J., Ukoumunne, O., Rogers, M., Whear, R., Newlove-Delgado, T.V., Logan, S., Morris, C., Taylor, E., Cooper, P., Stein, K., Garside, R., & Ford, T. J. (2015). Non-pharmacological interventions for attention-deficit/hyperactivity disorder (ADHD) delivered in school settings: systematic reviews of quantitative and qualitative research. *Health Technology Assessment (Winchester, England)*, *19*(45), 1–470. https://doi.org/10.3310/hta19450

Rief, S. F. (2016). *How to reach & teach children & teens with ADD/ADHD*. (3rd edn). San Francisco, California: Jossey-Bass.

Rinn, A., & Nelson, J. (2009). Preservice teachers' perceptions of behaviours characteristic of ADHD and giftedness. *Roeper Review*, *31*(1), 18–26. https://doi.org/10.1080/0278319080 2527349

Rodríguez, C., Gonzalez-Castro, P., Garcia, T. et al. (2014). Attentional functions and trait anxiety in children with ADHD. *Learning and Individual Differences* *35*(147–152). https://doi.org/10.1016/j.lindif.2014.07.010

Rommelse, N., Luman, M., & Kievit, R. (2020). Slow processing speed: A cross-disorder phenomenon with significant clinical value, and in need of further methodological scrutiny.

European Child & Adolescent Psychiatry, 29(10), 1325–1327. https://doi.org/10.1007/s00 787-020-01639-9

Rowe, K. (Chairman) (2005). *Teaching reading report and recommendations: National inquiry into the teaching of literacy.* Canberra, Australia: Commonwealth of Australia. Retrieved from: http://research.acer.edu.au/tll_misc/5

Sciberras, E., Mulraney, M., Anderson, V., Rapee, R. M., Nicholson, J. M., Efron, D., Lee, K., Markopoulos, Z., & Hiscock, H. (2018). Managing anxiety in children with ADHD using cognitive-behavioral therapy: A pilot randomized controlled trial. *Journal of Attention Disorders, 22*(5), 515–520. https://doi.org/10.1177/1087054715584054

Selikowitz, M. (2021). *ADHD: The Facts* (3rd edn). Oxford University Press.

Slobodin, O., & Davidovitch, M. (2019). Gender differences in objective and subjective measures of ADHD among clinic-referred children. *Frontiers in Human Neuroscience,* 13(441). https://doi.org/10.3389/fnhum.2019.00441

Smith, Z.R., & Langberg, J.M. (2018). Review of the evidence for motivation deficits in youth with ADHD and their association with functional outcomes. *Clinical Child and Family Psychology Review, 21*(4), 500–526. https://doi.org/10.1007/s10567-018-0268-3

Tannock, R., & Martinussen, R. (2007). Promising practices in education for students with ADHD. *Orbit,* 37(1), 32–35. https://hdl.handle.net/1807/24453

Taylor, C. The Anxiety Puzzle. ABC News Online, 21 February, 2022. www.abc.net.au/news/2022-02-21/what-causes-anxiety-genes-diet-trauma-new-treatment/100836300

Taylor-Klaus, E., & Dempster, D. (2016). *Parenting ADHD Now.* Berkeley, California: Althea Press. www.understood.com website

Thorsen, A. L., Meza, J., Hinshaw, S., & Lundervold, A. J. (2018). Processing speed mediates the longitudinal association between ADHD symptoms and preadolescent peer problems. *Frontiers in Psychology, 8,* 2154. https://doi.org/10.3389%2Ffpsyg.2017.02154

Vukovic, R. (2018) (podcast) The research files episode 46: Practical Strategies to assist children with ADHD in the classroom. *ACER Teacher Magazine online.* www.teachermagazine.com/au_en/articles/the-research-files-episode-46-practical-strategies-to-assist-children-with-ADHD

Wassenberg, R., Hendriksen, J. G. M., Hurks, P. P. M., Feron, F. J. M., Vles, J. S. H., & Jolles, J. (2010). Speed of language comprehension is impaired in ADHD. *Journal of Attention Disorders,* 13(4), 374–385. https://doi.org/10.1177/1087054708326111

Yoshimasu, K., Barbaresi, W. J., Colligan, R. C., Killian, J. M., Voigt, R. G., Weaver, A. L., & Katusic, S. K. (2011). Written-language disorder among children with and without ADHD in a population-based birth cohort. *Pediatrics, 128*(3), e605–e612. https://doi.org/10.1542/peds.2010-2581

Young, S., Adamo, N., Asgeirsdottir, B. B., Branney, M., Beckett, M., Colley, W., Cubbin, S., Deeley, Q., Farrag, E., Gudjonsson, G., Hill, P., Hollingdale, J., Kilic, O., Lloyd, T., Mason, P., Paliokosta, E., Perecherla, S., Sedgwick, J., Skirrow, C., Tierney, K., van Rensburg, Woodhouse, E. (2020). Females with ADHD: An expert consensus statement taking a lifespan approach providing guidance for the identification and treatment of attention-deficit/ hyperactivity disorder in girls and women. *BMC Psychiatry,* 20, 404. https://doi.org/10.1186/s12888-020-02707-9

Autism Spectrum Disorder (ASD)

Rhonda Filmer and Trevor Clark

VIGNETTE

Ainslie, a gifted young autistic woman, is currently working with Autism Spectrum Australia (Aspect) to assist with the inclusion of autistic people into its workplace. Her school years were not happy because she was not understood and there were frequent incidents of being bullied for being 'odd' and different. However, she went on to university.

She completed a Bachelor of Education degree, and has partially completed degrees in law, accounting, business studies and arts (ancient history). If the partial degrees were totalled, they would be the equivalent of several bachelor's degrees.

Ainslie was asked,

'Why did you not complete the degrees?'

'They were not in the field of my special interests.'

She is currently studying Japanese at university as Japan is one of her special interests.

Ainslie loves to learn but she must have a really passionate connection to the subject, or she cannot motivate herself to work hard. As an identified 2e autistic student her strengths and passions are integral to her completion of studies.

This chapter will firstly describe autism spectrum disorder (ASD) as a condition, then as a component part of a twice exceptional (2e) profile, its impact on a gifted student's skills and achievements and what to do about it. Two case studies are included that demonstrate the complexity of the school experience for autistic students giving insights into how to understand and effectively teach children with these learning needs.

DOI: 10.4324/9781003404972-9

What it is

Aspect Australia's website states that: 'Autism is a condition that affects how a person thinks, feels, interacts with others, and experiences their environment. It is a lifelong disability that starts when a person is born and stays with them into old age. Every autistic person is different to every other. This is why autism is described as a "spectrum".'

The American Psychiatric Association's Diagnostic and Statistical Manual of Mental Disorders (DSM-5-TR, 2022) definition of Autism Spectrum Disorder (ASD) includes:

A. Persistent deficits in social communication and social interaction across multiple contexts
B. Restricted, repetitive patterns of behaviour, interests, or activities in at least two of the following:
   - Stereotyped or repetitive motor movements, use of objects of speech (e.g., lining up toys or flipping objects, echolalia, idiosyncratic phrases)
   - Inflexibility in adherence to routines or ritualised behaviour
   - Fixated interests that are abnormal in intensity or focus
   - Hyper–or hypo-reactivity to sensory input (e.g., apparent indifference to pain/temperature, adverse response to specific sounds or textures, excessive smelling or touching of objects, visual fascination with lights or movement).

Symptoms cause clinically significant impairment in social, occupational, or other important areas of current functioning. Many autistic people experience atypical sensory processing with a wide range of symptoms and severity.

ASD is associated with or without accompanying intellectual impairment, with or without accompanying language impairment, associated with another neurodevelopmental, mental, or behavioural disorder, and may be associated with a known medical or genetic condition or environmental factor.

Most autistic people have other related characteristics; however, autistic children may not have all or any of the behaviours listed as examples here.

Behaviours may include:

- Delayed language skills
- Delayed movement skills
- Delayed cognitive or learning skills
- Hyperactive, impulsive, and/or inattentive behaviour
- Epilepsy or seizure disorder
- Unusual eating and sleeping habits
- Gastrointestinal issues (for example, constipation)
- Unusual mood or emotional reactions
- Anxiety, stress, or excessive worry

■   Lack of fear or more fear than expected
(National Centre on Birth Defects and Developmental Disabilities,
Centres for Disease Control and Prevention)

It should be noted that the DSM-5-TR no longer includes individuals with a well-established DSM-4 diagnosis of autistic disorder, Asperger's disorder, or pervasive developmental disorder not otherwise specified, and are instead included in the diagnosis of autism spectrum disorder with three levels of severity:

Level 1
'Requiring support'
Level 2
'Requiring substantial support'
Level 3
'Requiring very substantial support'
Desk Reference to the Diagnostic Criteria from DSM-5-TR.
Washington, DC, American Psychiatric Association, 2022 pp 27–28)

Along with the deficits outlined above, strengths and gifts are also associated with autism and these abilities will be discussed in the 'Going Deeper' section of the chapter. It is important to note, that there is a significant number of autistic gifted students who are not being identified because of the masking effects of either giftedness or autism, the lack of agreement of the definition of these strengths observed in autistic students, and the lack of teacher professional learning in twice-exceptionality and autism (Cain et al., 2019; Ronksley-Pavia, 2020).

Why it is relevant to twice-exceptionality

The prevalence of Autism Spectrum Disorder has increased significantly over the past 20 years – from 1 in 150 in 2000, to 1 in 36 eight-year-olds in 2020 (Centre for Disease Control and Prevention, 'Autism Spectrum Disorder – Data and Statistics', US Department of Health, and Human Services. Autism and Developmental Disabilities Monitoring (ADDM) Network.), although there is high variability in reported prevalence with autism organisations generally accepting around 1 in 70. The result of this increasing prevalence is higher numbers of school-aged autistic students in classrooms today. Hand-in-hand with this, is the increasing number of autistic students who are also gifted, that is, 'twice exceptional (2e)'. It should be noted, it is highly likely that autistic students who were diagnosed previously as having Asperger's Disorder, are in fact, twice-exceptional.

What you will see in the classroom

The presence of the characteristics listed below is linked to the autistic student's level of severity across the spectrum.

Social awkwardness

An autistic student might:

■ not be able to maintain eye contact with you and/or peers

■ display a limited range of facial expressions or use facial expressions that don't match what a person is communicating

■ have only limited speech or remain non-speaking

■ speak in unexpected or unusual ways, e.g., very formally or very informally, in a monotone, in an accent, etc.

■ have difficulty responding to the tone of voice being used by others, or to non-verbal social cues such as facial expressions and body language.

■ have difficulty in following conversations, with a tendency not to pick up on non-literal language like sarcasm or metaphor.

■ have difficulty following instructions with more than one or two steps.

■ not talk about feelings or answer personal questions

■ be rigid in setting and following rules, whether in the classroom or during play.

In the playground and informal settings, the student might:

■ have trouble initiating interactions with other children or developing and maintaining friendships with peers

■ dominate conversations or have trouble taking turns

■ try to dominate play when engaging with others

■ prefer spending time with younger children or with adults, rather than with children of the same age

■ prefer to play on their own rather than playing with others/avoid group activities

■ may be reluctant to develop close friendships

■ not easily recognise other people's personal space

■ focus conversation on subjects that interest them/reluctance to engage in other topics.

Repetitive or restricted behaviour, interests, or activities

An autistic student might:

■ show an intense focus on unusual hobbies, such as keeping lists or memorising statistics, on toys or more unusual objects

■ demonstrate repetitive behaviour, such as arranging objects or toys in a precise way

■ demonstrate sensory differences by objecting to wearing clothes made from certain fabrics, hate loud noises, or only eat certain foods based on their texture. Sensory differences can result in sensory overload and triggering extreme reactions

- not respond to some sensory experiences, such as heat, cold or pain
- closely following routines and become upset when plans change, or routines aren't followed.
- feel anxious or upset when in social situations with which they aren't familiar
- find it difficult to solve problems or apply skills they have learned in different contexts
- feel overwhelmed or upset about going to school, or regularly refusing to go
- make unusual body movements, such as hand clapping, hand flapping or rocking
- find it difficult to sit, stand or be still, or constantly fidgeting
- make unusual noises such as grunts or squeals, or frequently clearing their throat.

Some behaviours that may particularly pertain to autistic *girls* include:

- masking the social and sensory challenges they perceive
- being seen as excessively shy
- inclination to keep emotions under control in social settings but prone to 'meltdowns' at home
- having a very limited number of close friendships
- a strong sense of justice that means they stand up for others
- a highly developed imagination and enjoyment of fiction and fantasy
- intense interests focused on art, people, music, and animals
- advanced interests for their age
- a 'fussy' eater.

These characteristics have been derived from lists on the website of Autism SA. See https://autismsa.org.au/autism-diagnosis/autism-symptoms/signs-of-autism-in-children/

Observable characteristics of ASD pertaining to gifted and high potential autistic children

- delayed social maturity and social reasoning
- immature empathy
- difficulty making friends and often teased by other children
- difficulty with the communication and control of emotions
- unusual language abilities that include advanced vocabulary and syntax but delayed conversation skills, unusual prosody (rhythm, stress, and intonation of speech) and a tendency to be pedantic
- a fascination with a topic that is unusual in intensity or focus
- difficulty maintaining attention in class
- an unusual profile of learning abilities
- a need for assistance with some self-help and organisational skills

- clumsiness in terms of gait and coordination
- sensitivity to specific sounds, aromas, textures, or touch.

(Attwood, 2008, p. 33)

What do I do about it?

The learning supports and practices included in this section have proven effective in not only the education of autistic students but in better post-school opportunities and quality of life outcomes.

- *Individual Learning Plan (ILP)*

Develop an individual learning plan involving the student, parents, and all stakeholders in his education. For 2e autistic students the ILP should include goals for coping strategies, talent development and intervention for skills development if necessary. The writing and delivery of effective ILPs is explained in Chapter 11.

- *Inclusive Classrooms (Models of Practice – MoPs)*

The Models of Practice describe ways to set up and manage the inclusive classroom, how to relate to the students including the modelling of social skills and social problem-solving and how to teach students where their learning needs are not neurotypical. This site is an excellent, one-stop starting place for good evidence-based advice.

Two models were developed:

- one for the Early Years (K and Year 1)
- one for the Middle Years (7 and 8).

Beamish, Clark et al (2021) and teachers in NSW, Queensland and Victoria developed the MoPs which were trialled, evaluated, and endorsed through a collaborative process. Teachers reported that they felt more knowledgeable, confident, and self-efficacious to teach students with ASD following the process. Details can be found on the website, *inclusionED* under *Core Research Projects* with instructional videos and teacher-friendly resources.

Free evidence-based teaching practices in *inclusionED* are underpinned by the underlying principles of Universal Design for Learning in the areas of:

- Classroom management
- Sensory considerations
- Social/emotional wellbeing
- Career and self-discovery
- Adjustments and scaffolds
- Behaviour support
- School Connectedness.

■   *Sensory differences*

Your School Counsellor or Psychologist will have access to *screeners for ASD*. It is important that the child's sensory profile is assessed, not only the social and communication problems, and that interventions are found that do not just ameliorate the child's behavioural responses but attempt to address the underlying sensory hyper–or hypo–sensitivities. Aspect Australia's website has a form for how to develop a *Sensory Plan* (see Resources) for your autistic student. Like all such tools, it takes time to collect and collate information, but it is an important investment that allows a child to function in your classroom by bringing his sensory processing needs into his Individual Learning Plan.

■   *Strength-based approaches*

Success-O-Graph (Lanou et al., 2011) is an innovative program that illustrates the successful inclusion of strengths and interests for autistic 2e students. The program was developed for a student with anxiety and challenging behaviour who displayed exceptional mathematical abilities and who had an excellent sense of humour. The student was taught to self-monitor his own behaviour by recording his successes on the *Success-O-Graph*, a two-quadrant coordinate grid posted above the student's desk. A significant reduction in anxiety and outbursts of challenging behaviour occurred because of this differentiated program.

Savant Skill Curriculum is a differentiated educational program developed specifically for autistic students who display savant skills and incorporates many of the gifted and 2e programming recommendations outlined previously in the book (Clark, 2001). It is an example of an evidence-based talent development program that is inclusive of gifted education strategies (i.e., acceleration, enrichment, and mentorships) and goals to support social communication skills, sensory difference, and behaviour.

Evidence-based instructional strategies for the classroom

The difficulties of establishing what is an evidence-based practice from multiple, replicable studies is clearly articulated by Wong, Odom, Hume et al (2015) who, from an initial search, of 29,105 articles found 456 studies that met their criteria for inclusion. They then found 27 intervention practices that qualified as 'evidence-based' practice (EBPs). Classroom practices that qualified were well supported for their efficacy across a rigorous process.

Author note: Many of the EBPs have not been included here because they require small group or individualised off-curriculum instruction, service providers or out of school settings.

A cross-referenced list of evidence-based practices from multiple sources has been compiled below. Note that the Stokes et al. (2017) study used surveys by school principals and journal entries by teachers stating 'what works' with one particular ASD Level 1 student in each class. Quality research on EBPs is not readily available and there is a need for much more, ideally involving class teachers in the school setting.

1. *Classroom management structure*
   - *Antecedent management strategies* (Marks et al, 2003) are classroom strategies that assist to prepare the classroom and lesson materials for the lessons ahead in order to minimise challenging behaviours resulting from frustration and confusion. Fleury (2014, p. 73) uses the term 'priming' to describe the covering of lesson content prior to delivery to reduce concerns about unrehearsed material and tasks. Wong et al (2015) endorse this approach and all have found that these strategies reduce behavioural problems. Concrete instructions for all activity should be clear and explicit with consistency in routines (Stokes et al, 2017) with all children prepared for a change in routine where possible.
   - *Task analysis* is the division of all activity into small, manageable steps. Beamish, Clark et al. (2021) include it in the MoP Middle Years table. 'Explicit strategy instruction' (Fleury, 2014, p. 73) Specific techniques can be taught such as a step-by-step routine or a mnemonic to be followed even when working independently. *Author Note*: All tasks and especially assignments, should be 'chunked' so that each step, can be clearly understood, followed and completed. The act of 'crossing off' each step is satisfying and rewarding.

2. *Pedagogy*
   - *Modelling* (Wong et al., 2015) means the demonstration of a behaviour which then leads to the behaviour being learned e.g. 'model positive interactions' and 'model emotional literacy' (Beamish & Clark et al., 2021). Video modelling allows a student to call up a video of how to perform a particular skill. This will allow further exposure to the teaching of the skill and assist a student who finds it difficult to learn in a social setting. *Author note*: This method works with the rote memory and visual strengths of students and is applicable to curriculum content such as MathsOnline where a student can call up an instructional video of a Maths technique.
   - *Peer-mediated instruction* (Wong et al., 2015) is where neurotypically developing (NT) peers interact and assist the acquisition of new skills, behaviour, and social skills. Pairing or small group matching with peers trained to adapt instruction, provide feedback and promote communication with classmates is undertaken. At its best this overt strategy will increase the social contact of students with ASD. (Fleury, 2014). *Author note*: There should be measurable outcomes for the NT peers engaged in this activity or it is unconscionable.
   - *Prompting* (Fleury et al., 2014; Wong et al., 2015; Beamish & Clark et al., 2021) can be visual, using gestures or verbal prompts and it aims to give cues and assistance as a child with ASD attempts to use a skill.
   - *Provide an outline* (Marks et al., 2003) to aid with comprehension and attention. The student has a logical summary onto which can be placed additional points.
   - *Reinforcement* (Wong et al., 2015) is positive feedback as encouragement aiming to increase the behaviour/skill in the future.

- *Response interruption/redirection* (Wong et al., 2015) is defined as 'Introduction of a prompt, comment or other distracters, when an interfering behaviour is occurring, that is designed to divert the learner's attention away from the interfering behaviour and results in its reduction (p.1960).' *Author note*: One application here is the use of pre-prepared questions/visuals or items that motivate thought toward special interests/comfort zones as a distraction.

- *Self-management* (Wong et al., 2015; Fleury et al., 2014). Students are encouraged to self-monitor and to internally evaluate their effort and performance as well as reward themselves for appropriate behavioural choices. *Author note*: See the 'self-talk' strategy employed with students with ADHD and executive function weaknesses in Chapters 6 & 10.

3. *Visual aids*

Commonly used techniques observed in classrooms which have been validated by research and classroom practice over time, can assist with differentiation of the curriculum by displaying group expectations, tasks and questions.

- The possible language and/or comprehension weaknesses of autistic students and their visual-spatial orientation are supported by visual aids such as graphic organisers:

Venn diagrams
flowcharts
tree diagrams
mind maps
behaviour charts
number charts
'anger scales'

(Stokes et al., 2017, p. 199)

- Visual schedules, maps, labels and timelines can be used as alternative products for a research assignment if the writing task is too difficult. *Author note*: Visual supports can be used to work to the strengths of ASD students who tend to be 'bottom-up' thinkers with details as their focus (See Going Deeper). With well instructed use, the connection of details in a meaningful way using a graphic organiser, can support growth in comprehension skills.

4. *Growth of rapport and understanding between teacher and student*

- Stokes et al. (2017) report that improvement in behaviour and motivation occurred with the use of praise and rewards, teacher flexibility and preparedness to modify the environment, by demonstrating acceptance of the child while not giving undue special attention and by bringing the autistic child's special interests into the classroom.

Differentiation of learning activities

From a comprehensive understanding of the autistic student's learning strengths and weaknesses comes the need to differentiate each activity for that student. Smith, Bryant and Bryant (2019) propose a framework to guide a teacher on the choice of adaptations/adjustments of curriculum for a particular student using the research validated ADAPT framework:

'**A**sk "What am I requiring the student to do?"
Determine the prerequisite skills of the task.
Analyse the student's strengths and struggles.
Propose and implement adaptations from among the four instructional categories of *content, materials, delivery, and activity.*
Test and determine whether the adaptations helped the student to accomplish the task (p. 191).'

This framework allows for quick differentiation of a topic once the student's learning profile is well known.

Behaviour Support

According to Gonzales (2020):
Even when there has been prior assessment and careful planning to meet a student's individual needs, behaviour challenges may occur.
A quick checklist of causes may include:

■   'misunderstanding of verbal instruction or direction
■   difficulty standing or sitting still for a long period of time
■   misunderstanding of non-verbal cues
■   lack of motivation
■   short attention span and poor memory
■   difficulty in planning (in writing or attempting a work task)
■   difficulty in self-starting (needs assurance that she is doing the right thing)
■   lack of patience due to poor self-control (executive function)

(Chap 11, p. 164).'

Be ever mindful that challenging behaviour is most often an outward expression of an inward dysfunction, concern, or overload. Your frame of mind will assist you to gain a deeper understanding of the individual's inner lived experience. As a teacher, the wisdom to know what wilful behaviour is, and what it is not, can only develop with observation, experience, and time.

Going deeper

Background to the education of autistic twice-exceptional (2e) students

It is more likely now that a teacher will encounter a gifted or high potential student with aspects of ASD, in her mixed ability classroom, as the prevalence rises, nuanced diagnosis occurs, and classrooms become more inclusive and that she is completely unprepared from her pre-service training to teach this student. Morrier et al (2011) found that in a study of 90 teachers fewer than 15% had received training in how to teach students with ASD in their teacher preparation programs. They cite several studies when they assert that pre-service teacher training on special education is usually short, perhaps only a single course, giving instruction on legislative requirements and diagnostic criteria without going into detail about ASD students' social and academic needs nor the proven strategies that work with them. Nor is there instruction on how to integrate such strategies into the mixed ability classroom and teachers need this practical understanding.

Increasingly, inclusion of children with special education needs, including ASD, is being expected in mainstream classes. The concept of *inclusion* has shifted from the idea of a child with disabilities being present for some time, to one of a child being enrolled full-time with expectations that maximal achievement of all students in the class will occur. Chung, Chung, Edgar-Smith, Palmer, DeLambo and Huang (2015) made this observation along with reporting from previous surveys that teachers have concerns for their typical students when autistic students are integrated into inclusive classrooms because their behaviours may be disruptive. If given appropriate training, resources, and support staff levels then inclusion may be justifiable but to simply integrate without these provisions is to court underachievement for all students and a potentially stressful setting for teachers. Unsurprisingly, in all their cited studies, they found that teachers with special education training were far more positive about their inclusion than teachers without that training!

However, the work of Bandura (1997) has shown that our capacity to perform a task is based more on our self-efficacy, or self-belief about what we can achieve as teachers than on what is objectively true. Love, Toland, Usher et al. (2019) found that teacher self-efficacy for teaching autistic students was positively related to general teaching self-efficacy, job satisfaction and self-regulation and that contextual factors were important. Love, Findley, Ruble and McGrew (2020) found a positive and significant relationship between teachers' self-efficacy, engagement and student IEP goal achievement. If teachers believed they could teach autistic students and they engaged with learning how to do it, then their autistic students actually achieved better outcomes. Beamish, Clark et al. (2021) note that change in teacher classroom practice is more likely to occur when teachers can engage actively in collaboration with other educators about the practicalities of the classroom. The inference can be drawn that even short-term, whole-school initiatives to build staff knowledge of instructional strategies for the inclusive classroom, would support the general self-efficacy of capable, mainstream classroom teachers.

When students (of any profile) challenge your knowledge and capacity to manage their learning, ask yourself …

Who else is here to do this?
Who is better than me, at this time??

Know that you can help them if you apply what you know, read whatever reliable sources you can find and discuss your understanding with trusted colleagues.
No teacher can understand *everything* about the complex functioning of autistic students or those with any other condition.

It is possible that an autistic child in your class has very proactive parents who have seen multiple professionals, received excellent advice, and have gradually put many intervention programs and support people into the child's life. The child may be registered and receiving support from the National Disability Insurance Scheme (NDIS) which can financially support therapy services and equipment. Parental advice can help you to understand their child, so it is wise to invite both parents/ significant carers, if possible and available, for a meeting early in the first weeks of Term 1 or, ideally, to have made plans for the transition to your class in the previous year. An understanding of the child's individual learning profile, gained before problems arise in class, is of enormous benefit. An early meeting will ascertain if the parents are active or passive in the management of the child and their attitude toward you and school.

Conversely, it is possible that you are the first to notice particular symptoms in a child and you may suspect autism. Very young children, in Kindergarten to Year 2, may have behavioural characteristics that are excused by reasons of poor parenting, that she is just quirky or that he is shy. It takes time and observation to sort out an appropriate response to some behavioural traits of young children because of their varying rates of development.

The information following should help:

Autism SA (South Australia)'s website https://autismsa.org.au has very specific lists for

The first signs of Autism:

A Checklist for Babies and Toddlers
A Checklist for Children
A Checklist for Girls and Women
A Checklist for Boys.

Aspect Australia (see www.autismspectrum.org.au) has excellent information on getting a diagnosis, early intervention and how to navigate the NDIS. You can lead a child's parents to Aspect's resources, initially to the Autism Connect Helpline at 1300 308 699 without overtly suggesting a diagnosis which is not the role of a teacher.

It is beyond the scope of this book to describe ASD in its fullest range of symptoms since it is the presence of ASD in the gifted that is of our concern. Therefore, the possible characteristic of intellectual impairment will not be explored here.

Exceptional skills and autism

Strengths and gifts are associated with autism along with the previously discussed deficits. These abilities may be classified as relative strengths, savant skills, and giftedness.

Clark (2021) in an interview on the program *A different brilliant* with Orion Kelly (see www.youtube.com/watch?v=K8BFay40x70) defined the presence of exceptional skills in people with autism in the following way:

Savant skills are special abilities that exceed the general level of ability in that autistic person, and which sometimes exceed those in the general population. It is generally accepted that the skills fall into the range of memory, visual-spatial skills, calculation, drawing or music. The presence of relative strengths and savant skills in school-aged autistic students was reported in a recent study involving a survey of parents, students and teachers of autistic school-aged students in autism-specific schools in New South Wales, Australia (Clark et al., 2023). Memory and hyperlexic skills were the highest reported savant skills. Quoting several studies, Happe (2018) concluded that children demonstrating savant talents tended to show more autistic traits and to notice more details that others miss. Autistic children with higher level savant skills may not be in the mainstream classroom, in fact, they may even be non-verbal or intellectually impaired thus requiring that they be educated in special settings with highly trained teachers. The principles of gifted education would

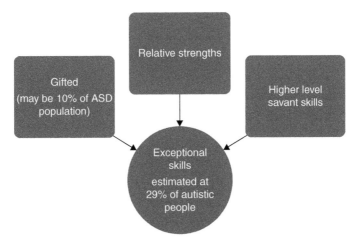

FIGURE 7.1 Map showing conceptualisation of the range of exceptional skills demonstrated by people with ASD (Clark, 2021, in interview). Some will have higher-level savant skills, some will have relative strengths and perhaps 10% will be gifted. Figure proposed by Gagne, see Chapter 4.

apply where possible. The talent should be acknowledged, nurtured, celebrated and enriched in the school setting.

My experience of gifted autistic students is that they appear to become more gifted as they grow older. Where a child has co-morbid ADHD she is unlikely to demonstrate high ability through written testing while still young. Mastery of self may be a pre-requisite for the exhibition of consistent talent in these students.

This is the story of a young man who presented for assistance in Year 4:

Case study

Blake

Blake was diagnosed with Asperger's Syndrome under the DSM-4 (now known as ASD Level 1) at age 5 and with ADHD at age 6 years. At age 9 years and 9 months his WISC-4 results were as follows in Table 7.1.

Summary of Scores

TABLE 7.1   Blake's WISC 4 results at 9 years and 9 months

WISC-IV	Percentile Rank	Confidence Interval Range	Classification
Verbal Comprehension	99	123–139	Very Superior
Perpetual Reasoning	92	111–127	Superior
Working Memory	55	93–110	Average
Processing Speed	97	114–133	Superior
General Ability Index	97	121–134	Superior

In Year 3 he had recorded Band 6 results in all areas of NAPLAN but for Persuasive Writing. In Year 5 his results were in Band 8 or above for all areas but Writing where he scored in Band 7. Blake was demonstrating his ability in this context but not consistently in class.

He has always found difficulty making friendships. He is very frank and unfiltered in his comments. Characteristically, he is excluded rather than bullied from his desired social settings while his relationships are comfortably made with older people and very young children. He is empathic and kind with them while harbouring a deep sadness, almost to the point of obsession, about his incapacity to make enduring friendships with young men of his age.

With the attainment of a black belt in martial arts and swimming achievements Blake has gained physical proficiency. He has not only excelled in martial arts but also in performance arts where he has held a position in the NSW Department of Education Arts Unit's Cello Ensemble and is Lead Cello in the local Youth Orchestra. But his real love is singing.

The following is a transcript of an interview with Blake, conducted when he was 16 years and 9 months old, in Year 11 at school. He is being educated in a NSW co-educational comprehensive high school.

Q: *At around what age or stage of school did you realise that your brain operated differently from the children around you?*

A: I realised that I was different around age 4 or 5 but my parents realised it when I started walking because I learned some things faster and other things not as quickly as other children. I was bullied pretty heavily from 4 onward so I learned that I was an outcast compared with the others.

Q: *How do you think and learn differently from most other children in your class?*

A: One example is that students in my trigonometry class, which I do for Maths Extension, mention things like 'I understand this concept' but for me it feels like there is a brick wall and it takes me time to see how one concept ties up with another. Yesterday in my trig class we mentioned the 'inverse tan' used to make symmetries using Pythagoras' Theorem. It took me the whole lesson to understand the first question while the others had it in 15 minutes. I understood it well after that, but it takes me a lot longer to 'get it'.

Q: *Do you miss out because of this?*

A: It depends on how accommodating the teacher is. My current teacher is kind and she writes it down for me.

Q: *Would it help if you had a video resource that could give you explanations on call?*

A: It is difficult to see how such a resource could contain all the questions I might need to ask.

Q. *If you could tell your teachers about the best ways to teach you when you were very young, what would you say?*

A: There was probably no good way to teach me when I was a child. I had massive behavioural issues, problems with authority, I'd be annoying and be all over the place. You could never 'pin me down'. There was nothing you could do except take me out of the environment where I was a problem.

Q: *Would it have helped if another person, a teacher's aide, could have worked with you and motivated you in the ways that you liked? Could you see that helping?*

A: Definitely.

Q: *Do you think that teachers and kids in your class know how clever you really are?*

A: I would say that I am not really clever in that sense. I have a different perspective from other people so it can be a problem. I would say that I feel just as intelligent as people around me but I do things differently from others.

[*Author note*: It became clear to me that Blake thought his need for more revisions when learning new concepts somehow discounted him from being 'highly intelligent'. I explained to him that his high intellectual ability and the way his autistic brain took time to process new information were somewhat 'asynchronous' characteristics of his but that it made no difference to the facts of his giftedness.]

Q: *What are your greatest learning strengths and abilities? What skills are you good at?*
A: I don't even know actually. Probably my strongest skill is keeping information in my memory for a long time. But I have such a lot of trouble getting it in because I want to master it before I use it. But once it is there, I have it.
I do love singing (and he sang for me in a beautiful untrained but well-modulated voice). It is a kind of a stim for me because it has become more like a habit.
I get the best results in performing arts and HSIE subjects although I enjoy STEM quite a bit. Music performance is my specialty. I enjoy all my work in different ways. My Chemistry class is too noisy and annoying. Distance Education Physics is annoying because of the IT problems.

Q: *Do you have other thoughts about school that you would be happy to share?*
A: The social climate of the school is like still water. If you have trouble making friends, like me, then the longer you wait to do that the more toxic it becomes, the more poisonous it feels to be moving around in it. It feels like I am being cut out from everyone else. One friend said I am quite confrontational and he doesn't know how to handle me and he feels annoyed with me.

Q: *The goal of my book is for teachers and parents to understand 'the twice-exceptional student'. Do you have insights or suggestions that you would like to share with this potential audience?*
A: That is a difficult question. Schools can cater to people better when they truly understand the problems and they create a place where they can help each other out.
I talk to people who are autistic but we don't talk about it in an academic sense. We need people who can understand what we are trying to ask. There is the age-old question of 'can you categorise autism'? If you can answer that then you can create a system around it.
A lot of teachers create a curriculum around the masses that leaves those twice-exceptional children behind. We need a change in the education system or in the way teachers teach. Both seem like a long task that would take years to achieve.
I try to see the counsellor at school sometimes, but they change so often that you have to start again, re-establish the connection again and again and I just feel like giving up on trying to talk to them.

The contrast between Blake at age 11 and at age 16 was remarkable. His greater self-awareness, ability to discuss emotions and his application to academic work is a legacy of his mother's perseverance, her advocacy and intuition and is not only accounted for through his adolescent development. Meeting him again confirmed that the development of apparent gifts into talents, in 2e children, builds self-efficacy, self-concept and well-being. I counselled Blake that his best friendships will probably develop through his favourite interests, activities and the finding of 'like-minded' companions. However, the knowledge of this possibility does not change the very lonely place he occupies currently at this very vulnerable stage of his life. He was very generous in choosing to share it with us all.

Presentation of ASD in women and girls

Aspect Australia states on its website that ASD is 'four times more common in boys than girls'. Is this actually the ratio of prevalence in the population or is it the rate of diagnosis currently occurring?

It is well documented that girls are more acculturated than boys and able to copy the actions of others, so when they are not able to manage well socially they imitate and mask their inner sense of incapability and anxiety. Girls can be so adept at mimickry that they are not diagnosed until much later than boys. Driver & Chester (2021), McDonnell & DeLucia et al. and Zener (2019) observe the low recognition of ASD in females in all settings and call for initiatives in clinical practice to increase awareness. A delayed diagnosis can mean that a young girl can wonder why she is so different from her age peers for many years, with consequent loss of self-esteem and skill development.

Autistic girls are often described as very shy or are not aware of how to conduct social relationships and how to play, sometimes acting in a controlling or bossy way. They internalise their anxiety while at school but may have strong emotional outbursts at home. Often, they will react to situations with extreme emotions. The common interests of autistic girls are noted as animals, people, nature, books and art and often their focus on a special interest will be extreme.

A part of this set of characteristics can be sensitivity to others, empathy, and a nurturing response. It is just not true that these girls will be uncaring. Rather, it should be assumed that they are 'clueless' about how to show their responses. Sometimes a girl will demonstrate perfectionism and yet be very disorganised with routines and possessions (see Spotlight on Girls with Autism, 2018).

What are the cognitive and sensory processing differences in autistic children?

Terminology

'Stimming' is short for 'self-stimulatory behaviours' – any movement or noise made, or any habit such as nail-biting, used to assist an individual to feel calmer. It may be done to allow focus or to reduce the effects of sights or sounds that are unwelcome.

Consider: In your classroom you may wish to stop strange or potentially disruptive stimming, but this is controversial amongst the autistic community. As with all matters of unusual behaviour in children, the wise move is to discuss the matter with the child's parents and to decide what behaviours can occur that will assist the child without undue disruption to the learning of other children in the class. New ways of expression or self-soothing may be found in collaboration with the child and family.

'Gestalt' is a configuration, pattern, or organised field having specific properties that cannot be derived from the summation of its component parts; a unified whole (dictionary.com). Gestalt perception where 'sensory information is received in infinite detail and holistically at the same time' can be a problem for people with ASD (Bogdashina, 2016, p. 60).' She notes that this 'unfiltered perception (p. 59)' is overwhelming and very difficult for the brain to process.

It has taken some time for the non-autistic world to understand the cognitive and sensory underpinnings in the lived experience of the autistic person. Donnellan et al. (2013) emphasise that the professional world has placed a social interpretation on the behaviours of autistic people which has detracted from a full understanding of their inner experience. ASD can pervade all areas of cognitive functioning. If given a neurological interpretation involving the individual's capacity to manage overwhelming or underwhelming sensation and involuntary movement then a more empathic response can occur from the rest of the population. The personal stories in Donnellan's article are interesting and insightful. Delacato (1974), was ahead of his time when he suggested that abnormal perceptions might give rise to a high level of anxiety and lead to obsessive, compulsive behaviours and social and communication problems. But it was not until 2013 that the DSM-5 included sensory responses as possible manifestations of the criterion: 'Restricted, repetitive patterns of behaviour, interests or activities.' Included for the first time in the DSM was 'Hyper – or hypo –reactivity to sensory input or unusual interest in sensory aspects of the environment (e.g., apparent indifference to pain/temperature, adverse responses to specific sounds or textures, excessive smelling or touching of objects, visual fascination with lights or movement (p. 28).'

> Indeed, the overwhelming and enduring tidal wave of sensations garnered by a hug may contribute to a ricocheting cascade leading from socialisation problems to mood disorders. And you can't afford to socialise while engaging in a hostile environment that assaults your senses.
>
> (p. 11 Casanova in the Foreword to Bogdashina 2016)

Sensory processing difficulties may cause the person to over-respond with strong, negative, or distressed behaviour or to under-respond with a very slow or non-response. This will manifest in varying sensory and movement behaviours.

And the impact of these behaviours in the classroom can bring further distress to the ASD child, can be frightening for his peers and certainly socially isolating in the peer group.

Memory in autistic students

The issues of attention and memory are fundamental to all learning. Nola Norris (2022) found from her PhD research that there are distinctive differences in the memory systems of autistic people. Three areas of long-term memory available to neurotypical (NT) learners are unevenly distributed in those with autism:

Episodic Memory is a weakly connected neural network. Because it is based on recollection of personal experience and requires strength in the areas of central coherence, executive function (EF) and abstracted reasoning it is not strong in the autistic person.

Semantic Memory is relied upon by autistic students. The features of semantic memory are:

- facts, general knowledge
- 'black & white' thinking
- focus on detail rather than the 'big picture'
- little interest in the factor of context
- reliance on rote memory.

Teachers can adapt the curriculum for these students by using quizzes, by allocating roles in research investigations according to student strengths and by praising factual recall. Ideally, pairing students with a trusted friend with complementary skills would work as an adjustment for autistic students who are being recognised for their semantic memory strengths.

Perceptual Memory is also strongly connected and is reliant on the perceptions of 'being in the moment'. Some autistic students have highly enhanced perception which can be valued as students are encouraged to share their responses.

The theory that autistic people are 'bottom up' thinkers is discussed frequently in the literature, that is, they tend to be focused on details rather than the 'big picture' ('top down') thinking, so can be weak on the metacognitive elements of comprehension, by missing the overall thematic development or an inferential interpretation of text.

Cognitive profile differences in ASD compared to Neurotypical (NT). What are the educational needs of autistic students?

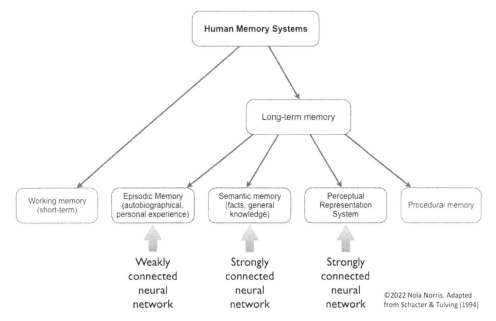

FIGURE 7.2 Cognitive profile differences in memory systems in autistic people compared to neurotypical. Used with permission by Nola Norris.

Instructional strategies for teaching reading skills

The implications of differences in memory in students with autism apply to the development of literacy. The term 'hyperlexia' has been applied to some autistic children where a child spontaneously learns to read early and beyond expected levels but the reading comprehension is below the standard of the word reading accuracy skills. Nation et al (2006) describe this phenomenon as 'a general mismatch between proficient reading accuracy on the one hand and the presence of cognitive and social deficits on the other (p. 918)'.

Of course, strong comprehension skills are the foundation of every aspect of learning, beginning with the oral listening comprehension needed for following instructions and attending to learning experiences, to understanding complex fiction and non-fiction texts from the literal meaning to the inferential and encompassing the devices of sarcasm, humour in the form of irony, jokes, riddles and witticisms. As has been established, for the autistic student, problems with reading comprehension flow from a predisposition to attend to the details in a passage with weaknesses in 'big picture' thinking, of context and the gestalt narrative.

With the increasing recorded prevalence of autistic students there has been a proliferation of research studies involving autistic students' reading proficiency and adjustments.

Twice-exceptional students with autism tend to have less severe language deficits, but not always. Nation et al. (2006) confirmed in their study of 41 autistic students that overall, their decoding skills fell into the average range, but their reading comprehension was often impaired. Norbury & Nation (2011) found that students who were proficient with language would need help to develop their skills in reading comprehension to the level of their school curriculum requirements.

So, it will be necessary to check carefully the range of reading comprehension skills of the autistic student.

Do not assume, because of observed verbal precocity, that the 2e autistic student has no deficit in reading comprehension

---

Reading Comprehension (RC) = Word Recognition X Language Comprehension

Gough & Tunmer (1986) The Simple View of Reading

Westerveld (2017) and her team found that RC in autistic students could be predicted by the degree of severity of their autism, their nonverbal cognition (NVIQ) and their spoken communication. But their 'word recognition' knowledge (decoding/letter & sound knowledge) was not dependent on these variables. While most autistic students will be able to learn to recognise words, many will struggle with RC, with gifted students predictably doing better if their language and vocabulary development is progressing well.

Note: Chapter 5 has presented the research on how to teach reading. Comments here pertain to how autistic characteristics add additional barriers to the development of RC proficiency.

1. *In emergent readers (Pre-school – Year 2)*
   Westerveld and her team recommend that when doing shared book reading for growth in meaning, therefore developing RC …

   ■ explain the meanings of unknown words carefully (for growth in vocabulary)
   ■ engage in conversation about the story with many prompting questions for understanding …What is happening in this story?
   ■ Have fun while reading. Motivational elements are enhanced this way.

2. *In Primary and Secondary School Children:*

TABLE 7.2 Use of the instructional strategies, Direct Instruction (DI) and Collaborative Strategic Reading (CSR), with autistic students who have reading comprehension difficulties

Step 1: Comprehensive assessment of comprehension using tools such as DIBELS to measure all aspects of word recognition fluency. Also, the use of reading inventories to check both literal and inferential comprehension. If possible, gain a thorough understanding of the impact of a student's underlying language skills from a speech pathology assessment. Note: Language ability is a powerful predictor of RC (Tárraga-Mínguez et al, 2021). Students need to be able to find the Main Idea of a text as a pre-requisite of RC development.

Step 2: See the table below explaining the use of two instructional strategies which were found to be effective [reported from several studies in Chang, Menzies & Osipova, (2020), Fleury et al (2014) and Tárraga-Mínguez et al, (2021).]

See: The National Institute for Direct Instruction (www.nifdi.org/) for a full explanation of the method. Reading Mastery is their product.

See: Brum et al (2019) for a clear explanation of how to use CSR with high school students. Download a PDF at https://journals.sagepub.com/doi/abs/10.1177/0040059919878663

INSTRUCTIONAL STRATEGY **Direct Instruction (DI)**	**INSTRUCTIONAL STRATEGY** **Collaborative Strategic Reading (CSR)** **Cooperative Learning, Guided and Shared Learning (peer tutoring, class-wide peer tutoring, small groups)** Note: students will need to be prepared for this social interaction and to work with trusted peers. Activities may require direct instruction prior to group activity**.**
ASD characteristic that is addressed when using this method:	
Weaknesses in observational learning and capacity to infer. Provides: • review of previously learned material • high degree of structure in the lessons • new material introduced systematically • in-built practice • feedback and error correction • clear guidance for action can be used for RC, vocabulary growth and for improvements in fluency.	*Weaknesses in social communication limiting the capacity to take a 'perspective' on a piece of text and to notice the structure of a text.* Provides: • opportunities to highlight the social aspects and value of reading. Tasks can include graphic organisers to record a character's feelings, the strength of emotions and interpretations of facial expressions. Shared tasks can include discussion about the illustrations in the text.

Incapacity to use 'prior knowledge' to support RC in a new text.	*Weaknesses in understanding how pronouns are being used (anaphoric cueing)*
• use Discussion questions to evoke application & sentence stems to practise new vocabulary usage (See Cravalho et al, 2020, p. 33) *Poor reading fluency & prosody.* • Follow an 'I do, you do, we do' approach, offering feedback.	• use a cloze activity and a list of pronouns to insert in the spaces • graphic organiser – a list of the pronouns used in the text for each character and why they changed according to the context in the passage.

Difficulty discerning emotional vocabulary, figurative language, spatial words and multiple meanings of words

• Visual supports and thinking maps to identify these words and graphic organisers to group them into categories.
• Colour-coding in the text to show the motivations of characters and their points of view, to show what is the main idea and what are the supporting details. (Can also be used to develop sequence by locating and noting antecedent events.)

Intepe-Tingir & Whalon (2022) improved understanding of target emotion words in six-to-seven-year-old autistic students after repeated reading of storybooks that illustrated the words.

Latest research in ASD and twice-exceptionality (2e)

Australian National Education Survey

An Autism Cooperative Research Centre (ACRC) research project, the Australian Autism Educational Needs Analysis (Saggers et al., 2018) involved a national survey of 1,468 Australian respondents who were educators, specialists, autistic students aged 11–18 and parents of autistic students found that the following characteristics had the most impact and required the highest levels of support, assistance, adjustments or accommodations in educational settings:

1. Social – emotional needs.

2. Sensory needs, particularly noise.

3. Behavioural and mental health needs
   ■ anxiety
   ■ learning difficulties
   ■ executive function skills such as attention to the task, personal organisation of their time and their belongings, and their thoughts (ASD is highly co-morbid with ADHD)
   ■ co-morbid conditions such as auditory processing disorder and language disorder

4. Transitions throughout the school day.

5. School connectedness.

6. Technology.

7. Students' perspectives of the level of challenge of activities experienced at school.

Educators, specialists, and parents stated that a lack of funding was the major barrier to supporting the complex needs of autistic students in schools. This was demonstrated in a consequent lack of time, lack of suitable education and training of teachers and assistant teachers and a lack of specialist support.

The survey identified several difficulties experienced by autistic students who were asked to indicate how hard or easy they felt a range of different settings were for them. On average, the top 10 most difficult activities autistic students experienced at schools included:

1 planning for assignments;

2 working as part of a group;

3 handwriting and being neat;

4 coping with change;

5 coping with bullying or teasing;

6 the speed at which they completed handwriting;

7 copying information from the board;

8 doing homework;

9 staying calm when other kids annoyed them; and

10 staying calm when the classroom is very noisy.

Overall, the executive function, social and emotional and fine motor challenges students experienced at school rated highly as difficulties.

Educational experiences of gifted autistic adults

A study recently undertaken by the UNSW and the Aspect Research Centre for Autism Practice (ARCAP), investigated the educational barriers and facilitators of twice-exceptional, intellectually gifted autistic adults (Townend, G., Jung, Jae. Y. J., Clark, T., Robinson, A., Merrington, H., 2022). Participants reflected upon, and reported their lived experiences during their school years and how such experiences were barriers or facilitators for strength recognition and talent development. The research aimed to support the improvement of talent development for this population. Findings of the study show that understanding and acceptance by families, teachers, and the community alongside material support for both giftedness and autism (i.e., programming, curriculum, and interventions) were highly influential for these participants. The findings allow for a clearer and a more complete understanding of the lived experiences of twice-exceptional autistic students in school settings and how such experiences supported or hindered the development of their strengths and talents as adults.

Given time to develop a trusting relationship with you, older autistic students will learn how to start telling you about their needs. But sometimes the needs are so complex and disguised under multiple layers of anxiety and low self-esteem that the child is a young adult before she can comprehend and interpret her own experience and find a way of verbalising it to the adults in her life. Nicholas has agreed to let you into his world as it unfolded.

Case study

Nicholas

NICHOLAS is a gifted young man with enormous empathy, with sensitivity to others and very high intellectual ability. He was diagnosed with ADHD while in primary school but his journey to an ASD diagnosis and the capacity to express his inner experience was long and painful.

Here is Nicholas' story in his own words:

It's hard to pinpoint when I realised I wasn't like other kids. In primary school, I feel that you can certainly get away with being the odd one out more, but I never really had trouble making friends. It wasn't until I started at a new school in year 5 (a boys-only school that ran from year 5 through to year 12) that I really felt like something was 'wrong with me'. This new school had a very high and harsh standard when it came to studying and academic performance. Whenever we were told to write something that was on the board, other students wrote two pages when I'd barely written two lines. I simply couldn't stay focused or on top of this new standard. I did feel that I was slower at working than my peers in my previous school – but it didn't feel anywhere near as dramatic and I often felt ahead of them in many other regards, leaving me more easily feeling bored in class and resorting to daydreaming.

Going into year 6 and being taught under a more interactive and engaging teacher made me begin to realise that the way I had been taught in year 5 simply did not suit me at all. Where my year 5 classes were more focused on copying and memorising uncompressed information, my year 6 classes allowed me to see that there were different ways to learn. *I preferred to have things explained step-by-step – the slower, the better. Instructions for tasks and explanations of new concepts had to be very specific and broken down into bite-sized chunks.*

However, my performance in exams at this time was still lacking as I often daydreamed without control. The exams I sat in year 5 and 6 were similar to high-school exams and a step up from what I had been doing previously. I found it incredibly hard to focus on the exams – particularly if I hit a snag with a question I didn't understand, and almost always found myself unable to move on. I think I had a hard time wrapping my head around the fact that there was something I perhaps didn't know in the exam, so I would get frustrated, then distracted by my own daydreaming.

Getting my exam results back, where I often didn't make it even most of the way through an exam, would leave me feeling distressed and often result in me breaking down and crying in class. In an all-boys school, this put an extra target on my back, as if simply being socially inept wasn't already enough. I had become a target for relentless bullying.

Entering high school only further exacerbated these issues. Due to my exam results, I was put in classes of academically low-scoring individuals whose only focus in class was to make my life hell, since they knew I was quite different and very emotionally sensitive – prone to crying and mental breakdowns where I would babble angrily. I understand now that this is rather typical behaviour for someone on the autism spectrum at that age, but at the time, I had only been diagnosed with ADHD.

Throughout these first few dark years of high school, the teachers were often ignorant of or simply didn't care enough to do anything about the bullying happening on the playground or in the classroom – be it subtle or blatant. I wish I could ask those teachers why they didn't do anything, why it seemed like they didn't care. If I could go back in time and ask the teachers anything it would be: 'Why didn't you do anything? It was happening right in front of you – did you not care? How could you not know what was happening?'

Eventually, I changed schools. I started term 4 of year 9 at a co-ed school that my older sisters had attended in the past, and it was an extraordinarily different experience. The teachers seemed more enthusiastic, more understanding, and the school culture as a whole was far friendlier. Learning tasks were varied and interactive, accommodating for various learning styles. During these years, I was confronted by how much people in this new high school complained about the school's 'strict' standards, despite it being far less strict than what I had experienced at my previous school. For convenient reference: a teacher at this new school was infamous for being particularly strict and old-fashioned, but he had previously been a teacher at my previous high school where he was renowned for being friendly and personable. The difference was not in his behaviour, but in the standards the students had developed.

However, the new school was not all sunshine and roses. The learning support there made a few hiccups that were detrimental to my mental health, and bullying still found its way to me, though not nearly as badly as my previous school. Furthermore, due to my experience at that previous school regarding their aggressive and belittling response to my exam results, I had developed chronic anxiety regarding exams. I would be unable to think clearly in exams or complete them due to the sheer anxiety that sitting an exam would give me – sometimes I would even throw up, or simply be in too much anxiety-induced nausea or pain to be productive at all. This would result in me getting terrible exam scores and further feed my anxiety for the next exam. As the years went on, this only got worse – and when it came time for the HSC, things were at their worst. My school and teachers put tonnes of pressure on students to perform well in the HSC and would hammer into us that our HSC results would essentially determine how successful we would be in life – our 'be-all-or-end-all'. I was therefore unable to sit my HSC exams due to the severity of my anxiety symptoms.

However, it was certainly not the end of my academic pursuits. I attained a diploma in counselling from TAFE and I am now studying for my Honours in Psychology at university, where I have so far maintained high grades. Rather than be limited by my ATAR, I embarked on a different route through university that has made me more experienced than many of my peers studying alongside me. I have thrived in university due to my freedom to learn what I want, how I want, and with my grades and results being answerable to only myself – not some scolding teachers. In fact, my lecturers and tutors at university have been nothing but encouraging and give students plentiful resources for us to study and learn. So, while my psychiatrically diagnosed specific phobia of exams still haunts me, the special provisions I am given, the lack of pressure from teachers, and the abundant independent learning opportunities have allowed me to achieve ongoing academic success at university. What's more, I've become actively involved in the extra-curricular aspects of my university – becoming an active member of the university's sports, student association and participating in many events.

Beyond university, I hope to work as a psychologist – in a clinical or research setting. I'm easy about either pathway because a major reason I embarked on this journey is so mental health issues and psychological disorders are better under-stood and treated, so either path will take me to either option. Not everyone is as privileged as I am to have been supported by understanding or caring people– there are too many stories I hear of people who find no understanding in their experience, no credible or feasible assistance for their needs, or who feel their issues aren't treatable. For me, I've always had the money, opportunity, and good fortune to receive the right support and treatment – but that is not a story as common as it should be. Nobody should be deprived of support based on their needs–learning disability or not. I'm just thankful to the people I've met along my journey who've allowed me to become who I am now – the teachers who cared, the specialists who looked deeper, and my mother who never stopped fighting for me.

Update: At the end of 2023 Nick finished the bachelor's degree part of his quali-fication. He is enrolled in the full Honours course with an eminent professor who will supervise him through his PhD. Nick has worked with this highly productive academic in the area of positive psychology for a year-and-a-half as his research assistant. This man has seen Nick's capacity and his passion for this area of psych-ology and offered him this very prestigious position. Nick was also student presi-dent at his university for nearly a year until this current contract arose.

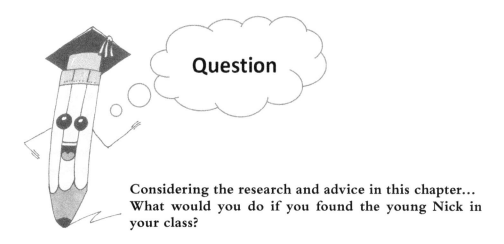

Considering the research and advice in this chapter...
What would you do if you found the young Nick in
your class?

'Go to' resources

The resources here should assist you to understand and differentiate your programs giving you evidence-based strategies to utilise. Of course, the efficacy of early intervention is indisputable so any perceived delays in speech, social, linguistic or movement skills should be noted and assisted separately and immediately. In NSW, parents will have to outsource these services as they are not routinely provided in schools.

The Alternate Achievement Literacy (AAL) and Collaborative Strategic Reading: High School (CSR-HS) can be downloaded at Brum, C., Hall, L. J., Reutebuch, C., & Perkins, Y. (2019). Reading comprehension strategies for high school students with autism spectrum disorder. *TEACHING Exceptional Children*, *52*(2), 88–97. https://journals.sagepub.com/doi/abs/10.1177/0040059919878663

To Be Gifted & Learning Disabled. Strengths-Based Strategies for Helping Twice-Exceptional Students With LD, ADHD, ASD and More (2017). Susan M Baum, Robin M. Schader, and Steven V. Owen. Prufrock Press, Waco, Texas. A book that contains user-friendly practical strategies for home and across the range of twice exceptional student groups.

Tony Attwood website. See
https://tonyattwood.com.au/

Found on this website is:
Attwood and Garnett events. See
https://attwoodandgarnettevents.com/2021/10/19/recognising-early-signs-of-a-meltdown-for-an-autistic-child-in-the-classroom/

■ Tip sheet for Recognising the Early Signs and Triggers of a Meltdown for an Autistic Child in the Classroom. This is an excellent resource.
■ Weekly newsletter with offers of available courses.

See https://attwoodandgarnettevents.com/2022/02/01/how-to-recognise-autism-in-girls/

- How to Recognise Autism in Girls
- There is a link to Questionnaires developed to assist the diagnosis of girls with autism, which usually does not occur until 12 to 13 years of age.
- An excellent list of 'signs of autism to look for in autistic girls'.

Australian Autism Cooperative Research Centre (ACRC) which investigated the promotion of school connectedness for students on the spectrum and has excellent resources for teaching and assisting autistic people across the lifespan. This video gives you the background and context. See www.youtube.com/@autism-crc

On the website www.autismcrc.com.au you will find the *Australian Autism Educational Needs Analysis* and the Executive Summary (PDF available) which will give you access to original, high-quality, Australian research (see citation below). See the three PowerPoint presentations: Teacher-Generated Strategies – Tier 1, Tier 2, Tier 3.

There is a link to free webinars for early career teachers (produced by inclusionED) that qualify for CPD hours. Create an account with InclusionED at www.inclusioned.edu.au for access to research-evidenced, highly practical tips and templates.

Autism Awareness Australia. See www.autismawareness.com.au/

A website funded by the Australian Government Department of Social Services with a wide array of resources including a vetted reading list.

Find on the *Educational Resources* page:

- a series of films 'What are you doing?' to explain ASD and to use with your class to explain the condition of autism.
- *Autism Classroom* contains information and ideas about building the skills that 'bring out the best in students'. There are links to low cost 'printables' for teaching social skills and behaviour skills.
- Under the heading *Teach* is a guide for setting up an 'autism classroom'.
  Author Note: This website may be overwhelming on one level but by scrutinising the ideas you may be prompted how some, even minor, adjustments to the setting and curriculum may assist in your differentiation purposes.
- Sensory Form Instruction Sheet. See www.autismspectrum.org.au/uploads/documents/Aspect%20Practice/SensoryFormWithInstructions.pdf Tools such as headphones, a low-lit space or a quiet area may be needed.

Autism and Girls
See www.yellowladybugs.com.au/
Spotlight on Girls with Autism PDF, produced in collaboration with the Department of Education and Training Victoria and a group of stakeholders. An excellent resource.
Points made are:

- Boys are four times more likely to receive a diagnosis of autism than girls
- The average age of diagnosis of a girl is nine years, but many are much older.

- Girls are better at masking their difficulties than boys because they are better acculturated and able to imitate the skills of other girls and they are more motivated to socially adjust and disguise their insecurities and skill deficits.

Autism Speaks – Visual Supports and Autism by Loring, W., & Hamilton, M. (2011). Visual supports and autism spectrum disorders. See www.autismspeaks.org/sites/default/files/2018-08/Visual%20Supports%20Tool%20Kit.pdf

Autism SA See https://autismsa.org.au/autism-diagnosis/autism-symptoms/signs-of-autism-in-children/

An autistic woman's lived experience: Grandin, Temple. See www.templegrandin.com.
Author Note: This website contains the story of this remarkable, high achieving, autistic woman through her short articles and links to her books and advice. It may be helpful for encouraging gifted autistic students to be inspired and to persevere.

Beyond Exceptional. See www.beyondexceptional.com.au
Beyond Exceptional provides individual and group bespoke services to support the unique learning needs of gifted and twice exceptional neurodiverse individuals and their networks, delivered remotely or in-person. The website 'Resources' page provides a forum for gifted and 2e people to share their achievements along with the latest research and practice information. Trevor Clark is a principal in the consultancy.

InclusionED. See www.inclusioned.edu.au
   This site is extraordinary with instructional videos from class settings to demonstrate practices described on this site. One example of this is:
   Under *Practices > Latest releases > Incorporate special interests in the classroom*. The video and explanation is clear.
   I think the instruction is strong enough to begin using the practice without further explanation!
Author Note: The Models of Practice described in the Beamish, Clark et al. (2021) reference are the practices described. So you can be sure that each one is research-evidenced and has been used in schools previously.

Indiana Resource Center for Autism
Visual Supports for School, Home and Community See www.iidc.indiana.edu/irca/resources/visual-supports/index.html
You will find a set of free, downloadable, printable visual support cards ready to use categorised under the headings 'Behaviour and Emotions', 'School', 'Schedules.' etc. They are very useful.

Myles, B.S., Hagen, K., Holverstott, J., Hubbard, A., Adreon, D., Trautman, M. (2016) *Life Journey through Autism: An Educator's Guide to Asperger Syndrome*, Organisation for Autism Research (OAR), reprint from original (2005).
The PDF is available online at https://researchautism.org/wp-content/uploads/2016/11/An_Educators_Guide_to_Asperger_Syndrome.pdf
Author note: As noted previously, the DSM-5-TR does not use the term 'Asperger Syndrome' but can encompass the characteristics of gifted/high potential autistic student in a diagnosis of ASD.

'Simple View of Reading' explanation can be found at: www.readingrockets.org/article/simple-view-reading
START: Strategies for Improving Literacy for Students with ASD (PDF) can be found at www.gvsu.edu/cms4/asset/64CB422A-ED08-43F0-F795CA9DE364B 6BE/asd_literacy_strategies_with_color.pdf This comprehensive guide from Grand Valley State University, Michigan, USA, is an excellent resource for teachers of students in the K-6 grades.

The Neurodiversity Hub. See www.neurodiversityhub.org/home
Author note: While there is a list of strategies for teachers, the best course of action is to negotiate their use with parents and to document their use from conversations in parent-teacher meetings.

■   Sensory Processing Disorder and Neurodiversity In Primary School: How It Can Affect Learning: a brief, visual explanation of how sensory processing differences affect learning. See https://static1.squarespace.com/static/5a88ab00f 43b552a84c3b7c9/t/601e2c6dcc2902327df72e7a/1612590192273/2.+SENS ORY+AND+STUDENT+LEARNING.pdf

University Coursework:

■   A short course, lasting four weeks at the Basic Level and called *Good Practice in Autism Education* is available through the University of Bath. There is a free, limited access option for those who merely want to experience the course materials. www.futurelearn.com/courses/autism-education

■   A quick search has revealed that courses on teaching students with autism are currently available at most universities. I cannot help with recommendations for particular courses, unfortunately.

Wong, M., Ratcliffe, B., & Li, S. (2018, July). Teacher-delivery of the Westmead Feelings Program: Emotion-based learning for children with autism spectrum disorder with and without co-occurring mild intellectual disability in primary schools. In *Proceedings of the 2018 Australian Association of Special Education National Conference: Creating Connections: Developing Personal and Social Capabilities* (pp. 8–10).

■   The Westmead Feelings Program (WFP) was developed and trialled at the Children's Hospital Westmead, New South Wales, Australia and is available as a kit and certification course from ACER.

Bibliography

American Psychiatric Association: Desk Reference to the Diagnostic Criteria From DSM-5-TR. Washington, DC: American Psychiatric Association, 2022, pp. 27–30

Bandura, A. (1997). Editorial. *American Journal of Health Promotion, 12*(1), 8–10. https://doi. org/10.4278/0890-1171-12.1.8

BBC News. (2013, June 5). Ouchlets. Stimming: What autistic people do to feel calmer. *BBC News.* Retrieved from www.bbc.co.uk/news/blogs-ouch-22771894

Beamish, W. & Clark, T. et al (2021). Models of practice for teachers of students on the autism spectrum. In Carrington, S., Saggers, B., Harper-Hill, K., & Whelan, M. (Eds.). *Supporting students on the autism spectrum in inclusive schools: A practical guide to implementing evidence-based approaches.* (1st edn). Abingdon: Routledge. https://doi.org/10.4324/9781003049036

Bogdashina, O. (2006). *Theory of mind and the triad of perspectives on autism and asperger syndrome: A view from the bridge.* London: Jessica Kingsley Publishers.

Bogdashina, O. (2016). *Sensory perceptual issues in Autism and Aspergers syndrome: Different sensory experiences – different perceptual worlds.* (2nd edn). London: Jessica Kingsley Publishers.

Bryant, B. R., Bryant, D. P. & Smith, D. D. (2019). *Teaching students with special needs in inclusive classrooms.* United States: SAGE Publications.

Cain, M. K., Kaboski, J. R. & Gilger, J. W. (2019). Profiles and academic trajectories of cognitively gifted children with autism spectrum disorder. *Autism: The International Journal of Research and Practice, 23*(7), 1663–1674. https://doi.org/10.1177/1362361318804019

Center for Disease Control and Prevention, 'Autism Spectrum Disorder – Data and Statistics', US Department of Health and Human Services. Autism and Developmental Disabilities Monitoring (ADDM) Network. (2020).

Chang, Y-C, Menzies, H. M. & Osipova, A. (2020). Reading comprehension instruction for students with autism spectrum disorder. *The Reading Teacher, 74(3)*, 255–264. https://doi.org/10.1002/trtr.1929

Chung, W., Chung, S., Edgar-Smith, S., Palmer, R. B., DeLambo, D. & Huang, W. (2015). An examination of in-service teacher attitudes toward students with autism spectrum disorder: Implications for professional practice. *Current Issues in Education, 18*(2), 1–10.

Clark, T. (2016). Curriculum to support students with autism and special talents and abilities. In *Exploring Giftedness and Autism* (1st edn, pp. 60–104). Abingdon: Routledge. https://doi.org/10.4324/9781315733388-3

Clark, T. (2019). A curriculum to support students with autism and special talents and abilities. In R. Jordan, J. M. Roberts, & K. Hume. (Eds). *The SAGE Handbook of Autism and Education* (pp. 315–320). SAGE Publications Ltd. https://dx.doi.org/10.4135/9781526470409.n25

Clark, T. (2021). In Interview. A different brilliant with Orion Kelly www.youtube.com/watch?v=K8BFay40x70

Clark, T., Yup Jung, J., Roberts, J., Robinson, A., Howlin, P. (2023). The identification of exceptional skills in school-age autistic children: Prevalence, misconceptions, and the alignment of informant perspectives. *Journal of Applied Research in Intellectual Disabilities* (pp. 1–12). Wiley & Sons. https://doi.org/10.1111/jar.13113

Cravalho, D. A., Jimenez, Z., Shhub, A. & Solis, M. (2020). How grades 4 to 8 teachers can deliver intensive vocabulary and reading comprehension interventions to students with high-functioning autism spectrum disorder. *Beyond Behavior, 29*(1), 31–41. https://doi.org/10.1177/1074295620907110

Delacato, C. H. (1974). *The ultimate stranger: The autistic child.* New York: Doubleday.

Donellan, A. M., Hill, D. A. & Leary, M. R. (2013). Rethinking autism: Implications of sensory and movement differences for understanding and support. *Frontiers in Integrative Neuroscience, 6*, 124. doi:10.3389/fnint.2012.00124

Driver, B. & Chester, V. (2021). The presentation, recognition and diagnosis of autism in women and girls. *Advances in Autism, 7*(3), 194–207. https://doi.org/10.1108/AIA-12-2019-0050

Fletcher-Watson, S. & Happé, F. (2019). *Autism: A new introduction to psychological theory and current debates* (2nd edn). Abingdon: Routledge. https://doi.org/10.4324/9781315101699

Fleury, V. P., Hedges, S., Hume, K., Browder, D. M., Thompson, J. L., Fallin, K., … & Vaughn, S. (2014). Addressing the academic needs of adolescents with autism spectrum disorder in secondary education. *Remedial and Special Education, 35*(2), 68–79. https://doi.org/10.1177/0741932513518823

Frith, U. (1994). Autism and theory of mind in everyday life. *Review of Social Development, 3*(2), 108–124. https://doi.org/10.1111/j.1467-9507.1994.tb00031.x

Frith, U. (2012). The 38th Sir Frederick Bartlett Lecture Why we need cognitive explanations of autism. *Quarterly Journal of Experimental Psychology* (2006), *65*(11), 2073–2092. https://doi.org/10.1080/17470218.2012.697178

Gonzales, M. (2020). *Systems Thinking for Supporting Students with Special Needs and Disabilities: A Handbook for Classroom Teachers.* Springer Publishing. https://doi.org/10.1007/978-981-33-4558-4

Gough, P. B. & Tunmer, W. E. (1986). Decoding, reading, and reading disability. *Remedial and Special Education*, *7*(1), 6–10. https://doi.org/10.1177/074193258600700104

Happé, F. (2018). Why are savant skills and special talents associated with autism? *World psychiatry: Official Journal of the World Psychiatric Association (WPA)*, *17*(3), 280–281. https://doi.org/10.1002/wps.20552

Harrop, C. (2015). Evidence-based, parent-mediated interventions for young children with autism spectrum disorder: The case of restricted and repetitive behaviors. *Autism: The International Journal of Research and Practice*, *19*(6), 662–672. https://doi.org/10.1177/1362361314545685

Intepe-Tingir, S. & Whalon, K. (2022). Teaching emotion vocabulary to children with autism spectrum disorder. *Journal of Special Education*, *56*(4), 193–207. https://doi.org/10.1177/00224669221083341

Kaffemaniene, I. & Kulese, Z. (2021, May). Ways of individualization of education for children with autism spectrum disorders: The experience of special pedagogues'. *Society. Integration. Education. Proceedings of the International Scientific Conference*, *3*, 37–50. https://dx.doi.org/10.17770/sie2021vol3.6410

Kouklari, E.-C., Tsermentseli, S. & Auyeung, B. (2018). Executive function predicts theory of mind but not social verbal communication in school-aged children with autism spectrum disorder. *Research in Developmental Disabilities*, *76*, 12–24. https://doi.org/10.1016/j.ridd.2018.02.015

Lanou, A., Hough, H. & Powell, E. (2012). Case studies on using strengths and interests to address the needs of students with autism spectrum disorders. *Intervention in School and Clinic*, *47*, 175–182.

Love, A. M. A., Findley, J. A., Ruble, L. A. & McGrew, J. H. (2020). Teacher self-efficacy for teaching students with autism spectrum disorder: Associations with stress, teacher engagement, and student IEP outcomes following COMPASS consultation. *Focus on Autism and Other Developmental Disabilities*, *35(1)*, 47–54. https://doi.org/10.1177/1088357619836767

Love, A. M., Toland, M. D., Usher, E. L., Campbell, J. M. & Spriggs, A. D. (2019). Can I teach students with Autism Spectrum Disorder?: Investigating teacher self-efficacy with an emerging population of students. *Research in Developmental Disabilities*, *89*, 41–50. https://doi.org/10.1016/j.ridd.2019.02.005

Lukito, S., Jones, C. R. G., Pickles, A., Baird, G., Happé, F., Charman, T. & Simonoff, E. (2017). Specificity of executive function and theory of mind performance in relation to attention–deficit/hyperactivity symptoms in autism spectrum disorders. *Molecular Autism*, *8*(1), 60–60. https://doi.org/10.1186/s13229-017-0177-1

Koegel, L. K., Koegel, R. L., Ashbaugh, K. & Bradshaw, J. (2014). The importance of early identification and intervention for children with or at risk for autism spectrum disorders. *International Journal of Speech-Language Pathology*, *16*(1), 50–56. https://doi.org/10.3109/17549507.2013.861511

McDonnell, C. G., DeLucia, E. A., Hayden, E. P., Penner, M., Curcin, K., Anagnostou, E., … & Stevenson, R. A. (2021). Sex differences in age of diagnosis and first concern among children with autism spectrum disorder. *Journal of Clinical Child & Adolescent Psychology*, *50*(5), 645–655. https://doi.org/10.1080/15374416.2020.1823850

McGillicuddy, S. & O'Donnell, G. M. (2014). Teaching students with autism spectrum disorder in mainstream post-primary schools in the Republic of Ireland. *International Journal of Inclusive Education*, *18*(4), 323–344. https://doi.org/10.1080/13603116.2013.764934

Maras, K., Norris, J. E. & Brewer, N. (2020). Metacognitive monitoring and control of eyewitness memory reports in autism. *Autism Research: Official Journal of the International Society for Autism Research*, *13*(11), 2017–2029. https://doi.org/10.1002/aur.2278

Marder, T. & de Bettencourt, L. U. (2015). Teaching students with ASD using evidence-based practices: Why is training critical now? *Teacher Education and Special Education*, 38(1), 5–12. https://doi.org/10.1177/0888406414565838

Marks, S. U., Shaw-Hegwer, J., Schrader, C., Longaker, T., Peters, I., Powers, F. & Levine, M. (2003). Instructional management tips for teachers of students with autism spectrum disorder (ASD). *Teaching Exceptional Children*, *35*(4), 50–54. http://dx.doi.org/10.1177/004005990303500408

Montgomery, D. (2015). *Teaching gifted children with special educational needs: supporting dual and multiple exceptionality* (1st edn) Abingdon: Routledge. https://doi.org/10.4324/9781315712321

Morrier, M. J., Hess, K. L. & Heflin, L. J. (2011). Teacher training for implementation of teaching strategies for students with autism spectrum disorders. *Teacher Education and Special Education*, *34*(2), 119–132 https://doi.org/10.1177/0888406410376660

Narzisi, A., Alonso-Esteban, Y., Masi, G. & Alcantud-Marín, F. (2022). Research-Based Intervention (RBI) for autism spectrum disorder: Looking beyond traditional models and outcome measures for clinical trials. *Children (Basel, Switzerland)*, *9*(3), 430. https://doi.org/10.3390/children9030430

Nation, K., Clarke, P., Wright, B. & Williams, C. (2006). Patterns of reading ability in children with autism spectrum disorder. *Journal of Autism and Developmental Disorders*, *36*(7), 911–919. http://dx.doi.org/10.1007/s10803-006-0130-1

National Centre on Birth Defects and Developmental Disabilities, Centres for Disease Control and Prevention, Retrieved 31 March 2023. www.cdc.gov/ncbddd/

Norbury, C. & Nation, K. (2011). Understanding variability in reading comprehension in adolescents with autism spectrum disorders: Interactions with language status and decoding skill. *Scientific Studies of Reading*, *15*(3), 191–210. https://doi.org/10.1080/10888431003623553

Norris, N. *Neurodiversity and the Nature of Learning: Memory and the Autism Spectrum*. Presentation at The Research Conversations online conference, 23 October 2021, hosted by St Andrew's Cathedral School, Sydney.

Norris, N. G. (2023). How does my student learn? Neurodiversity and the nature of learning in autism. *International Journal of Christianity & Education*, *27*(1), 65–87. https://doi.org/10.1177/20569971221084350

Randi, J., Newman, T. & Grigorenko, E. L. (2010). Teaching children with autism to read for meaning: Challenges and possibilities. *Journal of Autism and Developmental Disorders*, *40*(7), 890–902. https://doi.org/10.1007/s10803-010-0938-6

Reutebuch, C. K., El Zein, F., Kim, M. K., Weinberg, A. N. & Vaughn, S. (2015). Investigating a reading comprehension intervention for high school students with autism spectrum disorder: A pilot study. *Research in Autism Spectrum Disorders*, *9*, 96–111. https://doi.org/10.1016/j.rasd.2014.10.002

Ronksley-Pavia, M. (2020). Twice-exceptionality in Australia: Prevalence estimates. *Australasian Journal of Gifted Education*, *29*(2), 17–29. https://doi.org/10.21505/ajge.2020.0013

Saggers, B., Klug, D., Harper-Hill, K., Ashburner, J., Costley, D., Clark, T., Bruck, S., Trembath, D., Webster, A. A. & Carrington, S. (2018). *Australian Autism Educational Needs Analysis – What are the Needs of Schools, Parents and Students on the Autism Spectrum? Full*

Report and Executive Summary, version 2. Cooperative Research Centre for Living with Autism, Brisbane.

Schacter, D. L. & Tulving, E. (1994). What are the memory systems of 1994? In D. L. Schacter & E. Tulving (Eds), *Memory Systems 1994* (pp. 1–38). Cambridge MA: MIT Press.

Scheeren, A. M., de Rosnay, M., Koot, H. M. & Begeer, S. (2013). Rethinking theory of mind in high-functioning autism spectrum disorder: Advanced theory of mind in autism. *Journal of Child Psychology and Psychiatry, 54*(6), 628–635. https://doi.org/10.1111/jcpp.12007

Stenhoff, D. M., Pennington, R. C. & Tapp, M. C. (2020). Distance education support for students with autism spectrum disorder and complex needs during Covid-19 and school closures. *Rural Special Education Quarterly, 39*(4), 211–219. https://doi.org/10.1177/87568 70520959658

Stokes, M. A., Thomson, M., Macmillan, C. M., Pecora, L., Dymond, S. R. & Donaldson, E. (2017). Principals' and teachers' reports of successful teaching strategies with children with high-functioning autism spectrum disorder. *Canadian Journal of School Psychology, 32*(3), 192–208. https://doi.org/10.1177/0829573516672969

Tárraga-Mínguez, R., Gómez-Marí, I., & Sanz-Cervera, P. (2021). Interventions for improving reading comprehension in children with ASD: A systematic review. *Behavioral Sciences, (Basel, Switzerland), 11*(1), 3. https://doi.org/10.3390/bs11010003

Taylor, A., Beamish, W., Tucker, M., Paynter, J. & Walker, S. (2021) Designing a model of practice for Australian teachers of young school-age children on the autism spectrum. *Journal of International Special Needs Education, 24*(1), 1–13. https://doi.org/10.9782/JISNE-D-18-00017

Thye, M. D., Bednarz, H. M., Herringshaw, A. J., Sartin, E. B. & Kana, R. K. (2018). The impact of atypical sensory processing on social impairments in autism spectrum disorder. *Developmental Cognitive Neuroscience, 29*, 151–167. https://doi.org/10.1016/j.dcn.2017.04.010

Van Der Steen, S., Geveke, C. H., Steenbakkers, A. T. & Steenbeek, H. W. (2020). Teaching students with Autism Spectrum Disorders: What are the needs of educational professionals? *Teaching and Teacher Education, 90* (103036). https://doi.org/10.1016/j.tate.2020.103036

Westerveld, M. (webinar) Literacy profiles and literacy predictors for early learners on the autism spectrum. (2017, Sept. 25) www.youtube.com/watch?v=k4OZvYpmPS4

Williams, D. (2010). Theory of own mind in autism: Evidence of a specific deficit in self-awareness? *Autism: The International Journal of Research and Practice, 14*(5), 474–494. https://doi.org/10.1177/1362361310366314

Wong, C., Odom, S. L., Hume, K. A., Cox, A. W., Fettig, A., Kucharczyk, S., … Schultz, T. R. (2015). Evidence-based practices for children, youth, and young adults with autism spectrum disorder: A comprehensive review. *Journal of Autism and Developmental Disorders, 45*(7), 1951–1966. https://doi.org/10.1007/s10803-014-2351-z

Wu, I.-C., Lo, C. O. & Tsai, K.-F. (2019). Learning experiences of highly able learners with ASD: Using a success case method. *Journal for the Education of the Gifted, 42*(3), 216–242. https://doi.org/10.1177/0162353219855681

Zener, D.(2019). Journey to diagnosis for women with autism. *Advances in Autism, 5*(1), 2–13. https://doi.org/10.1108/AIA-10-2018-0041

Developmental Coordination Disorder/Dyspraxia

Rhonda Filmer

VIGNETTE

Alistair is the 'go to' authority on Roman history, algebra, general knowledge and trivia quizzes. Everyone in the class wants to sit near him when the problem-solving activities start. For his current history unit on early American colonisation he has read everything in the school (and local) library, on the *Best History Websites* and on *Encyclopedia Britannica*. Alistair has an incredible memory for facts and argument.

Yet, he walks with an unusual gait that is quite awkward and he sometimes slurs his speech. This has not changed since he started at the school despite appropriate therapy with his occupational therapist.

His whole class in Year 6 has accepted that he will field in softball but he won't bat and he will never enter the house competition for cross-country running. Alistair is great fun and he is a popular classmate because, from the beginning of school, his diagnosis of DCD has been accompanied by pro-active, resourceful parenting and appropriate therapies enabling him to develop a rare combination of self-acceptance and resilience.

What it is

According to the DSM-5-TR, DCD, historically referred to as dyspraxia, affects a child's capacity to execute coordinated motor skills such that they are:

'substantially below that expected, given the individual's chronological age and opportunity for skill learning and use' (p. 39)

DOI: 10.4324/9781003404972-10

The condition is characterised by:

- affected movement and co-ordination in fine motor or in gross motor activity or both
- problems with executive function and visuo-spatial working memory (from studies cited in Opitz et al, 2020; Leonard & Hill, 2015; Saban, 2014; Feng et al, 2012 and Alloway & Archibald, 2008)
- performance speed problems along with completion of tasks
- being present in children of any intellectual ability.

In order to qualify for a diagnosis of DCD a child **must not**:

- exhibit intellectual disability
- have visual impairment
- present with some other neurological condition that has an effect on motor activity (such as cerebral palsy or muscular dystrophy).

Why it is relevant to twice exceptionality

The gifted/high potential student may not actually develop her intellectual or creative potential if her impaired accuracy of motor skills, participation in physical development activities, reading, handwriting and practical skills are affected by DCD which is undiagnosed and untreated. As a consequence, without appropriate and effective therapy, the 2e student will also develop poor self-efficacy and self-consciousness affecting his social relationships and enjoyment in his school years.

What you will see in the classroom

'Difficulties are manifested as:

clumsiness (for example, dropping or bumping into objects) as well as

slowness and inaccuracy of performance of motor skills (for example, catching an object, using scissors or cutlery, handwriting, riding a bike or participating in sports)' (DSM-5-TR p. 39).

lower than expected outcomes in spelling and reading

up to 95% of students with DCD will have handwriting difficulties (Barnett & Prunty, 2020). Problems with opening lunch containers, art and craft storage and science equipment.

There are *three stages in the performance of a task* according to Christmas & Van de Weyer (2019, p. 8):

Ideation – thinking about what the body needs to do

↓

Motor planning – organising the body to do the actions

↓

Execution – actions which happen 'automatically' in a non-DCD person occur following a conscious decision in response to the environment. Practice leads to the development of less conscious monitoring.

The movements of children with DCD will be:

- slower
- less accurate
- more effortful (Cacola, 2014, p. 102).

The impact of this disorder will be significant in the life of the school-age student. It may affect involvement in physical activities such as games, sports, dance and social activities along with handwriting and the neatness of book work, the capacity to type, even to paint or do leisure activities. Academic results will be affected in the organisation and completion of work on time. It is not hard to see how an average or bright student with DCD will have poorer school outcomes than his intellectual peers.

As with every disability, it will manifest in specific difficulties for each individual and at a varying level of severity.

What do I do about it?

1. All students with DCD should have *early intervention* so speak to your grade supervisor or school counsellor as soon as you notice any abnormalities in a student's physical abilities, including handwriting.

2. The problems your student is facing should be brought to the attention of his parents. If there has not been a previous diagnosis then a recommended Occupational Therapist can do a *diagnostic assessment* and offer *intervention activities* to maximise the student's motor skills outcomes.

3. Seek subtle ways to *modify PE activities*.

4. Allow time for the student to *move about in the room* to prevent the discomfort of sitting for long periods.

5. Avoid situations where students choose their team members for outdoor games.

Possible adjustments for students with DCD

Exercise physiologists and physiotherapists often have specialist training in paediatrics. While providing therapy that develops the skills required for playground and leisure activity, they can present recommendations for how to modify Physical Education (PE) activities for a student and in cohort with parents.

TABLE 8.1 Practical strategies for the classroom as suggested by Christmas & Van de Weyer (2019, pp 10–13)

DCD Problem	School Adjustment
Child cannot work across the mid-line of the body	Student should be seated facing the teacher to avoid the need to turn or twist, also allowing her to observe the teacher's 'body language'.
Handwriting problems	Ensure that the student's feet are on the ground when sitting at a desk. Allow space to place the whole arm on the desk surface. Promote a tripod grip. Use moulded pen grips.
Poor organisation and sequencing skills	Use a visual timetable – replicated at home and at school. Give a two-minute warning for transitions.
Poor gross motor skills	Subtle differentiation of activities Allow for additional practice time to gain mastery.
Over-reactivity when touched or nudged by others	Place the student at the head of any queue.
Reduced awareness of how much 'force' they use, for example, a reduced sense of touch may lead to a lack of awareness of injury.	Monitor carefully.
Discomfort from sitting for a long time	Choose the student to do class tasks such as giving out papers or light equipment, allowing for movement.

The M.A.T.C.H. model was developed in the OT setting by Dancza, Missiuna & Pollock (2017) aimed at optimising children's participation and involvement in class activities by:

THE M.A.T.C.H. MODEL

> **M**odifying the task
> **A**ltering their expectations
> **T**eacher strategies
> **C**hanging the environment
> **H**elping children feel understood and supported.

They recommend:
> *'Identifying situations where participation is valued more highly than performance and where children with DCD perceive there is a good match between performance expectations and their own abilities will therefore support children's psychosocial well-being, build self-efficacy and encourage their participation.'*
>
> (Dancza, Missiuna C & Pollock, 2017, p. 39)

Excellent practical resources setting out exactly what to do at each grade level of school for particular symptoms of DCD (Grades 1/2 →Adolescent) with the M.A.T.C.H. model can be found at: www.canchild.ca/en/resources/123-m-a-t-c-h-flyers-a-resource-for-educators. Download the flyers immediately!

Going deeper

Developmental Coordination Disorder (DCD) is not commonly cited in the profiles of 2e students unless it is a severe level of presentation but with prevalence rates reported by Zwicker et al (2012), Cleaton, Lorgelly et al (2019), Licari, Williams et al (2020) and Barnett & Prunty (2020), in fact agreed upon across the literature, at *up to 6% of school age children*, this condition is bound to be more common than it is being diagnosed. At a mild to moderate level, it is probably overlooked for diagnosis in a child with other disabilities.

DCD is under-diagnosed because symptoms are encompassed in co-morbid conditions

In a previous time 'clumsiness' was included on the list of symptoms for dyslexia but the definition of the International Dyslexia Association (IDA) is 'a specific learning disability that is neurobiological in origin. It is characterised by difficulties with accurate and/or fluent word recognition and by poor spelling and decoding abilities. These difficulties typically result from a deficit in the phonological component of language that is often unexpected in relation to other cognitive abilities and the provision of effective classroom instruction. Secondary consequences may include problems in reading comprehension and reduced reading experience that can impede growth of vocabulary and background knowledge.' (This is fully explained in Chapter 2.)

We can see that *students with dyslexia and co-morbid 'clumsiness' most probably have DCD*. With a more specific understanding of the presenting symptoms of both SLD dyslexia and DCD and more precise diagnoses, the needs of the child can now be better understood and treated.

Interestingly, Bhat (2020) reports the prevalence of *motor impairments in ASD* at 50%–85% yet, in her study of 11,814 parents of children with ASD only 31.6% were receiving physical therapy services. The DSM-5-TR has broad and complex presentations for ASD involving motor impairment so that rarely do children receive a dual diagnosis of ASD and DCD.

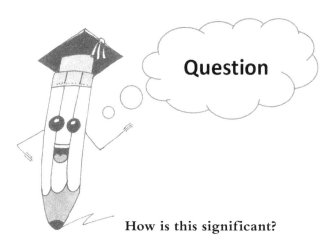

How is this significant?

It may be that the physical and motor impairments that children with ASD are experiencing are not receiving adequate early intervention because of under-diagnosis. Kangarani-Farahani et al (2023) confirmed this in their meta-analysis of 27 suitable studies on this topic and found that 92.5% of the articles agreed with Bhat's figure of 50–85% on standardised measures. Yet, only 15% of the papers described the problems as DCD. It certainly appears to be under-diagnosed in this population.

Problems with executive function and visuospatial working memory

Visuospatial working memory (VWM) is a component of working memory responsible for the holding of information about the visual characteristics of an object, its textures and colour and for the location of features in space, for example, particular buildings, furniture and personal items. VWM deficits have been linked with poor motor skills for tasks associated with a sequence of actions, for example, tying shoelaces. (It is no wonder that Velcro strapped shoes are very popular for young children!)

Like all working memory components, information may only be held briefly. Wangkawan et al (2020) conclude from research studies that visuospatial working memory is strongly linked to academic achievement in children particularly in mathematics and arithmetic problem solving.

> If a student is unable to recall the sequence of steps for performing algorithms and procedural activities because of Visuospatial Working Memory deficits, then her attention and progress will be inhibited.

Studies cited in Opitz et al, 2020; Leonard & Hill, 2015; Saban, 2014; Feng et al, 2012 and Alloway & Archibald, 2008, found a clear link between visuospatial working memory and executive function. Alloway et al (2008) report that students with low visuospatial memory skills performed relatively poorly in literacy and numeracy tasks at all levels of IQ (Alloway, 2007b, cited in Alloway et al, 2008). They claim that working memory tasks and the active motor elements in visuospatial memory tasks required for learning put high demands on the processing systems of students with DCD. Feng, Pratt & Spence (2012) saw the similarity in visuospatial working memory and attention, finding support for the idea that attention and VWM share the same processing resources in overlapping brain regions.

Task avoidance

With weaknesses of this kind it is understandable that students with DCD will avoid settings where they feel unable to manage or where they risk receiving comments from others. The consequences for these students are often 'reduced fitness levels; increased risk of being overweight or obese; difficulties with executive functioning; reduced educational achievement; poor social functioning; increased risk of negative self-concept and increased risk of mental health difficulties, particularly anxious and depressive symptoms' (Cleaton & Kirby, 2018 cited in Cleaton et al., 2020, p 29).

Ferguson et al. (2015) used the term *visuo-manual coordination*, including the actions of reaching for objects or catching a ball, to describe the difficulties of students with DCD whose performance during these tasks 'lacks fluency and precision' (p. 13). They often cannot regulate the accuracy nor the force with which they execute such tasks. Green and Payne (2018) found that these students were usually quite correct in their self-assessment of motor competence and were prone to unfavourable self-comparison with their peers leading to low self-esteem.

Known strengths

When reporting from a survey on the severe negative impacts of a child with DCD on families, Cleaton et al. (2019) noted that a lack of support from medical and educational professionals was a major source of stress. They also report from cited research that individuals with DCD have been noted for their empathy, resilience, humour and creativity. As teachers looking for a 'way in' to growing relationships with students demonstrating these characteristics, authentic praise and appreciation can be the basis for building strengths and self-efficacy (see Chapter 10).

Whereas it was once seen as an affliction of childhood, DCD is now generally accepted as a lifelong disorder requiring early intervention and accommodations for optimal outcomes.

The Impact for DCD in Australia (2020) Report, the result of the largest survey in the world on DCD conducted in 2018–2019, examined the lived experiences of children with DCD and those of their families. Participants were the families of 443 children from across Australia whose average age was 9.2 years and who were experiencing movement difficulties that were not cerebral palsy or muscular dystrophy. It gave a voice to families along with identifying critical data leading to recommendations for ways to improve all aspects of life with DCD.
Key findings are:

■ 'Teacher awareness of DCD was the greatest challenge at school' (p. 6).

■ The condition is underdiagnosed and the impact of movement difficulties is underrated. 'Within Australia, the process of identifying children at risk for DCD is simply not occurring' (p. 9).

- DCD frequently co-occurs with other neurodevelopmental conditions (70% of children in the survey had one diagnosed co-morbidity and 40% had at least two co-occurring disorders). The most common co-morbidity was Childhood Apraxia of Speech, followed by ADHD and Autism.

- Perceived negative impacts of the condition on the student's education were reported by 82% of parents. Only half of the children in the survey had an individual learning plan in place.

- There are significant associated mental and physical health impacts which often lead to avoidance of physical activity which may result in a child failing to acquire better physical skills.

- Physical clumsiness and awkwardness impact the holding of a pencil, cutting with scissors, opening and closing containers and eating lunch. Students with DCD feel fatigue from the effort of keeping up with the requirements of learning and the classroom.

- Two-thirds of the students surveyed scored clinically significant levels of emotional problems and peer relationship issues. Many were anxious about going to school.

- Students afflicted in this way are often the victims of bullying in the school playground impacting on their sense of belonging to a group and the lowering of general self-esteem.

Among its recommendations, the report *called for the development of resources* that would assist teachers to adjust the curriculum and activities so that students with DCD could access learning at their intellectual level and find school more enjoyable.

The report can be found at: www.telethonkids.org.au/globalassets/media/documents/projects/impact-for-dcd-report.pdf.

Throughout their resource for teachers, Christmas & Van de Weyer (2019) provide suggestions for how to address the detailed symptoms involved in problems of balance/touch/body position which may cause a student to under-register or over-register stimulus. But the condition of DCD is complicated in its restrictions on a student's movement involving systems of the body that are not within the training or sometimes the understanding of classroom teachers.

Allied health professionals' reports can recommend complex factors that are not easily adjusted within the classroom and become the domain of therapeutic intervention.

> Be discerning about what you can do and request *teacher aide time* to assist you to deliver manageable adjustments.

It may be necessary to offer an exemption from a particular course or skill requirement depending on a student's capacity, ensuring it is recorded clearly in his Learning Plan.

In a 2e student with moderate to severe motor incapacity, be certain to include *intellectually stimulating* material in all coursework.

Handwriting problems

A reduced capacity to record information and thought has a profound effect on the achievement of students. Keyboard skills will be reduced also. Barnett & Prunty (2021) claim that up to 95% of children with DCD will struggle with handwriting. They note that valuable working memory resources are often exhausted in the process of handwriting, leaving little for the complex task of actually expressing oneself in written form and attending to the presentation of ideas, the application of correct sentence structure and the conventions of written English. (This, of course, is another context in which cognitive load theory appears to prevail.)

Barnett & Prunty observed in students with DCD:

- more pausing in handwriting
- lack of automaticity
- more errors in letter formation than peers without DCD
- more difficulty regulating the size of letters
- often chose an unjointed letter style which was interpreted as an attempt to simplify and reduce the demands of a handwriting task.

IT adjustments

Dictation software has improved over time, but it takes time and skill development to use it correctly with the required results. A concerted effort with a teacher/IT support person in the initial phase of implementation is needed, especially if a student has difficulty pronouncing the words she wants to use or has limited working memory resources to dictate with fluency and to give commands.

This article by Martin (2023) in Understood.org gives a general overview of details. It can be found at:

www.understood.org/articles/dictation-speech-to-text-technology-what-it-is-and-how-it-works

In all circumstances, it is necessary for students to have a *written plan* for each task and to test the software for its suitability and effectiveness, evolving how it should be used.

Occupational therapists will most likely be aware of innovations in IT software and equipment ahead of schools.

Some people seek Alternative Therapies

Many of my clients have independently sought the diagnostic and treatment services of *kinesiologists* and many have sung their praises as a part of their children's intervention regimes. Kinesiology evaluates health by exploring the biofeedback from muscles. It claims to study the mechanics of bodily movements and to use a model of disease as a disturbance of energy flow in the body. Anecdotally, it is said to be effective as an intervention technique for motor problems. There is just not sufficient good scientific research to support the claim that kinesiology is a research-evidenced therapy so I cannot recommend it.

There have been some very controversial therapies in use. The DORE program, originally named Dyslexia Dyspraxia Attention Treatment (DDAT) claimed that a series of exercises could address the problems of the immature cerebellum in the brain which was said to be the underlying problem for all these disabilities. It was discredited as a treatment for dyslexia several decades ago. Yet, several clients claimed that it was helpful … Could it have been effective for a dyslexic child's undiagnosed, co-morbid DCD but without specific scientific research?

The research cited in support of The Arrowsmith Program was insufficient to validate claims of its efficacy. There is a critique of the claims and research around this program at: https://codereadnetwork.org/arrowsmith-program-what-has-chan ged-not-an-awful-lot/

However, therapies like these will continue to appear as people seek to find a simple fix for disabilities which are actually complex and often diverse in their presentation making their diagnosis long, often protracted, and treatment often expensive and time-consuming. Parents may be aware of the passing of time and opportunity to intervene in their child's problems and can be influenced by per-suasive marketing spiels. Alternate therapies abound but it is easier than ever to find research and reviews online.

My approach to the use of therapies that are not scientifically validated is to explain this to parents suggesting that it is their decision to begin a therapy once they are aware of the facts. Symptoms can sometimes be relieved even if a therapy does not address underlying causes. Sometimes the lack of evidence is because there has been insufficient funding to support research in the field. I always suggest that parents seek relevant research and if they cannot gain access through a univer-sity library then they should use websites like the National Library or their State Library databases. They can create an 'alert' on www.googlescholar.com. This way, they will be aware of available research and, hopefully, of problems that have been reported with any particular therapy.

Our knowledge and discernment as teachers can guide and support our families during their very vulnerable times.

'Go to' resources

Christmas, J., & Van de Weyer, R. (2019). *Hands on Dyspraxia: Developmental Coordination Disorder: Supporting Young People with Motor and Sensory Challenges* (2nd edn). Abingdon: Routledge. https://doi.org/10.4324/9780429438998
Code Read Network. See https://codereadnetwork.org/.
Google Scholar See www.googlescholar.com.

Martin, J. (2023, 12 May) Dictation (speech-to-text) technology: What it is and how it works. Understood.org (website). See www.understood.org/articles/dictation-speech-to-text-technology-what-it-is-and-how-it-works.

Centre for Childhood Disability Research (CanChild) M.A.T.C.H. Flyers: A Resource for Educators. See www.canchild.ca/en/resources/123-m-a-t-c-h-flyers-a-resource-for-educators. Resources are downloadable and are prepared for all stages of schooling to adolescence. I highly recommend them.

Bibliography

Addy, L., & Dixon, G. (2004). *Making Inclusion Work for Children with Dyspraxia: Practical Strategies for Teachers*. London: Routledge. https://doi.org/10.4324/9780203561546

Alloway, T. P., & Archibald, L. (2008). Working memory and learning in children with developmental coordination disorder and specific language impairment. *Journal of Learning Disabilities, 41*(3), 251–262. https://doi.org/10.1177/0022219408315815

American Psychiatric Association: Desk Reference to the Diagnostic Criteria From DSM-5-TR. Washington, DC: American Psychiatric Association, 2022, pp. 39.

Barnett, A. L., & Prunty, M. (2021). Handwriting difficulties in Developmental Coordination Disorder (DCD). *Current Developmental Disorders Reports, 8*(1), 6–14. https://doi.org/10.1007/s40474-020-00216-8

Bhat, A. N. (2020). Is motor impairment in autism spectrum disorder distinct from developmental coordination disorder? A report from the SPARK study. *Physical Therapy, 100*(4), 633–644. https://doi.org/10.1093/ptj/pzz190

Cacola, P. (2014). Movement difficulties affect children's learning: An overview of developmental coordination disorder (DCD). *Learning Disabilities, 20*(2), pp. 98–106. http://dx.doi.org/10.18666/LDMJ-2014-V20-I2-5279

Cleaton, M. A. M., Lorgelly, P. K., & Kirby, A. (2019). Developmental coordination disorder: The impact on the family. *Quality of Life Research: An International Journal of Quality of Life Aspects of Treatment, Care and Rehabilitation, 28*(4), 925–934. https://doi.org/10.1007/s11136-018-2075-1

Cleaton, M. A. M., Lorgelly, P. K., & Kirby, A. (2020). Developmental coordination disorder in UK children aged 6–18 years: Estimating the cost. *British Journal of Occupational Therapy, 83*(1), 29–40. https://doi.org/10.1177/0308022619866642

Dancza K., Missiuna C., & Pollock N. (2017). Occupation-centred practice: When the classroom is your client. In Rodger, S., & Kennedy-Behr, A. *Occupation-centred Practice with Children: A Practical Guide for Occupational Therapists* (2nd edn). Hoboken: Wiley.

Feng, J., Pratt, J., & Spence, I. (2012). Attention and visuospatial working memory share the same processing resources. *Frontiers in Psychology, 3*, 103. https://doi.org/10.3389/fpsyg.2012.00103

Ferguson, G., Duysens, J., & Smits-Engelsman, B. C. (2015). Children with developmental coordination disorder are deficient in a visuo-manual tracking task requiring predictive control. *Neuroscience, 286*, 13–26. https://doi.org/10.1016/j.neuroscience.2014.11.032

Green, D., & Payne, S. (2018). Understanding organisational ability and self-regulation in children with developmental coordination disorder. *Current Developmental Disorders Reports, 5*(1), 34–42. https://doi.org/10.1007/s40474-018-0129-2

Jelsma, D., Targino Gomes Draghi, T., Cavalcante Neto, J., & Smits-Engelsman, B. (2023). Improved attentional abilities after playing five weeks of active video games in children with and without Developmental Coordination Disorder. *Applied Neuropsychology. Child*, 1–9. Advance online publication. https://doi.org/10.1080/21622965.2023.2190024

Kangarani-Farahani, M., Malik, M. A., & Zwicker, J. G. (2023). Motor impairments in children with Autism Spectrum Disorder: A systematic review and meta-analysis. *Journal of Autism and Developmental Disorders*. Advance online publication. https://doi.org/10.1007/s10803-023-05948-1

Kennedy-Behr A, Rodger S, & Mickan, S. A (2013). Comparison of the play skills of preschool children with and without Developmental Coordination Disorder. *OTJR: Occupational Therapy Journal of Research*, 33(4), 198–208. https://doi.org/10.3928/15394492-20130912-03

Leonard, H. C., Bernardi, M., Hill, E. L., & Henry, L. A. (2015). Executive functioning, motor difficulties and Developmental Coordination Disorder. *Developmental Neuropsychology*, 40(4), 201–215. https://doi.org/10.1080/87565641.2014.997933

Leonard, H. C., & Hill, E. L. (2015). Executive difficulties in developmental coordination disorder: Methodological issues and future directions. *Current Developmental Disorders Reports*, 2(2), 141–149. https://doi.org/10.1007/s40474-015-0044-8

Licari, M., Williams J., & the Impact for DCD Team. (2020). *National Survey Evaluating the Impact of Developmental Coordination Disorder in Australia: Summary of Results.* Telethon Kids Institute, Perth, Western Australia. www.telethonkids.org.au/globalassets/media/documents/projects/impact-for-dcd-report.pdf

Livesey, D., Lum Mow, M., Toshack, T., & Zheng, Y. (2011). The relationship between motor performance and peer relations in 9–to–12-year-old children. *Child: Care, Health & Development*, 37(4), 581–588. https://doi.org/10.1111/j.1365-2214.2010.01183.x

Masi, L., & Gignac, M. (2015). ADHD and comorbid disorders in childhood psychiatric problems, medical problems, learning disorders and developmental coordination. *Clinical Psychiatry*, 1(1), 1–9. https://doi.org/10.21767/2471-9854.100005

Opitz, B., Brady, D., & Leonard, H. C. (2020). Motor and non-motor sequence prediction is equally affected in children with Developmental Coordination Disorder. *PloS One*, 15(11), e0232562–e0232562. https://doi.org/10.1371/journal.pone.0232562

Prunty, M., Barnett, A. L., Wilmut, K., & Plumb, M. S. (2016). The impact of handwriting difficulties on compositional quality in children with developmental coordination disorder. *British Journal of Occupational Therapy*, 79(10), 591–597. https://doi.org/10.1177/0308022616650903

Prunty, M., & Barnett, A. L. (2020). Accuracy and consistency of letter formation in children with Developmental Coordination Disorder. *Journal of Learning Disabilities*, 53(2), 120–130. https://doi.org/10.1177/0022219419892851

Sartori, R. F., Valentini, N. C., & Fonseca, R. P. (2020). Executive function in children with and without Developmental Coordination Disorder: A comparative study. *Child: Care, Health & Development*, 46(3), 294–302. https://doi.org/10.1111/cch.12734

Snapp-Childs, W., Mon-Williams, M., & Bingham, G. P. (2013). A sensorimotor approach to the training of manual actions in children with Developmental Coordination Disorder. *Journal of Child Neurology*, 28(2), 204–212. https://doi.org/10.1177/0883073812461945

Tal Saban, M., Ornoy, A., & Parush, S. (2014). Executive function and attention in young adults with and without Developmental Coordination Disorder – A comparative study. *Research in Developmental Disabilities*, 35(11), 2644–2650. https://doi.org/10.1016/j.ridd.2014.07.002

Thomas, L. *News Medical Life Sciences*. www.news-medical.net/health/What-is-Kinesiology.aspx Retrieved 24 March 2022.

Thoren, A., Quennerstedt, M., & Maivorsdotter, N. (2021). What physical education becomes when pupils with neurodevelopmental disorders are integrated: a transactional understanding. *Physical Education and Sport Pedagogy*, *26*(6), 578–592. https://doi.org/10.1080/17408989.2020.1834525

Viholainen, H., Aro, T., Purtsi, J., Tolvanen, A., & Cantell, M. (2014). Adolescents' school-related self-concept mediates motor skills and psychosocial well-being. *British Journal of Educational Psychology*, *84*(2), 268–280. https://doi.org/10.1111/bjep.12023

Wang, T.N., Tseng, M.H., Wilson, B. N., & Hu, F. C. (2009). Functional performance of children with Developmental Coordination Disorder at home and at school. *Developmental Medicine and Child Neurology*, *51*(10), 817–825. https://doi.org/10.1111/j.1469-8749.2009.03271.x

Wangkawan, T., Lai, C., Munkhetvit, P., Yung, T., & Chinchai, S. (2020). The development and psychometric properties of the Visuospatial Working Memory Assessment (VWMA) for children. *Occupational Therapy International*, 8736308. https://doi.org/10.1155/2020/8736308

Zwicker, J. G., Missiuna, C., Harris, S. R., & Boyd, L. A. (2012). Developmental coordination disorder: A review and update. *European Journal of Paediatric Neurology*, *16*(6), 573–581. https://doi.org/10.1016/j.ejpn.2012.05.005

Giftedness/high potential and multiple co-morbidities

Rhonda Filmer

VIGNETTE

Mathematics is Lucy's 'achilles' heel', proving to be her hardest subject to conquer. She explained to Mr Lorenzo in the second week of Year 8 that he does not explain maths *in the way my brain learns* and that sometimes,

> *You will just have to explain it to me again so I can understand, Sir.*

Her tirades at home increased in intensity as she struggled with algebra, annoyed that he could not make it clear to her.

During a parent-teacher interview Lucy told him it was his responsibility to answer her questions so she 'gets it'. Looking bewildered yet sympathetic, he said,

> *Lucy, ask your questions more specifically so I can see where the problem lies!*

Lucy's diagnosis of ASD came late in Year 7, following much earlier findings that her IQ is in the 140 range and she has ADHD (PIP). Her mother provides a strong level of example and she has developed unusual self-efficacy for her age. She works hard, determined to succeed despite her perceived weakness in mathematics.

By Week 8 of Term 1 the dialogue between teacher and student had aligned and Lucy had developed deep respect for Mr Lorenzo despite giving him a challenging time when new topics were introduced. With patience, he came to understand that Lucy's mental rigidities and working memory weaknesses were real while expecting her to refine her questioning to communicate effectively. Their working relationship was harmonious as he learned new ways to reach neurodiverse students in his classes.

DOI: 10.4324/9781003404972-11

The purpose of this short chapter is to explore how the presence of co-existing conditions (co-morbidities) along with giftedness/high potential can affect a 2e student's learning profile. It summarises the observable characteristics of students with these conditions and assists you to cross-reference and 'map' an individual student's profile. Research is presented that furthers the discussion on the effects of multiple co-morbidities resulting in the conclusion that each 2e student is unique. Professional judgment is required to work through the recommendations for pedagogical methods and curriculum adjustments that have been found in research. This discussion concludes with a Case Study which demonstrates the efficacy and importance of strengths-based education for the 2e student.

> A comprehensive understanding of a student's underlying conditions
> **'learning profile'**
> assists in identifying his strengths and challenges which, in turn,
> helps to build deep rapport between teacher and student.

Use the chart below (Figure 9.1) to 'map' and document the combination of giftedness and co-morbidities in the 2e student. Reflect on the implications of this combination and the functional impact that each learning difficulty has on the student's giftedness/high potential.

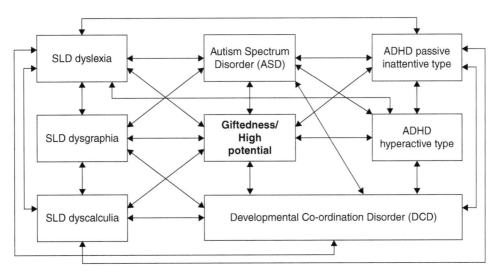

FIGURE 9.1 Any combination of characteristics can occur to make up the *learning profile* of an individual 2e student which guides teacher choices on curriculum adjustment decisions.

TABLE 9.1 Compilation summary of observable characteristics of conditions. For details and full references go to the lists of characteristics in the appropriate chapters indicated

A Summary of Observable Characteristics of Conditions

Intellectually Gifted Characteristic	Specific learning Disability (SLD)	Attention Deficit Hyperactivity Disorder (ADHD)	Autism Spectrum Disorder (ASD) (Observed with high ability)	Developmental Co-Ordination Disorder
Ref: Chap 4	Ref: Chap 5	Ref: Chap 6	Ref: Chap 7	Ref: Chap 8
Advanced vocabulary	**Dyslexia** Weak phonemic awareness	**Hyperactive type** Fidgeting, Squirming in the body	Delayed social maturity & social reasoning	Clumsiness–bumping into or dropping objects
Sophisticated sense of humour	Weak sound–letter correspondence	Inappropriate movement – leaves his seat constantly	Immature empathy	Slow & inaccurate motor skills: – catching an object
Prefers company of older children or adults	Slow progress to reading accuracy	Talks excessively	Difficulty making friends & often teased	– using scissors or cutlery – handwriting – riding a bike
Outstanding memory	Poor reading fluency remains effortful	Poor impulse control, calls out in class, can't wait his turn	Difficulty with emotional control	– participating in sport
Broad knowledge base	Persistent confusion of vowel sounds	Interrupts or intrudes in others' space	Unusual language – advanced vocabulary & syntax	– processing delay
Sees possibilities	Poor reading comprehension	Cannot engage quietly in activity	Unusual prosody (rhythm & intonation of speech)	
Connects disparate ideas	Avoidance of reading	**Inattentive type** Careless errors Overlooks detail	Unusual interests – intense focus	
Develops intuitive 'theories'	**Dysgraphia** weak spelling	Difficulty sustaining attention to tasks, conversations or sustained reading	Tendency to be pedantic	
Asks questions	Multiple grammatical, punctuation errors	Seems distracted & often distracted by external stimuli	Delayed conversation skills	
Curiosity	Poor paragraph organisation	Does not follow through with instructions	Sensitivity to specific sounds, aromas, textures or touch	
Thrives on complexity	Lack of clarity in expression	Disorganised, non-sequential		

TABLE 9.1 (Continued)

Intellectually Gifted Characteristic	Specific learning Disability (SLD)	Attention Deficit Hyperactivity Disorder (ADHD)	Autism Spectrum Disorder (ASD)	Developmental Co-Ordination Disorder
Emotional investment in interests	Handwriting difficulties (motor dysgraphia) – illegible and slow	Poor time management		
Displays original ideas	**Dyscalculia** Poor number sense	Forgetful in daily activities		
Flexibility in problem solving	Difficulty learning number facts & recalling procedures			
Emotional depth sensitivity when young	Difficulty with maths reasoning (application)			
Achievement in top 10% of age cohort (or not, if underachieving)	Counting on fingers Cannot subitise (estimate visual arrays)			

Research into the effects of multiple co-morbidities

An unidentified co-morbid condition may be present that:

- affects a student's capacity to learn requiring changes to adjustments
- complicates the management of a student
- increases the potential for anxiety

The … importance of a correct classification is that this special-needs population of students can only be properly served if, first, they are correctly identified and diagnosed. (Pfeiffer & Prado, 2021, p.2)

… experience suggests that the high-ability student presents with an admixture of maladaptive symptoms and quirky behaviours and, at times, two or even more distinct co-occurring disorders (Pfeiffer & Prado, 2021, p.6).

I concur with their analysis, after 20 years of working with the 2e population, that few 2e students present with only one very specific disorder. Often there are insufficient characteristics to warrant a full and clear second diagnosis but, with knowledge, you can observe closely and make professional judgments about appropriate curriculum, adjustments and management of each 2e student.

A note on *quirkiness*. It can simply be an environmentally learned style of behaviour or personality trait, often associated with the creatively gifted. Parental characteristics, lifestyle, socio-economic factors and childhood history are important factors in a child's life that can inhibit or enhance *quirkiness*.

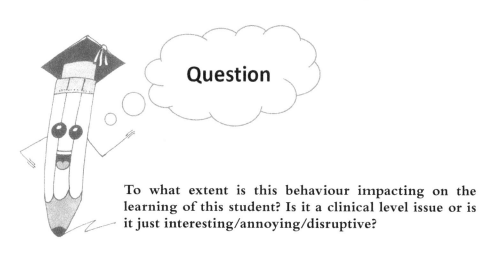

Question

To what extent is this behaviour impacting on the learning of this student? Is it a clinical level issue or is it just interesting/annoying/disruptive?

It is important to note that:
    Each disability can **manifest differently** in the presence of **a co-morbid condition** thus changing its functional impact on a gifted/high potential student.
    Your observations from a position of knowledge will assist you.

An example of the effects of multiple co-morbidities

The problems with ASD-ADHD co-morbidity are wide-ranging and may affect areas such as social skills, language skills, attention, activity levels, and compulsive behaviours of an individual… rated to have more severe anxiety symptoms compared to other groups (Lien, Kuo et al., 2023, p.3).

In a study using standardised checklists, Cremone-Caira, Trier et al. (2021), showed that children with the co-morbidities of ASD and ADHD showed greater difficulty carrying out goal-directed behaviours and inhibiting behavioural responses than those with one diagnosis. In a single case study research project with a 2e student gifted in mathematics, Lien, Kuo et al. (2023) found from analysed observational and performance data from teachers that computer-assisted, project-based learning instruction helped a student to increase classroom concentration, mathematical concepts and problem-solving skills. It was found that misbehaviour decreased from around ten times per class to less than three times per class.

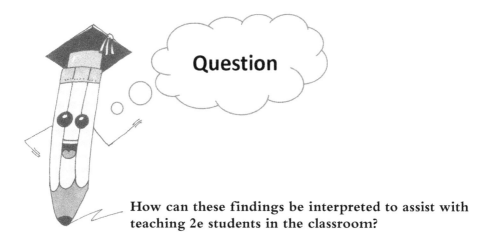

How can these findings be interpreted to assist with teaching 2e students in the classroom?

1. Know your student well through observation over time and analysis.

2. Be aware that the student's full profile may not have been identified or diagnosed.

3. Seek intervention/remediation for skills deficits.

4. Apply your knowledge to working with her strengths, understanding that they can be masked by unusual behaviours.

5. Be informed and brave when choosing suitable formats, approaches and research questions in a differentiated curriculum.

Strengths-based strategies for teaching

It is not necessarily intuitive to work to a person's strengths in schools and workplaces but the intention is that it motivates and enlivens through the recognition and expression of positive abilities particularly in the presence of learning difficulties. Unfortunately, within the education field, 'strengths-based education' is sometimes used to denote giving attention *only* to a student's strengths and not to the ability/skills deficits therefore implying no intention to remediate. I am philosophically and ethically opposed to that view as demonstrated throughout this book.

In a study by Reis, Gelbar and Madaus (2023) successful 2e high school students with ASD identified the strategies that worked for their success.

They said,

■ it was particularly important that their **strengths and talents were recognised** by their teachers

■ most students learned to **structure their time** around sport and extra-curricular activities that developed their interests

■   **advanced level classes taught them rigour** while opportunities for advanced, interest-based academic experiences; participation in residential programmes during high school; strong and positive relationships with teachers and counsellors taught them how to **work with their strengths, overcome anxiety and build social connections**.

Lopez & Louis (2009) clarify 'strengths-based education' as a "philosophical stance" (p.1) derived from research in the field of education, psychology, social work and behaviour and involving the five principles of:

1. measurement of achievement, **learner characteristics and strengths** and, interestingly, **teacher strengths** – from a position of personal knowledge of one's own strengths, a teacher can maximise her own efficacy while modelling how to work with the following principles …

2. individualization – taking into account the **setting of goals based on strengths** while providing feedback and promoting ongoing discussion on goal achievement; involves options for choices and discussion on how to demonstrate achievement capitalising on strengths

3. networking – **older students can mentor others** whose perceived strengths align, bringing the learning context into a more relational, real-world, perspective

4. deliberate application of strengths brings about **new learning behaviours** – students' awareness of self leads to more effective ways to achieve goals, using strengths to leverage the development of, and compensation for, weaknesses.

5. **Intentional development of strengths** through seeking out novel experiences that will require effort and build skills through extracurricular activities, strategic course selection (for senior high school and university students) and targeted opportunities.

    Dweck's (2006) mindset theory applies here where students with a 'growth mindset' learn that results come from effort as opposed to those with a 'fixed mindset' who believe that putting effort in will only reveal that they are not smart! It is not hard to imagine that a 2e student may be more likely to have a 'fixed mindset' regarding his personal strengths because of the effects of the learning difficulty. Through mentoring about the effects of goal setting for strengths, a 2e student can learn to grow in talent.

Case study: Josie

Josie, in Year 12, is now a very high-achieving 2e student with dyslexia and dysgraphia, excelling in English Extension and Ancient History. Her self-identified gifted strengths are definitely spoken language and critical and lateral thinking. Josie was asked to comment on Louis & Lopez's principles and on how she learned to use her gifted strengths to bring about high achievement results.

Background

Josie was enrolled in a high school known for its inspired, hard-working learning diversity department. At her entrance interview it was obvious that her past school and professional reports had been read and understood and that her allocated teacher mentor was fully aware of her learning profile. From day 1 in Year 7 Josie's programme reflected the full range of her learning strengths and weaknesses. For example, Josie was offered a scribe and a reader so she could speak some parts of her assessments.

> *I opted to speak in assessments and exams where I could. Over time I taught myself to compose on the spot keeping colloquialisms out of the more formal exam setting. I just intuitively worked on building skills in my strength areas.*
>
> *We were taught well and I have grown to love Philosophy because of the critical and lateral thinking we practised.*
>
> *It helped that we were coached well in debating. I joined Debating in Year 7 and by our senior years we were winning inter-school competitions. Many times the adjudicators would comment that it was our lateral thinking in our case interpretation, argued powerfully, that won it for us. That was often my contribution in the prep room.*

On Principle 2: **Individualisation**

> *It is too hard for teachers to individualise in secondary school but Year 7 is not too late for remediation. There is a re-set after primary school and everyone is on the trajectory of gaining new skills. Teachers are trying to challenge the gifted/high achievers and bring the slower students up. Year 7 teachers need to know how to identify children with learning difficulties. Find those who are excelling and extend them and find those who are falling behind and bring them up to speed.*

Josie has been the recipient of 1:1 tutoring for reading, spelling, writing, mathematics and anything she requested, over a long period of time, and passionately believes in its importance for 2e students.

On Principle 3: **Networking**

> *The Librarians at school have helped enormously and the learning diversity department has encouraged dyslexic kids to support each other and to share successes building mentoring relationships and friendships.*

On Principle 4: **Deliberate application of strengths**

> *It is so important to speak up for yourself in every respect, especially when advocating for yourself in class and for exam settings. My oral ability has been very useful.*

On Principle 5: **Seeking out novel experiences** to build strengths

> *I have seriously sought to develop elevated language and interpersonal skills. My mum took me to adult social events and invited me into the conversation from a young age, so*

I learned how to speak with adults. Joining drama classes outside school from Year 7 was great fun, raising my skills over all the years of doing it. Now I am sitting the HSC in Drama and still loving it!

One teacher took me to extra-curricular activities for gifted students and we hosted extension extra-curricular groups at my school. They were wonderful in so many ways.

I have learned to use rest break accommodations well in exams. I use them to control anxiety if I feel myself escalating.

Josie has learned how to use her strengths to overcome the effects of her significant specific learning disabilities and consequent anxiety to build self-efficacy and confidence. Interestingly, it was through discussion that occurred over time with her tutor/mentor that she realised what was holding back her achievements in primary school. She learned to find another way to realise her goals while being given opportunities from Year 7 to practise how to do exams using a scribe and reader.

As is often the case, it was Josie's networking and influential mother who encouraged her and who sourced opportunities for her from a very young age. The effects of her strong family structure for nurturing, support and for bringing reality appropriately, into her young life, should not be undervalued.

The professional decisions made by her high school's learning diversity department were the result of individual teachers building a collective culture that nurtures 2e students in this way. To that extent, it is within the power of all teachers to build a culture of understanding, rigour, skills development and high expectations upon a foundation of knowledge in any school!

In Section 3, you will read about the principles used to build 2e students' executive function skills in Chapter 10, then Chapter 11 brings together everything that has been discussed before to apply that knowledge to classroom teaching. Chapter 12 containing Longitudinal Case Studies concludes this book.

References

Amran, H. A., & Majid, R. A. (2019). Learning strategies for twice-exceptional students. *International Journal of Special Education, 33*(4), 954–976.

Coleman, M. R. (2005). Academic strategies that work for gifted students with learning disabilities. *Teaching Exceptional Children, 38*(1), 28–32. https://doi.org/10.1177/0040059 90503800105

Cremone-Caira, A., Trier, K., Sanchez, V., Kohn, B., Gilbert, R., & Faja, S. (2021). Inhibition in developmental disorders: A comparison of inhibition profiles between children with Autism Spectrum Disorder, Attention-Deficit/Hyperactivity Disorder, and comorbid symptom presentation. *Autism: the International Journal of Research and Practice, 25*(1), 227–243. https://doi.org/10.1177/1362361320955107

Dweck, C. S. (2006). *Mindset: The new psychology of success.* Random House.

Gierczyk, M., & Hornby, G. (2021). Twice-exceptional students: Review of implications for special and inclusive education. *Education Sciences, 11*(2), 85. https://doi.org/10.3390/educ sci11020085

Josephson, J., Wolfgang, C., & Mehrenberg, R. (2018). Strategies for supporting students who are twice-exceptional. *Journal of Special Education Apprenticeship, 7*(2), n2. https://schol arworks.lib.csusb.edu/josea/vol7/iss2/8

Lien, K.-M., Kuo, C.-C., & Pan, H.-L. (2023). Improving concentration and academic performance of a mathematically talented student with ASD/ADHD: An enrichment program. *Education Sciences, 13*(6), 588. https://doi.org/10.3390/educsci13060588

Lopez, S. J., & Louis, M. C. (2009). The principles of strengths-based education. *Journal of College and Character, 10*(4), https://doi.org/10.2202/1940-1639.1041

Madaus, J., Reis, S., Gelbar, N., Delgado, J., & Cascio, A. (2022). Perceptions of factors that facilitate and impede learning among twice-exceptional college students with Autism Spectrum Disorder. *Neurobiology of Learning and Memory, 193*, 107627. https://doi.org/10.1016/j.nlm.2022.107627

Margari, F., Craig, F., Petruzzelli, M. G., Lamanna, A., Matera, E., & Margari, L. (2013). Parents psychopathology of children with Attention Deficit Hyperactivity Disorder. *Research in Developmental Disabilities, 34*(3), 1036–1043. https://doi.org/10.1016/j.ridd.2012.12.001

Masi, L. & Gignac, M. (2015). ADHD and comorbid disorders in childhood psychiatric problems, medical problems, learning disorders and developmental coordination. *Clinical Psychiatry, 1*(1), 1–9. www.primescholars.com/articles/adhd-and-comorbid-disorders-inc hildhoodpsychiatric-problems-medicalproblems-learning-disordersand-developmental-coordina-104677.html Retrieved 5 November 2023.

Pfeiffer, S. I., & Prado, R. M. (2021). Diagnostic challenges in working with the twice-exceptional student. In F. H. R. Piske, & K. H. Collins (Eds), *Autismo, superdotação e dupla excepcionalidade*, Juruá 95–108.

Reis, S., Gelbar, N., & Madaus, J. (2023). Pathways to academic success: Specific strength-based teaching and support strategies for twice-exceptional high school students with autism spectrum disorder. *Gifted Education International, 39*(3), 378–400. https://doi.org/10.1177/02614294221124197

From understanding to implementation for 'twice-exceptional' students

Teaching/coaching to improve executive function skills

Rhonda Filmer

VIGNETTE

Hannah brought home her Gold Certificate for Academic Achievement in Year 3. She was proud of it because this year had been so great! Mr Sim did the best lessons, her two best friends had been in her class, she had represented the school in swimming, chess, tag league and dancing and she really loved school.

Hannah wanted to put the prized award into a safe place to keep. But her bedroom was littered with possessions; clothes, toys and games covered the entire floor space. She tripped on her toy box lying upended on the floor and hit her head on the side of the bookcase. The certificate lay crumpled in her hand.

Hannah immediately began to scream and cry at maximum volume.

Like so many girls with ADHD, Hannah has been able to disguise her Executive Function deficits at school so far. But they are patently obvious to her family. Her mother's clear and firm guidance and support has enabled Hannah to function strongly at school but at the end of the school day when she comes home fatigued, her emotional dysregulation and personal disorganisation impact severely on her life bringing stress to her family. Young girls can often manage to conform and excel at school while aspects of their lives are disordered at home. In a family where at least one parent has strong Executive Function skills a child has a role model and a support system. But children need to learn strong skills for themselves if they are to thrive at school and in life.

In Chapter 6 on ADHD, Executive Function (EF) skills were explained as the deficits that occur with ADHD. Deficits in these skills are common to many conditions as discussed widely in the research literature: ASD, SLD, DCD and in children with acquired brain injury or sometimes as a result of abuse/deprivation.

DOI: 10.4324/9781003404972-13

Whether the Executive Function deficits are inherent within those conditions or there is co-morbid ADHD is inconclusive in the research.

In this chapter you will read about the principles of Executive Function coaching and how to teach them in both the classroom and the 1:1 setting. I want you to understand how 'executive function' differs from the intellectual ability of a student and why students need to set goals to learn new skills about how to rationally respond to situations that have caused stress, negative outcomes and failure in the past. In order to ensure that this chapter is practical and that the principles are well demonstrated I have used vignettes and illustrations throughout.

This field has grown enormously with terminology sometimes used imprecisely amongst writers bringing with it the potential for confusion. I chose the comprehensive list of executive skills used by Dawson & Guare (2012) as the underlying structure in my coaching and the teen version of their Executive Skills Questionnnaire (used with permission). I augmented it with materials from research and I have presented that with examples from my own coaching practice in this chapter.

Insofar as their coaching model is 'built on a theoretical foundation well-grounded in the behavioural literature' (p. ix) they claim that it is evidence based. I am not aware of their questionnaires being piloted or checked for validity and reliability, but I have had excellent responses from their use with follow-up coaching and the subsequent growth in self-efficacy in the students with whom I have used them.

A brief survey of an online bookshop's offerings in 'executive function skills in the classroom' brings an array of creditable references and models to peruse. The purpose of this chapter is to demonstrate one particular way that has worked.

What it is and why it is needed

Executive Function (EF) – what it is

Many students without diagnosable conditions may experience Executive Function deficits at low levels depending on their environmental circumstances and many other factors. Challenging circumstances in life such as sickness, grief or high stress can demonstrate to us all just how our locus of control and self-regulation can shift.

Barkley (website, 2021) suggests there is no definitional consensus for Executive Function in the field and he prefers the definition, 'those neuropsychological processes needed to sustain problem-solving toward a goal (p. 2)' emphasising that self-regulation is the primary deficit in ADHD.

Foster and Cooper-Kahn (2013) offer this definition:

'Executive Functioning is an umbrella term for the mental processes that serve a supervisory role in thinking and behaviour. It incorporates a number of neurologically based operations that work together to direct and coordinate our efforts to achieve a goal' (p. 7).

Harvard University's Center for the Developing Child uses the analogy of EF skills as an 'air traffic control system'. See https://developingchild.harvard.edu/resources/building-the-brains-air-traffic-control-system-how-early-experiences-shape-the-development-of-executive-function/

The need for Executive Function coaching

The need for coaching in Executive Function skills is often lost behind poor, acting-out behaviours that take the attention of teachers from the weakness and incapacity to place it firmly on a distracting situation. Whether the intention to create a diversion is wholly conscious or simply the cry for help of a child forced 'into a corner' from which he cannot emerge with dignity is not always obvious at first.

But be aware that a student who can orally discuss the multiple causes for the success of the imperial goals of the Roman Empire, may not be able to turn on his computer, find its charger, log in and answer a written question before he loses his concentration to a more interesting aspect of the classroom. It will nearly always look like intentional, disobedient behaviour until it is observed and investigated.

We are in the early days of neuroscience and at some time in the future our knowledge of neural pathway impairments will be able to explain neurodevelopmental conditions with more nuance and specificity. We may not need to use all the labels objected to by Baum & Olenchak (2002) who refer to 'the "alphabet child" whose diagnoses contain more letters than wisdom (abstract)'. We will talk in the field of Education about the appropriate interventions for the functional impairments children display, with knowledge, understanding and compassion and we will all look for how to enrich, extend and challenge students with high intellectual potential. Initial Teacher Education courses will universally educate student teachers about how to teach literacy and about the diverse needs of children so that all new teachers will go into schools expecting that at least 20% of the children in their classes will have learning needs that require differentiation of the curriculum. Schools will be mini-research fields collecting and interpreting relevant data on what interventions work and the results will be routinely circulated to all staff in the school within a vibrant learning community. There will be sufficient teachers to do this work and to support Response to Intervention Tiers 2 and 3 in every grade of every school. Morale will be very high among teachers because they know their efforts are bringing creditable results for their students and they will be respected and paid appropriately according to the high status they deserve.

That is my dream.

But for now, we have to work with the resources we have and a knowledge of Executive Function coaching will assist you ...

For a greater understanding of the motivation (and lack of it) experienced by some children click on this link: https://developingchild.harvard.edu/resources/the-brain-circuits-underlying-motivation-an-interactive-graphic/. Harvard University has created this interactive infographic to explain the Brain Circuits that build motivation. We can see that repeated positive experiences that bring good feelings will motivate the development of positive behaviour and future good choices. By creating positive experiences and new strategies for learning and behaving a child learns how to repeat them.

Coaching principles

Experience has taught me to **assume** that most 2e students will benefit from Executive Function coaching and that the starting point for intervention with each one will not be immediately obvious.

> The principal goal of Coaching is *not* to develop Independence immediately.
> That will be a long time coming!
> … after targeted input and the prior development of
> *self-regulation* and *impulse control.*

> **Our goal is to develop self-efficacy**

which is the belief that you can achieve a task well.

Bandura (1994) was a pioneer in the concept of self-efficacy:

> *Perceived self-efficacy is concerned with people's beliefs in their capabilities to exercise control over their own functioning and over events that affect their lives. Beliefs in personal efficacy affect life choices, level of motivation, quality of functioning, resilience to adversity and vulnerability to stress and depression. People's beliefs in their efficacy are developed by four main sources of influence.*
> *They include:*

> - *mastery experiences*
> - *seeing people similar to oneself manage task demands successfully*
> - *social persuasion that one has the capabilities to succeed in given activities*
> - *and inferences from somatic and emotional states indicative of personal strengths and vulnerabilities.*

> *Ordinary realities are strewn with impediments, adversities, setbacks, frustrations and inequities. People must, therefore, have a robust sense of efficacy to sustain the perseverant effort needed to succeed. Succeeding periods of life present new types of competency demands requiring further development of personal efficacy for successful functioning.*
> *The nature and scope of perceived self-efficacy undergo changes throughout the course of the lifespan (p 16).*

You may choose to incorporate these coaching principles with a small group in your primary school class or in your secondary classes, particularly in Years 7–10. You may choose to do daily morning 'check-ins' just prior to school starting time with individual students. If you can weave them into your differentiated curriculum then your time is efficiently used and supported by the research that underpins the field of neurodiversity.

Illustration

TABLE 10.1 Excerpt from an Individual Learning Plan involving metacognition, an executive function skill

Goal:	Teaching Strategies
To assist with the development of metacognition	• Occasional use of a self-monitoring checklist at the end of the lesson • Explicit feedback to set self-monitoring goals in the next lesson

The principles are the same whether students are as young as Year 1 or ready to do the HSC.

The two components in coaching are both Environmental Modifications and Teaching Strategies.

Goal-directed persistence

Set small achievable goals. Asking children to 'do their best' is not effective as most students who need coaching, have no idea what that means!

> **VIGNETTE**
>
> After working through the Dawson & Guare EF Teen Questionnaire, Lee, a Year 4 student said that the amount of homework he has to do was causing him to 'melt down' most nights. I am negotiating with his teacher to reduce that homework load (an environmental modification) but meanwhile we discussed how he feels when he is getting more angry and escalating toward a meltdown. He decided that when he senses those feelings coming, putting his arms out in front of him, warding them off, he will say:
>
> *'I am not going there!'*
> As a distraction he will look for his dog for a cuddle,
> *'Where's Pepe?'*

By creating a *statement* a student has a ready tool to use when a situation is threatening the achievement of a personal goal.

I will monitor how often he has had a meltdown after school this week. How do I know if he is telling me the truth since he will want to please me? I have to ask his mother.

Further skills to be acquired are:

Planning/prioritisation

Planning requires strong Executive Function skills. Students with poor skills do not think sequentially or with a sense of priority. It has to be demonstrated and explicitly taught.

Illustration

Characteristically, a student with executive function deficits will write minimal length and detail into written expression. Amir, in Year 5, now produces a Brainstorm (detailed in Chapter 5) at home on the day before he is due to produce a written piece at school. He has placed a sequence (1st, 2nd, 3rd) onto the action ideas: ready to go. In class, during the writing lesson, he works his way through the sequence, writing two or three sentences for each point and crossing off the point on the Brainstorm as he goes. This is both an environmental modification and a teaching strategy. He is producing longer and more creditable texts than he has managed before, in a much shorter time. This small adjustment which we negotiated with his inspired teacher is making a big difference to his skill development and his progress toward self-efficacy.

For secondary students, when preparing an English essay, the Brainstorm can be done on Inspiration or other software, on a whiteboard or a large sheet of paper and all the elements of the question can be noted, e.g. How the author developed the themes could be colour coordinated to allow the PEEL★ paragraphs to be written from it. Secondary students need help to plan every step of an assignment across its content and across their available time to complete.

★PEEL is an acronym denoting the way to write a paragraph:

P... make your point

E... elaborate on the point

E ... give examples

L... link back to the question.

This is the simplest of techniques which can be further elaborated once a student has mastered the process.

Metacognition

Our NSW Department of Education has taken an interest in metacognition with this definition: 'Metacognition is an important thinking skill which is defined as 'thinking about thinking.' This involves any behaviour directly linked with a person's control and monitoring of their own learning and thinking, including emotion.'

See https://education.nsw.gov.au/teaching-and-learning/education-for-a-changing-world/thinking-skills/metacognition

Perry, Lundie and Golder (2018) reviewed 50 studies and there was strong evidence that the effective teaching of metacognition had a very positive effect on pupil outcomes. Dawson & Guare (2012) found that students can 'consider potential obstacles to achieving their goals and to think of ways to overcome obstacles (p. 50)'. But the Education Endowment Foundation report (UK, 2021) warns that there is little evidence to support the idea of teaching metacognitive skills in separated thinking skills lessons because pupils cannot transfer the learning from a general application to specific subject knowledge. A distinction needs to be made here between a classroom application and that in a tutoring/mentoring setting where a student's individual needs can be identified and addressed and there is student 'buy-in'. Their report, which can be accessed at https://educationendowmentfou ndation.org.uk/education-evidence/guidance-reports/metacognition is excellent in its research base, its clarity, brevity and applicability.

VIGNETTE

In an initial interview with a gifted Year 4 student who had failed to show what he knew in the Opportunity Class entrance tests and failed to reach the required standard to gain a place, I asked him,

What kind of thinking did you do in the test?

He looked at me quizzically.

Did you do the same sort of thinking and responding that you do when you play Super Mario (his favourite Nintendo game)?

What do you mean?

Did you act fast and race through the test or did you do a question, stop, think about it, check the answer, then move on to the next question?

He smiled at me, knowingly.

We had begun our conversation about metacognition and how to choose an appropriate way of thinking to approach learning (and testing) activities.

Organisation: prompts and charts

Young children tend to have parents/carers who will organise their time and lives, having them ready for the school day. Many families I know have morning routines that are clearly set out in pictures or text. Of course, this links clearly with issues of Time Management.

Organisational schemes need to be established. such as use of a diary, homework folders, notebooks and particular places for materials to be stored.

Jessica McCabe established her YouTube channel *How to ADHD* after trying to establish a working life. She created a video on how to use a Bullet Journal https:// youtu.be/jkZEEQG6IVE for the following reasons:

- The Bullet Journal works – many people are devoted to using it.
- Some high school students are floundering with online communication systems. They forget to look! Their schools might still issue diaries, but many schools do not effectively ensure their use.

ADDitude Magazine has put out a Free Guide which is available at:

www.additudemag.com/download/organize-your-adhd-home/. This provides tips on how to organise your home when you have ADHD. It contains some good tips for parents to model in the organisation of space and belongings in the home.

This e-magazine is excellent for its articles on many aspects of ADHD and EF.

Time management

Here is where the smartphone comes into its own: the timer, the alarm, the notes, the voice memos, the apps, the camera for recording something that hasn't been written down. Secondary students in schools where phones are confiscated during the day may need to gain permission to keep them … and then be disciplined enough to use them to assist with their time management and not as a source of distraction….

Students with ADHD have 'pleasure-seeking' brains so addiction to screens and videos is a distinct possibility. This is, in itself, a way of using up enormous amounts of time. I advocate controls over screen time, by parents, for the whole duration of a 2e student's time at school.

Flexibility

- scaffolding of tasks
- explicit instruction – coach can re-teach if instruction on assignments has been inadequate for that student
- overtly discuss ways of coping with change … make a list? Use a statement to prompt and avert a negative response to a change of plans.

Task initiation and sustained attention

- I use the Nike statement, 'Just do it', to prompt a student to recognise that it is time to start.
- Use of timer to prompt. I ask students to 'catch yourself dreaming' then perhaps use a timer at intervals over a short period.
- Self-talk. Teach and model the habit of talking through a sequence of steps for the execution of a task.
- Student can plan to give themselves a reward at pre-arranged intervals.

Response inhibition

- explicit teaching to seek the facts of a topic before forming an opinion
- perhaps the development of a new habit like '1, 2, 3' before calling out.
- 'Always raise your hand in class.'

Emotional control

- overt discussion about situations that provoke an emotional response and are hard to control, for example, a sibling or a particular child at school (who may, in fact, be bullying).

VIGNETTE

One student who is particularly bothered by her 'very annoying' younger brother's noisiness and activity and tired of her own escalated responses, says to herself …

Just ignore him …

… I need to do something.

She finds a distracting activity such as a word puzzle or sketching that she knows will keep her mind busy for some time while she settles herself.

Saline (2023) has developed an infographic on what to do when you are 'fired up' which is downloadable from www.additudemag.com/wp-content/uplo ads/2023/02/Anger-Management-Steps-and-Scripts.pdf

The process of executive function coaching

Applying what we know from the literature, to help academic progress.

> Coaching involves a student learning how to:
>
>   … modify and self-regulate behaviour. New skills and 'habits' are formed.
>
>   … set and reach goals (even though goal-directed perseverance might not develop for that person until they are in their 20's)

Steps to undertake at the outset

1. Administer the Dawson and Guare Executive Skills Questionnaire–Teen Version (2012) to gain an understanding of the student's own behaviour. https://iris.peabody.vanderbilt.edu/wp-content/uploads/modules/ss1/pdfs/ ss_01_link_Executive_Skills_Questionnair_Teen.pdf

   Expressive of her attitude toward herself: one young student of mine was laughing about how 'bad' she was at so many of the listed tasks … highly self-aware.

2. Observe the behaviour at school and/or gain reports from her other teachers.

3. Interview her parents.

4. Arrange an interview with the student (and parents depending on the age of the student and the setting).

5. After scoring the questionnaire, take the *three weakest skills* and discuss them. *Set Goals* with a time period for completion.

   Structure a 'statement' or pre-arranged thought that can be repeated when the time is right.

6. Organise adjustments in the classroom based on the question:

> **Is the performance of this task within the control of this child?**

Parents may need to be arbiters of this and to quietly inform teachers where the child is unable to perform a task, particularly on projects and complex homework. Parents can tell you about the turmoil that such activity causes at home. As teachers, we can interpret that the child does not have the EF skills or the 'micro-skills' to manage the requirements.

> … If a task is not within the control of a child then it is a risky choice to require it of him. It may highlight the child's lack of EF, allow stress and anxiety to develop and possibly ruin the connection you have with the child.
>
> A breakage in the connection you have with that child is actually a loss of trust in your care of him.

7. Parents and teachers can focus on the *process* of executing work practices rather than the *product* of the completed work. Without those skills, independence cannot develop.

8. The use of authentic and specific praise (more often than reprimands).

VIGNETTE

In my fateful first year of teaching, one of my students, Billy Rogers, in Year 3, had not progressed in reading and when I took the class he did not know the 'initial sounds' of English. I had no records nor background into why he had failed to thrive. I thought for days how to break into this child's world and to gain his confidence. The words of a very inspired lecturer from my Diploma of Education days, Mr Gordon Young, came to mind,

'Praise opens doors'

What can I praise Billy for? He was not able to attempt any work, nor did he seem concerned to try.

Then, looking at him one day with his lovely bright face I said,

'Billy, I love your smile!'

Honestly, that tiny statement made a world of difference. Billy smiled at me, at some point, during every day and he began to talk with me more. The resulting lift in his self-esteem allowed him to attempt tasks, to 'give it a go'. By the end of the year, one criterion by which my Principal judged my performance on that class was …

'Well, Billy Rogers is reading now!'

9. Develop the student's capacity to 'self-talk', which is not natural for students with ADHD who are generally weak on sequential processing. Encourage her

to plan the sequence of a task, out loud, while recording it on a graphic organiser/mind map.

Illustration: Jonathan (gifted with dyslexia and ADHD) and I looked at his teachers' comments on his Semester 1, Year 9 semester report. I asked him to highlight key phrases and to transcribe them into his study notes, in google.docs, for Semester 2.

They are now Jonathan's EF Goals.

Conversation between Jonathan and Coach analysing his report comments

TABLE 10.2 Conversation focusing on the executive function skills underlying his teachers' report comments

---

Teacher comments →focus on an executive function skill

English comment:

'Revise language features & read widely to practise this skill'→

Coach: We know that students who read widely perform better in English because of exposure to a variety of composition styles and acquisition of complex vocabulary and syntax. How many audiobooks have you listened to this year?

Jonathan: One or two.

Coach: Mmm … any thoughts on that?

Jonathan: Ok, I'll increase that, this semester. (goal–directed persistence)

Coach: It is fine to know the list of language features but it is a whole new dimension to encounter them in texts and have those 'Ah, ha' moments like …'that was delicious irony' or recognising a beautifully constructed analogy. Let's look at some fiction book titles that might interest you …

History comment:

'Use key words in order to make connections between the question and the content in essay writing'→

Coach: What do you think this comment means?

Jonathan: The teacher wants this so I should do it. (planning)

Coach: It makes your work more logical and sequential if you address it like this … (a quick sketch to re-iterate the logical order in which to address the relationship between key words and content – using a known graphic organiser)

Maths (which is his definite academic strength) **comment**:

'Should try to maintain this consistent revision and also by attempting more challenging questions'→

Coach: Not attempting challenging questions?

Jonathan: Sometimes I don't get up to them in class.

Coach: Any ideas about how to correct that?

Jonathan: Maybe I could ask my teacher if I could miss some easier questions and do these early in the lesson? (metacognition)

Coach: Good idea.

I know that despite Jonathan's high ability, his weaknesses in the Executive Functions of:

> Organisation
> Task initiation and
> Goal-directed persistence

mean that I must directly instruct him on what to do and I must reiterate frequently… using humour when I can.

As Jonathan's Coach I look for every appropriate setting to draw attention to metacognition and self-regulation.

'Stress is the gatekeeper of learning' (Goodrich, 2017)

A child may shut down under threat.

Ultimately, a student needs to develop tolerance for stress, again a very unlikely early skill for attainment. When coaching we can be protective of students and because we grow to know them very well from the quite personal conversations we have with them, we can see when the stress is too much and use our influence to stop it environmentally and/or behaviourally with new strategies.

Illustration: one technique for **Building on Strengths**

> Visualise a suitcase – everything that I will need is laid out on the bed before I pack it in the suitcase. A goal in itself.

There is a lot of effective work going on in secondary schools in terms of 'chunking tasks'.

The problem arises when the child also has a problem with motivation, activation and sustained effort. This is not always well understood because it looks to be disobedient and disrespectful.

Learn to discern where the student is currently placed on:

The Can't–Won't Continuum

CAN'T ⟵——————⟶ WON'T

- Consider this continuum quietly for every planned activity.
- Give the student the benefit of the doubt and stand by him until he teaches you to discern when he CANNOT do a step of the process (as opposed to Won't!).
- Stop and teach it, at the first opportunity.
- Walk him through it.
- Record the sequence of steps.

And don't be surprised when you find a skill that you just assumed the student could do.

The resource *Learning How to Learn: How to Succeed in School Without Spending All Your Time Studying* was found to be effective with a small group of junior high school students when used in a Book Club setting by Stephenson (2022). It is a lively and highly suitable, readable e-book for even the most reluctant 2e student. I recommend it.

As an Executive Function coach,
in whatever setting you are placed, be:

- prepared to be surprised
- ready and armed with strategies
- fully in the moment

and

Listen and observe **very carefully**.

'Go to' resources

ADDitude magazine Free Guide (online): How to Tidy Up Your Home Like a Pro. See
www.additudemag.com/download/organize-your-adhd-home/

Center on the Developing Child, Harvard University
https://developingchild.harvard.edu/resourcetag/executive-function/

McCabe, J. (2016, September) How to Create a Bullet Journal Plus My Top 10 Tips
https://youtu.be/jkZEEQG6IVE

McCabe, J. (2017, January) This is what it's really like to live with ADHD [Video]. TED Conferences.
www.ted.com/talks/jessica_mccabe_this_is_what_it_s_really_like_to_live_with_adhd_jan_2017/

Bibliography

Bandura, A. (1994). Self-efficacy. In V. S. Ramachaudran (Ed.), *Encyclopedia of Human Behavior* (Vol. 4, pp. 71–81). New York: Academic Press. (Reprinted in H. Friedman (Ed.) (1998). Encyclopedia of Mental Health. San Diego: Academic Press).

Baum, S. M., & Olenchak, F. R. (2002). The alphabet children: GT, ADHD, and more. *Exceptionality, 10*(2), 77–91. [abstract]

Cooper-Kahn, J., & Foster, M. (2013). *Boosting executive skills in the classroom: A practical guide for educators.* San Francisco, USA: John Wiley & Sons, Inc. (p. 7).

Dawson, P., & Guare, R. (2012) *Coaching students with executive function deficits.* New York, USA: The Guilford Press.

+ Resource to use with students: *Smart but Scattered* series, Guilford Publications. Versions are for children and for teens.

Education Endowment Foundation (2021). *Metacognition and Self-regulated Learning.* London: Education Endowment Foundation. https://educationendowmentfoundation.org.uk/education-evidence/guidance-reports/metacognition

Oakley, B., Sejnowski, T., & McConville, A. (2018). *Learning how to learn: How to succeed in school without spending all your time studying; a guide for kids and teens.* New York, USA: Penguin Random House.

Perry, J., Lundie, D., & Golder, G. (2018). Metacognition in schools: what does the literature suggest about the effectiveness of teaching metacognition in schools?. *Educational Review*, *71*(4), 483–500. http://dx.doi.org/10.1080/00131911.2018.1441127

Saline, S. (website, 2023) Anger management: Steps and scripts to use when you're fired up. www.additudemag.com/wp-content/uploads/2023/02/Anger-Management-Steps-and-Scripts.pdf

Stephenson, E. (2022) Presentation at St Andrew's Cathedral School online conference, *Research Conversations*, 29 October 2022. www.youtube.com/playlist?list=PL5q_Zb7lgyasov4Zr6cwfEkgqGLVSXMTO

Putting it all together for the 2e student in the classroom

Rhonda Filmer

VIGNETTE

Mei watched as her Year 4 class filed into the room. It is Tuesday at 9:00 am, Week 6 of Term 1. As she looked at the faces of this disparate class of 30 students she suddenly felt a sense of relief.

'I am nowhere near conquering the challenges of this group for maximal learning, but we are getting there.'

The children were purposeful, the mood was buoyant and every child was positive in demeanour. They all knew what to do next.

Mei, like every other teaching professional I know, had spent countless hours since several weeks before school began, reading her students' past records and preparing her class programme to fit with the known learning needs of her students. She knew that time spent 'setting up' conducive classroom management systems and curriculum adjustments would result in smoother processes that would make up for 'lost' time as the year progressed.

Initial time spent on preparing for the rest of the year is a *time investment*.

You may need a month, six weeks, a whole term or as long as it takes.

It will earn dividends over and over again

beginning with the growth of trusting relationships

between you, your 2e student/s and the whole class resulting in

quality differentiated programmes, appropriately adjusted

and self-efficacious learners!

DOI: 10.4324/9781003404972-14

This book has brought you to a place where you are primed with evidence-based knowledge and understanding about the range of learning strengths and needs of 2e students.

Now, this chapter is in three parts:

Part A will assist you to prioritise your valuable and limited time starting with the steps required to understand the 2e students assigned to you for this year. Two comprehensive case studies illustrate this process in practical terms.

Part B will navigate from where to begin when the new school year arrives, how to deliver curriculum in your classroom for the 2e student and the rest of the class and how to build classroom culture and climate.

Part C presents more on theories of curriculum differentiation and a warning to beware of the claims of some educational theories and schemes in the area of curriculum differentiation.

I am mindful that the vast majority of readers will be teaching in one or more mixed ability, inclusive classrooms at levels somewhere between the first and final years of schooling …

Part A

Prioritising learning and content

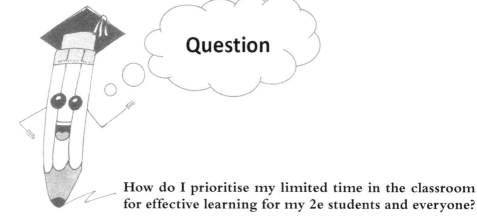

Question

How do I prioritise my limited time in the classroom for effective learning for my 2e students and everyone?

Start by …

thoroughly checking all your students'
achievement *levels* in all aspects of
LITERACY and NUMERACY

then develop their skills and knowledge to their maximal level

It needs to start with what we know from research:

- Use explicit instruction to teach reading and spelling through a Systematic Synthetic Phonics programme and growth in spoken and written language as outlined in Chapter 5, from Day 1 in Kindergarten, giving maximal time to those skills from K to Year 6. Use those strong foundations as a springboard to excellent skills of language analysis, composition and research throughout upper primary and secondary schooling while modifying your subject syllabus according to the capacity of individuals.
- Avoid class time interruptions. This needs to be a whole-school intention.
- Use Response to Intervention principles utilising Tier 2 and Tier 3 interventions for low progress students. Never give up.
- Introduce appropriate ICT support for written work when the need is clear but not till well into primary school. Keep handwriting going but allow the use of ICT for the composition of text.

And now to individual 2e students ...

The process of discovering the full learning profile of 2e students occurs over time. I have taken a walk through each of the following case studies demonstrating how to:

- interpret standardised test results
- draw conclusions about a student's learning profile, his strengths and needs
- apply adjustments for this student in the class setting and see the benefits for the whole class.

Case study 1

Sophie

Sophie was 11 years 3 months old and in Year 6 when she came to see me because her teacher said she is 'bright but not translating onto paper'.

In Kindergarten, Sophie had been able to spell some advanced words but she needed Learning Support in Year 1. She was given Reading Recovery and it took till Year 4 before she read well. Her Mum had her tested by a psychologist who found her IQ to be 120 (an underestimate in light of her later achievement.)

I administered the WIAT 2 Achievement test (current at the time) and the results were very interesting (see Table 11.1).

Wechsler Individual Achievement Test – 2nd Edition (WIAT–2)

Sophie Chronological Age 11 years, 3 months

TABLE 11.1 WIAT 2 results: Sophie C.A. 11:2 yrs

	Percentile Rank	Age Equivalent (year and month)	Year Equivalent (school year and month)
Reading			
Word Reading	30	10:4	5:4
Reading Comprehension	98	>19:11	>12:9
*Pseudoword Decoding	32	9:0	4:0
Composite Score	**63**		
Mathematics			
Numerical Operations	53	12:8	7:9
Maths Reasoning	94	>19:11	>12:9
Composite Score	**45**		
Written Language			
Spelling	50	12:4	7:5
Written Expression	73	14:00	9:5
Composite Score	**61**		

*The 'pseudoword decoding' subtest uses nonsense words to check a child's capacity to decode words carefully without the assistance of word meaning in context.

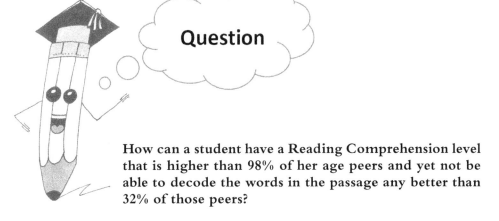

Question

How can a student have a Reading Comprehension level that is higher than 98% of her age peers and yet not be able to decode the words in the passage any better than 32% of those peers?

Sophie is *dyslexic* and has learned to be able to find meaning through visualisation of a context and by predicting outcomes. Her well *above average intellectual ability* has enhanced that capacity to foresee meaning, but it is only a form a 'clever guessing'. She would be termed an '*instructional casualty*', that is, a victim of an early reading programme that failed to teach her strong letter-sound correspondence and an intervention programme that is now outmoded and discredited. As a very bright girl she made a good start with Spelling through learning 'by gestalt', that is, the whole word, but she could not sustain learning that way as English has too many words and too many alternative ways of spelling the same sound (NB 44 sounds and 175 spellings). All students, but especially those who have the SLD, dyslexia, need to be directly instructed in letter-sound correspondence, the blending and segmentation of words into their sounds and later their syllables.

Looking at her Maths results, her Reasoning is in the 94th but her accuracy on algorithms, Numerical Operations, is the 53rd. Sophie's reasoning is very high but her results at school are in the average range. She is having trouble remembering facts and processes and her working memory is weak in mathematical calculations. This can be observed in children who count on their fingers or repeat the question you have asked out loud while they think of the answer. Sophie did both during the WIAT 2 testing.

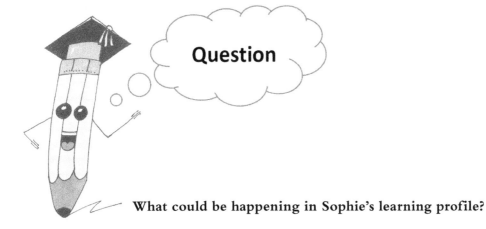

What could be happening in Sophie's learning profile?

Her Executive Function skills are weak. When asked, 'Do you catch yourself dreaming?' she replied, 'Oh yes, often.' She told me that she gets the work done at school but that she takes a long time. She finds that frustrating. Sophie is not hyperactive, but she forgets details and she has a problem with time. She is very conscientious, but she takes hours to complete set work.

I suspected ADHD, the 'passive inattentive' (PIP) type.

Sophie is artistic and demonstrates design ability.

She is a high potential learner/creatively and possibly intellectually gifted.
She certainly looks like a twice-exceptional learner, doesn't she?

In my assessment report to Sophie's school I wrote:

Sophie is a 2e learner and an 'instructional casualty'
New strategies need to be put into place to reduce the cognitive load that Sophie bears when she solves problems and interprets meaning.

A poor working memory when combined with a slow processing speed can cause considerable fatigue and stress in a young student. It certainly reduces the capacity to demonstrate the complexity of ideas and concepts that are intellectually synthesised especially when the requirement is a written task. It is important to reduce the cognitive load of students who have this learning profile through the use of graphic organisers and electronic planning devices. She also needs to be 'automatic', that is, showing mastery of all number facts so that her cognitive capacity is targeted on a Maths problem and not on trying to recall simple calculations.

This is so important! The 'crowded curriculum' of recent primary school syllabuses may have reduced class time for students to learn excellent recall of the 'friends of 10', addition and subtraction facts and all multiplication and division tables BUT for so many students quick recall builds efficiency, accuracy and self-esteem in Mathematics. 'Whole-language' and 'balanced literacy' methods in early reading instruction have meant that students may not have a precise and automatic mastery of sound-letter correspondence.

It is worth taking the time (or seeking teacher support) because you will make up time later!

Conclusions and follow-up

I summarised *Sophie's learning profile*:

- Excellent verbal comprehension and mathematical reasoning … gifted?
- Artistic and design ability … creatively gifted?
- Verbally precocious … gifted?
- Very conscientious … a motivated personality factor
- Report showing 'B' & 'C' levels in all subjects
- Tendency to be anxious
- Completes work slowly and inefficiently … slow processing speed
- Dyslexic … (individual programme to remediate skills + given extra time in tests)
- Concentration and WM weaknesses … eventually diagnosed with ADHD (PIP)

Sophie did an individualised programme with me over the Christmas holiday period in all of these matters and I taught her a whole range of Mathematics problem-solving strategies as well.

Sophie entered high school with the Individualised Learning Department fully informed about her 2e profile and her mother kept in touch with me. Sophie was an excellent self-advocate so that by Year 9 she was actually telling her teachers how her work needed to be adjusted for her. She was gaining very high levels in her subjects and excelling in Maths, Art and Technology subjects.

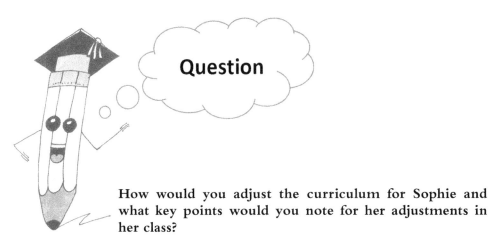

Question

How would you adjust the curriculum for Sophie and what key points would you note for her adjustments in her class?

TABLE 11.2 Summary of adjustments for Sophie's programme

Strengths	Key Points/Supports	Benefits for the rest of the Class
• Advanced English and Maths curriculum	* Curriculum compacting & vocabulary enrichment	→ Who else could be included? Is there a potential Cluster Group#?
	* Allow plenty of time on written tasks	→ Could the students learn to opt for a given time for their task?
	* Instruction in 'test taking skills'	
	* Executive Function (EF) goals and support – check specifics	→ Teacher time and attention given to observing EF details in students
	* Check for her understanding of instructions & the maths examples process after the class starts working	
• Speaking opportunities	* Non-verbal cue system if feeling anxious	
• Art, IT & design opportunities (formal and informal)		
• Highly motivated, enthusiastic	* May want to ask questions privately	

A cluster group, a term used by Brulles & Winebrenner (2019) is a group of identified gifted or high-potential students who are clustered in the classroom of one teacher who has had special training in gifted education. Their programme is differentiated for their needs among a variety of students with other learning profiles.

You can read the rest of Sophie's story, in Chapter 12, Longitudinal Case Studies.

Case study 2

Luke

Luke's profile in Year 1 looked like this:
Chronological age 7 years 3 months
IQ 96th percentile or the top 4% of students his age.
Wechsler Individual Achievement Test – 3rd edition (WIAT–3)

TABLE 11.3 WIAT 3 results: Luke C.A. 7:3 yrs

	Percentile Rank	Age Equivalent (year and month)	Year Equivalent (school year and month)
Reading			
Word Reading	98	9:8	4:2
Reading Comprehension	99	>19:11	12:1
Pseudoword Decoding	90	10:4	5:2
Mathematics			
Numerical Operations	99.7	9:8	4:2
Maths Reasoning	87	7:8	2:4
Written Language			
Spelling	81	7:8	2:4
Sentence Composition	82	8:0	3:1

These results are clearly those of a *gifted or high potential child*.

Let's look further:

Wechsler Intelligence Scale for Children – 5th edition (WISC–5)

TABLE 11.4 WISC-5 results Luke C.A. 7:3 yrs

Verbal Comprehension Index	99th percentile	Extremely High Range
Visual Spatial Index	93%	Very High Range
Fluid Reasoning Index	96%	Very High Range
Working Memory Index	16%	Low Average Range
Processing Speed Index	58%	Average Range
Full Scale IQ	96%	Very High Range
General Ability Index*	99%	Extremely High Range

It is here that we start to see the '*twice-exceptionality*' of this student. The first three indices are in the gifted range (top decile of 90–99.9th) but Luke's Working Memory and Processing Speed are in the Low Average and Average Range respectively.

In the WISC 5 the following definitions apply:

TABLE 11.5 WISC-5 definitions for working memory and processing speed

Working Memory Index (WM)	The ability to register information, to briefly focus attention, auditory discrimination and auditory rehearsal, transformation of information and mental manipulation. It also measures visual working memory. In short, it is the ability to hold information and to manipulate it at the same time. WM has been shown to be **a better indicator of academic success than IQ** by many researchers, but it is malleable and can be improved to around age 11 before it plateaus.
Processing Speed (PS)	Procedural and incidental learning, psychomotor speed, visual perception, visual-spatial scanning ability and discrimination, sustained attention, concentration, cognitive flexibility, inhibitory control and planning. Timed tasks are very difficult to complete for students with slow PS.

*The General Ability Index is his IQ if you factor out the WM and PS. This puts him in **the top 1% of learners his age.** We can see that level of result in the individual achievement performance test he did with the psychologist (WIAT 3) but is he gaining this level in school? I would expect not, for a variety of reasons that we will explore.

We have some of the psychometric data, now let's look at how this student performs in his daily life at school.

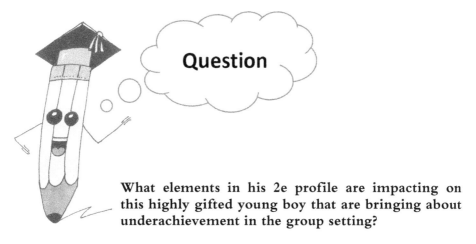

What elements in his 2e profile are impacting on this highly gifted young boy that are bringing about underachievement in the group setting?

I summarised *Luke's learning profile*:

- Avid reader with excellent literacy skills …   gifted
- Naturally curious–absorbed in interests–asks many questions …   gifted
- Large general knowledge …   gifted
- Verbally precocious …   gifted
- Report showing 'B' level in all subjects?
- Becomes overwhelmed ★★?
- Struggles in fast-paced environment – slow processing speed
- Somewhat perfectionistic and can be anxious ★?
- Struggles with handwriting?

There was more information from his paediatrician who tested for Autism relating to ★★ his tendency to be rigid, to become overwhelmed and his anxiety.

The results were as follows (see Figure 11.1 on page 198); look at Sensory Sensitivity, Behavioural Rigidity, Unusual Behaviours.

Luke demonstrates many of the symptoms of autism spectrum disorder, specifically Behavioural Rigidity (incapacity to adapt his behaviour to the social setting), some Social/Emotional Reciprocity (meaning he does not engage in two-way conversation with peers, easily). He meets the DSM-5-TR criteria for a diagnosis.

As was established in Chapter 7 on ASD, it is important to concentrate on the individual ASD characteristics demonstrated by Luke and their functional impact on his giftedness and not be overloaded by trying to understand the entire spectrum disorder.

In addition, he was shown to have Executive Function deficits particularly with tasks that require him to plan and organise information, work within specific time frames, make decisions, do problem solving and with 'thinking things through' (metacognition).

Luke *may have ADHD as well* judging from these symptoms.

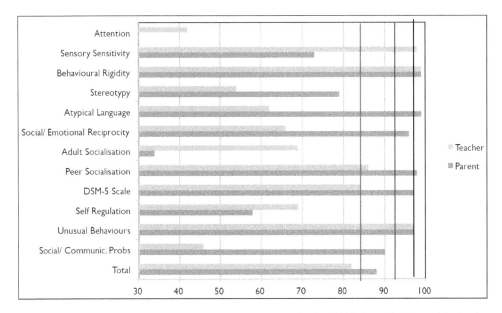

FIGURE 11.1 Luke's percentiles on the Autism Spectrum Rating Scales (ASRS) (ages 6–18 years) for teacher and parent.

The amended summary of Luke's 2e learning profile looked like this:

LUKE'S 2E STUDENT PROFILE:

GIFTED

Verbally talented, exceptional reading and mathematical ability.

AUTISTIC TRAITS

Rigid thinking, slow PS, becomes overwhelmed and tends to be anxious.

EXECUTIVE FUNCTION DEFICITS

Planning, organisation, timed tasks, decision making, problem solving.

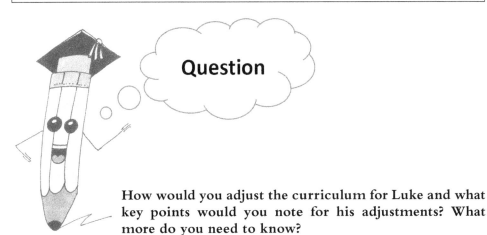

Question

How would you adjust the curriculum for Luke and what key points would you note for his adjustments? What more do you need to know?

TABLE 11.6 Questions to prepare for curriculum adjustments for Luke and the whole class

1. Get to know Luke	For the whole class
Questions:	
What are his greatest interests?	Administer an Interest Inventory – see appendix
Where does he have gaps in the skills that are required to do curriculum tasks? How long can he sustain activity?	→group class into Interest Groups
What students in the class could work well with him?	Prepare a sketch 'socio-gram' in the first weeks of term as preparation for grouping specific activities – find 'like-minds'
What opportunities can I give him to shine/to gain self-esteem from being recognised for his strengths in the class? Would he like to be a Resident Expert in some area?	Who shares his interests? What special interests are held by classmates?
2. Observe him in class	
Does he work best in a group? Is he able to make good choices when given options?	Who is ready to make sensible choices if I offer them?
How often is his attention wandering (as far as is observable!)?	Observe the class for concentration capacity. Does anyone need to be assessed?
3. Talk to him about his learning	
Questions:	
Are there any class activities that make you feel unsettled? What is the best way you like to learn? What would you love to learn about?	Create a culture of acceptance that allows for difference. Build classroom culture. See Tomlinson & Imbeau (2010, pp 78–91)

TABLE 11.7 Curriculum adjustments for Luke and the whole class

Strengths	Key Points/Supports	Benefits for the rest of the Class
Exceptional ability in English and Mathematics	*Curriculum compacting, enrichment and extension in all areas of English and Maths curriculum	→ Who else could be included?
	*Allow plenty of time on written tasks – Very slow if handwriting	Complete over multiple sessions in class or modify the activity for a small group → for everyone
	* Prioritise EF goals from these areas: – planning – organisation – awareness of time – making decisions – problem solving	
	*Non-verbal cue system if feeling anxious	→ clear routines & procedures ensure a smooth-running classroom
	* Perfectionistic – make expectations clear – for older children build them into the marking scheme – don't always use marks but rather, oral feedback	
	*Rigid with transitions – warn if routines will vary	

Curriculum differentiation/adjustments for Luke in his primary school class:

This information about Luke will inform the development of an Individual Learning Plan (ILP) which should involve all teacher stakeholders in Luke's development. Parental and student input should be collected prior to this meeting then a short meeting held to present the ILP, receive feedback and set the time for the review meeting (one/two term(s)?).

Luke (Year 2)

1.   Individual Learning Plan (ILP)

One-page Sample Summary for Classroom Practice:

TABLE 11.8 Summary of Luke's ILP classroom practices

Term 1

Classroom	Allow time – use buzzer/timer? Ask Luke what helps him
	Warn if variation to routine
	Eye and hand-signal cues – teach him unspoken signals
	Set a specific EF goal
	Explicit expectations on how to correct mistakes, use of erasers, time to colour in

Subject	**Adjustment**	**Notes**
English	Compact following pre-test Teach touch-typing (home & school)	Enrich in poetry See https://www.familyfriendpoems.com/poems/children/–choice of activity Compose a narrative/report on topic of interest–typed for ease
Maths	Compact curriculum following pre-test. Ensure automaticity of number facts Work with a buddy?	Enrich and extend in problem solving using: Joshua, A. (2006) Enrichematics (3rd Ed.) Book 3 *Becoming a Problem-solving Genius* HB publication

Remember ... This is a time investment!

■   Build trust and a strong relationship with him based on clear, fair expectations and a willingness to listen. With each planned activity, ask yourself, 'Could I be setting this child up to fail by asking him to do this? Can I modify this content better for him?'

■   The same principles will apply for all the work you adjust for Luke.

■   Over time, Luke will probably begin to tell you what works best for him.

Postscript on Luke

This information was presented at Luke's school on a professional learning (PL) day. It was de-identified and not noted as a real student. Without further in-service training the staff embraced an understanding of how to adjust and modify curriculum for a 2e student. His mother reported that since the PL day she noticed a significant shift in the approach taken toward her son. He was placed in the gifted and talented programme, in extension maths and receives support where he needs it. The teachers understand him better and accept him as he is, whereas he had been in trouble constantly, often coming home very upset. The staff have understood what it means to be smart but have challenges and they know how to manage him. She said that all the teachers he comes in contact with, not just his class teacher, are briefed on his ILP accommodations. Luke is happy and thriving in his school environment.

Important points here are:

1. *whole staff commitment* to working as a professional learning community where specialist and executive staff take on the task of owning and communicating appropriately the *learning profiles of students*

2. the student's *diversity of needs is understood* not only in the classroom but in the playground, the library and throughout the school

3. punitive responses for playground misdemeanours are avoided when observation, assistance and *understanding* are applied

Part B

In a new school year where do I begin with this class??

Begin at the beginning …

Step #1 Data gathering

Start with observations of your class/es and look for the asynchronous student, possibly 2e:

LOOK	for signs of *high potential or giftedness* in the student, in the school data records, school reports, anecdotal comments. If there is no documented evidence then seek comprehensive assessment (IQ + standardised achievement testing WISC 5 and WIAT 3, Woodcock-Johnson or other recommended psychometric testing) through the school counsellor. If there is a time delay before testing can occur, then use a screener as outlined previously.
MAP	the student's strengths (intellectual, physical, creative and social-emotional).
DOCUMENT	symptoms of possible *learning difficulties* SLD? ASD? DCD? ADHD? High anxiety? Does the existence of co-morbidities complicate the learning profile further?
OBSERVE	carefully for evidence of *executive function* weaknesses & seek other teachers' observations.
MEET	with the student's parents for their *perspective* on her strengths and weaknesses and for copies of past reports from

	psychological, medical or allied health professionals if not on file.
RECORD	details of the student's *learning profile*.
	How are the difficulties *functionally impacting* on this child's high intellectual ability?
CALL A MEETING	with *stakeholders*: parents, learning support teachers, gifted/ high potential students coordinator and class teacher/s.
PREPARE	an *Individual Learning Plan* including the 3 most important provisions or adjustments to curriculum
SHARE	successes with stakeholders about how the student's learning needs are being met in the classroom…. and with colleagues about how *adjustments* were done…. and the results.

Step #2 Planning for curriculum adjustments

Conceptualise 'groups' of students according to their curriculum adjustment needs

The particular pattern of *learning needs* in each student will intersect with others in the class. 'Group' these, *in your mind*, regardless of the student's diagnosed condition, for the purpose of organising adjustments when planning curriculum.

It is not suggested here that you should sit the students in groups with other students who have the same adjustments unless there are other reasons to do so. Of course, individual differences will apply and a student may need adjustments across several 'groups'.

Group 1: Handwriting difficulties

We can see that the *handwriting weaknesses* of students with motor dysgraphia and developmental co-ordination disorder may look similar in a classroom.

The student with handwriting weaknesses will need:

- a reduced quantity of handwriting activity
- to be allowed alternate ways to demonstrate knowledge such as the use of graphic organisers, oral responses, audio or video presentations
- use of assistive technology on tablets or computer for students in upper primary and high school, including Dictation software
- avoid copious copying from a whiteboard or presentation. *Prepared notes* can be given to an older child or an agreement with a 'buddy' might result in the sharing of notes by *photocopying* or *taking a screenshot*.

Group 2: Attention difficulties

The student with *attention* and *executive function (EF) weaknesses* – ADHD /ASD will need:

- teacher attention to *ensure the task is understood* following instructions given to class
- *non-verbal cues* to prompt return to task and *visual planners* for instructions and procedures where possible
- *Executive Function goal-setting* according to Dawson & Guare (2012) questionnaire & response
- pairing with a *buddy* who assists (without losing her learning time)
- negotiated *adjustments* for *product & pace.*

Group 3: Reading difficulties (decoding &/or spelling)

The student with *reading difficulties (decoding)* – SLD dyslexia will need:

- use of *audio books*, appropriate YouTube *videos* for information gathering
- reduced amount of material to read – a prepared summary
- not to be asked to read aloud in class
- *visual planners* for instructions and procedures
- in upper primary and high school, use of text to speech software, audio books and reading pens

(A structured synthetic phonics remediation programme with explicit instructions using decodable books in the early grades will help gain the greatest level of reading accuracy and fluency attainable.)

Group 4: Reading difficulties (comprehension)

The student with *reading difficulties (comprehension)* – a type of SLD dyslexia/ASD will need:

- *prior teaching* of new vocabulary, wherever possible
- use of an *online thesaurus* e.g. wordhippo.com. Student should highlight unknown words and find meanings before reading a passage of text
- additional supports: *graphic organisers/outlines* for recording meaning
- in upper primary and high school, use of Dictation software, audio books and reading pens

Group 5: Mathematics difficulties

The student with *mathematics difficulties* – SLD dyscalculia/ASD will need:

- use of maths *concrete materials/manipulatives*, times tables and hundreds charts
- use rehearsed 'silly statements' (Chapter 5) and procedure charts on the wall/desk to *prompt memory* for algorithm processes
- in upper primary and high school, use of calculators and software programs.

(A remediation programme teaching all facts & processes to mastery to the end of Year 6.)

Group 6: Writing difficulties

The student with *writing difficulties* (organisation & planning) – SLD dysgraphia will need:

- to be taught how to '*brainstorm*' to include full extent of ideas
  - advanced notice to give time to complete
  - to keep 'messy brainstorm maps' to demonstrate increasing complexity and capacity to map thought
- to use other *graphic organisers* for the '*sequencing*' or planning stage after the original brainstorm map has been completed (www.educationoasis.com)
- to break the task into 4 or 5 pieces to complete in multiple sittings
- to be allowed to present a researched project using multimedia

Group 7: Individual needs

The students with specific *individual needs* related to their particular conditions and co-morbidities will need adjustments suggested by medical or allied health professionals that are reasonable to administer in the classroom. Included in this group may be students with very high anxiety, emotional dysregulation at a high level, multiple co-morbidities such as ASD/DCD/ADHD or oppositional defiance so that management strategies are highly individualised and supported to assist the teacher … and, ideally, consistent in the whole school context.

Summary of conceptual 'groups':

Group 1: Handwriting adjustments
Group 2: EF goals and adjustments
Group 3: Reading adjustments (decoding)
Group 4: Reading adjustments (comprehension)
Group 5: Mathematics adjustments

Group 6: Writing adjustments
Group 7: Individualisation.

The gifted/high potential student will need *access to an advanced curriculum* and not be limited to a 'dumbed down' level of intellectual activity because of handwriting, reading, attention, processing speed or mathematics weaknesses.

A possible classroom scenario …

Out of a class of *30 students …*

Year/Stage-based programme will suit 80%	→	24 students
Substantial extension for gifted/HPL, 10%	→	3 students
Year/Stage-based program, specific adjustments for disabilities, recorded in an ILP, 5–10%	→	1 to 3 students

Substantial adjustment recorded in an ILP for 2e students
for extension *and* learning support, 2–5%   →1 to 2 students

(crossing into above categories)

Step #3 Creating ILPs

Create Individual Learning Plans for students requiring them

Your school's policy will dictate how adjustments for individual students should be recorded. It is reasonable that the assessed needs, goals and adjustments of 2e students should be recorded in an Individual/Personalised Learning Plan (ILP/PLP), but it should be recorded in brief form to avoid it being a time-consuming, onerous task for class teachers.

The ultimate goal for all students is to find an optimal match between the level of the learner and the level of the curriculum. VanTassel-Baska (2021) warns that no curriculum should be withheld from students who are capable of using it.

Adjustments are key provisions to allow access to curriculum for students with disability.

The NSW Department of Education website states that personalised learning (ILPs/PLPs) has four key elements:

- the assessed individual education needs of the student
- provision of adjustments to meet those needs
- review dates and impact statements
- evidence of collaboration between stakeholders including the student.

A thorough and ongoing process is of enormous support to the 2e student but not all schools create ILPs when giftedness is in the mix of learning needs. That is an oversight on their part.

Note: The following sample is a composite document. Secondary schools may hold this information electronically in various parts of the school's platform with not all teachers having access to all elements in the data. For example, the notes from a meeting held between the school counsellor and parents may not be made available for all staff to view.

TABLE 11.9 A composite sample template for an ILP/PLP

A sample template for an ILP/PLP:	
Student name, class & photo	
NCCD category: Physical/Cognitive/Sensory/Social-emotional	**Is there standardised testing on file? Yes/No**
Specific disabilities:	
Areas of giftedness Intellectual/Creative/Physical/Social-emotional	**Strengths/Interests:** Specific developing talents …
Sample conclusion: High potential learner with a disability (Twice–exceptional)	
Goals: S.M.A.R.T.	
Adjustments to instruction:	**Adjustments to classroom:**
Adjustments to assessment:	**Support:** Use of special equipment (e.g. text to speech software/C-pen)
Collaborative planning: Personnel involved Internal and external sources	
Dates and times of meetings	**Review period:** Say two terms

Step #4 Planning for curriculum differentiation

Thinking about curriculum differentiation for individual 2e students

The work of Tomlinson in curriculum differentiation (CD) over decades, holds at its heart the dignity of each learner and

- her right to a learning programme that meets her learning needs
- based on a comprehensive knowledge of the student from records
- by building relationships within the class.
- personalised knowledge of individual students promotes student engagement and motivation
- removes a student's barriers to learning.

Gibbs & Beamish (2021) found that teachers concur with CD principles and view CD in terms of student learning needs. However, they are restricted in its implementation by their training, experience, and for secondary teachers, by the limited time with students. All practising teachers will validate that restriction as problematic to the outcomes of 2e and all students.

The need for enrichment, extension and challenge is commonly met by project-based learning (PBL) yet throughout this book I have explained how 2e students may not have the underlying skills required to manage it well. Independence in learning may be a long time coming.

Beware of PBL projects for young 2e students!

IS THIS TASK BEYOND THIS 2E STUDENT'S CONTROL AT THIS TIME?

If you think he is ready, be sure to:

1. Negotiate the task requirements
2. Explain your expectations fully
3. Break the task into small, manageable pieces
4. Feedback frequently
5. Hold him accountable ... to show progress as planned.

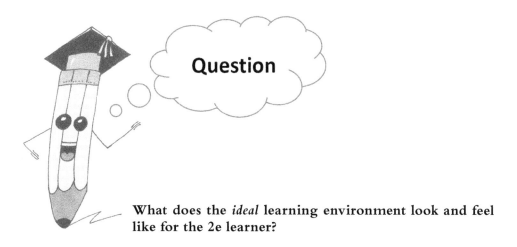

Question

What does the *ideal* learning environment look and feel like for the 2e learner?

1. A trusting, mutually respectful relationship between teacher and student in a class where individual differences including remediation for weaknesses are accepted and ability is celebrated, through 'strengths-based' principles (Lopez & Louis, 2009).

2. Clear and explicit expectations of courteous behaviour.

3. A self-advocating student who speaks about what works for her using respectful and appropriate language.

4. Choice/flexibility in learning, assessment and pace (Willard-Holt et al, 2013, p. 259).

5. Practices informed by both gifted education and special education while working collaboratively with parents (Coleman & Gallagher, 2015).

6. Individual Learning Plans for each 2e student with input from the student.

7. Freedom to choose available supports: graphic organisers, technology, concrete materials for mathematics in a classroom where all students can choose what they need and feel comfortable doing so with teacher observation and evaluation of choices.

8. Ultimately, student involvement in setting their own projects and products to align with curriculum expectations and clear and explicit details about the level of mastery required (Willard-Holt, 2013)

Step #5 Differentiating a unit of work

Differentiating the curriculum for the 2e student and the whole class

---

Effective evidence-based classroom practice is the foundation for all differentiated curriculum with group and individual adjustments:

High expectations
Explicit teaching
Effective feedback
Use of data to inform practice
Assessment
Classroom management
Wellbeing
Collaboration

CESE document *What works best 2020 update:*
https://education.nsw.gov.au/about-us/educational-data/cese/publications/research-reports/what-works-best-2020-update

Planning a unit of work

A unit of work is a plan of the intended teaching and learning for a particular class for a particular period of time. The duration of a unit of work could be for a number of weeks, a term or a semester (NSW Dept of Education website).

Choose the topic

Pre-Test

A key first step before designing differentiated curriculum is to find out *what students already know* by using one or more of these methods:

■   Give them the final factual Assessment Quiz or Activity, prior to beginning the unit of work.

■   Question the whole class and/or follow up your observations with further questioning of individual students.

■   Ask students to fill out a KW Chart for the topic. Some modelling of your expectations will be required including how to frame questions:

The K-W Chart

What I Know	What I Want to Know

- Use the Winebrenner (1992) strategy *Five Most Difficult First*. Ask the five most difficult questions about the topic, that you would ask at the completion of the unit, at the outset. Students' responses are indicative of prior knowledge and higher order thinking ability.
- Brainstorming 'What I know' on a mind-map and explaining it orally, individually or in a small group.
- Use Kahoot to find out what percentage of the class already knows the answer to particular questions.
- Use a Traffic Lights system: The teacher has a list of the expected knowledge and concepts for the unit of work on a column grid. Students indicate their understanding by holding up a coloured sign. Red for No Knowledge … Orange for Some Knowledge … and Green for Substantial Knowledge. Students indicating Green can be further questioned for more detail to inform your enrichment planning.

Beware of the 'ceiling effects' of tests. Allowing for a high ceiling or higher than expected ('off-level') scope to the test means that a gifted/2e student is more able to demonstrate the full extent of what he knows.

Use pre-test data to inform the starting point

Act on the information received from the Pre-testing. Students who already know facts or concepts should not be asked to waste time in class while others learn. 'Compact' the curriculum and plan for enrichment work for them. Reis and colleagues (2021) define enrichment pedagogy as 'the teaching methods that respond to students' academic strengths and interests (p. 2)' and their article comprehensively lists ideas for enrichment activity. For example, when teaching a mathematics algorithm type such as 'long multiplication' give problem solving applications using an additional process as well. In the Humanities subjects ask the student to use multiple sources, rather than one passage for information, and to synthesise a response.

At its simplest, begin the lesson as a whole class then differentiate the activity into small groups or individual work with appropriately levelled content and process. It requires forward planning and reference to those students whose needs are the most complex, first. The adjustments required for the groups (listed in Step #2) are built into the planning process of each specific unit of work. This will become easier and less time-consuming as the year progresses and you can observe the progress of students because the adjustments are allowing students to thrive.

Create and modify curriculum

Mandated curricula by education authorities and systems are the starting point but not the constraint when developing appropriate curriculum for your class.

It is impossible to overstate the usefulness of the Anderson & Krathwohl revised taxonomy with attention to the levels of knowledge. It is an evocative toolkit for differentiation across classroom activities. The Anderson & Krathwohl (2001) revision of Bloom's taxonomy (Wilson, 2016) was introduced in Chapter 4 on Giftedness/High Potential Learners with the cognitive processes of thinking defined as: Remembering, Understanding, Applying, Analysing, Evaluating, Creating.

Particularly important to know is how the levels of knowledge relate to the taxonomy:

The levels are:

Factual Knowledge →	the basic information one needs to be able to work within a discipline or to solve problems, knowledge of terminology
Conceptual Knowledge →	classifications, models, theories and important structural knowledge attached to any field of learning
Procedural Knowledge →	information that helps a student do something in an area of study. It may involve specific skills, formulae and *how* to do something
Metacognition →	awareness of what kind of thinking is needed to accomplish a task. It is strategic and reflective. (Note: it is a category in the Executive Function skills work. It is a long-term teacher goal for every 2e student with ADHD.)

This grid could be useful when developing and differentiating units of work:

TABLE 11.10 Wilson (2016). Anderson & Krathwohl revision of Bloom's taxonomy, cognitive processes

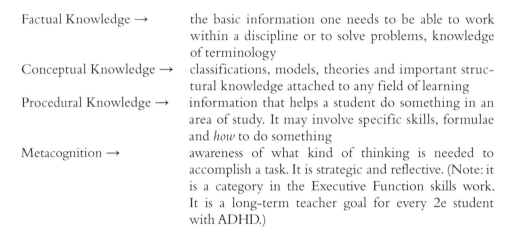

Cognitive Processes						
The Knowledge Dimensions	**1. Remember**	**2. Understand**	**3. Apply**	**4. Analyse**	**5. Evaluate**	**6. Create**
Factual						
Conceptual						
Procedural						
Metacognitive						

The question stems found in the following PDF are highly recommended: https://education.illinoisstate.edu/downloads/casei/5-02-Revised%20Blooms.pdf

An example of teaching procedural knowledge

Teaching long division to year 6

Remembering – *What do I do first? What do I do next?*

Understanding – *What would happen if I put the tens number here? How would you explain this error to warn a friend?*

Applying – Given a set of word problems in mathematics ...*Which problem requires a long division algorithm?*

Analysing – The wrong answer is found ... *What explanation do you have for this answer?*

Evaluating – Six people found this answer and it is wrong ... *What would you suggest they are doing wrong?*

Creating – *Compose a word problem that is challenging, involving the use of long division.*

Assessment

Assessment activity must allow the use of adjustments for all students that qualify:

- *Formative Assessment*

  Occurs during a learning cycle and informs both teacher and student of progress against the success criteria. Feedback – specific and informative, was found to have an ES of 0.70 and is one of the most valuable phases for learning which can be prompted by the questions (Hattie & Zierer, 2019, p. 88):

  Where are you going?
  How are you getting there?
  Where do you go next?

  Goals are set for the learning that will come next.

- *Summative Assessment*

  Informs the level of knowledge and skills acquired at the end of a unit or cycle and the next steps in learning. If a student's programme has been adjusted (for any reason) then his Assessment should be adjusted to reflect that change.

Step #6 Building a productive classroom culture

Building classroom culture and climate

- Build a (whole school) culture of acceptance and eventually celebration of difference. Start in your classroom.
- Teach students to accept and support individual differences, individualised programming and the use of curriculum adjustments.
- Utilise the visual-kinaesthetic wherever possible to assist *global, often non-sequential, learners.*
- *Creative use of* 'raps, rhymes, rhythms' (Winebrenner, 2003, p. 134).
- Establish *expectations* of effort, accountability & respect.
- Establish an orderly 'enabling' (vs 'restrictive') environment with routines and emphasis on the learning where students' learning needs are increasingly being met (Tomlinson & Imbeau, 2010, p. 75).
- *Big picture* first. Where does this part fit into our topic? How does this topic fit into scientific knowledge/the history of the western world/ the world of art/ the types of books written for children?

  Mind map concepts first, then details – connect all the parts of the topic schematically.

- Everyone sets *short-term goals* – utilise them.
- Can't or Won't? … consider this at every student obstacle to achievement.
- Limit homework in the K-6 years … so many reasons … Is it teaching anything? Can you be sure the student has learned enough in class to be able to do that homework? Is it creating stress in the home environment?
- Utilise *graphic organisers* – they are powerful.
- Pickett (2022) suggests the use of a *task slip* for students with auditory processing issues, working memory problems or anxiety. The subtle slip sits on the desk and after instructing the class the teacher or support teacher can fill in the first step of the instructions. The student completes it, ticks or crosses it off then asks for the next step (through verbal or agreed non-verbal cues).
- *Teacher's Toolkit* pp. 151–174 in Tomlinson & Imbeau (2010) (PDF) for building classroom community based on '*getting to know you*' activities.

Questioning – creating safety with intention and rigour

(See 'The power of good questioning' in Chapter 4)

- a highly effective method for eliciting thinking, targeted sensitively to individual students
- used cleverly it can be a vehicle for creating and building classroom climate: everyone is asked questions, but they must be targeted well ('safe' enough) to avoid anxiety in vulnerable students
- remember that whole-class questioning is 'public' and often spontaneous
- give appropriate questions to individual students either planned or impromptu
- the types of questions used during instruction influence the cognitive processes of students (Chin, 2007):
  - closed questions elicit information and simple responses
  - open-ended questions engage students in cognitively challenging conversations involving higher-order thinking and are especially appropriate to use with gifted and 2e students
- consider staggering the inclusion of 2e students into this setting, waiting until rapport is established and a student's strengths are well understood.

Building relationships

Positive relationships improve academic and affective development for students (Hattie, 2019) … Is this not true for the thriving of all humans in every stage of development?

Focus groups of gifted secondary students in a WA study by Capern & Hammond (2014) identified that the most important teacher behaviours that promote teacher-student relationships are promoting academic success through high levels of knowledge, understanding of student individual abilities and needs, feedback and encouragement, being approachable including allowing jokes, smiling and being courteous while treating all students equally and fairly. In the same study, students with emotional/behavioural disorders favoured teachers who had a warm and friendly disposition, were prepared to talk to and listen to students formally and casually, give feedback privately and support student learning by differentiating for their learning needs, for example, step by step instruction, patience when they don't understand, giving time for work to be completed because they care.

Giving feedback

There's a strong evidence base behind the impact of feedback. See the AITSL website www.aitsl.edu.au/teach/improve-practice/feedback#tab-panel-3 and the Spotlight article *Reframing feedback to improve teaching and learning*. Here, the Hattie and Timperley model of feedback (2007) is compared with the Black and Wiliam model of formative assessment (2009) with helpful guidance on the use of feedback.

Immediate feedback is considered to be ideal and especially for your 2e students but, of course, very difficult to achieve in real time.

I want to reiterate that subtle, non-verbal means of giving instant feedback are very effective with 2e and students with disability. A pre-arranged signal can be given to alert a student to an escalating problem behaviour or to note an error in written work that he is trying to avoid.

Bouwer & Dirkx (2023) used gaze data from eye-tracking, thinking aloud and text analyses to examine the depth at which secondary students responded to written feedback and found wide variations in how deeply and actively they engaged with it. They conclude that teachers should prioritise their feedback to higher-order elements of writing, such as structure and content to effectively assist students to improve their writing. They suggest that explicit instruction could be given on how other students and expert writers use feedback.

Goal setting

This is important in differentiated curriculum, the development of EF skills and in the growth of self-efficacy.

Much is written about SMART goals: Specific, Measurable, Attainable, Realistic and Time-based. It is worth taking the time to assist a student to make his goals fit the SMART criteria.

Students can start with one achievable, articulated goal in one subject; introduce goal setting slowly or at the 2e student's pace:

e.g. *I want 70% in my Maths test.*
I want to have mastered my 7 times tables by the end of term

Use of technologies

Teachers' skills greatly improved during remote-learning periods now enabling further differentiation in the classroom. Mahoney and Hall (2017) show how accommodations, differentiated instruction and individualised instruction can be provided using technology programmes: Plickers (for group formative assessment), Padlet, Storybird, Bookshare (for those with reading or visual impairment), Bubbl. us for mind maps, are just a few.

Web 2.0 technologies, in Bower (2012): *Pre-recorded video* may be used by a small group or as an adjustment for a student who likes to see multiple demonstrations of a Maths process or a science experiment. Video review of lessons: Hattie (2017) found an ES of 0.88. Kolber (2022) challenges teachers to explore the use of podcasts, videos and screencasts to challenge the currency of PowerPoints, worksheets, textbooks and novels as the media for learning. There is a place for every medium if it works for students in your class. Considering the literacy challenges of some 2e learners, I have noted their choices to search *YouTube* for source information before attempting to navigate a prose text. Overreliance on one source of information is limiting in skill development and potentially on the quality of information available to the student. *Text reading technology* is particularly helpful for older dyslexic students when reading large amounts of text for class or for editing where errors can be easily overlooked. Natural Reader is recommended: the voice is rather robotic, but in the upgrade at the premium level a better voice is used.

Teaching to improve weak executive function skills

(See Chapters 6 and 10)

- know where the barriers are for the 2e student
- include specific strategies into the ILP.

Case study: Michael

Michael, an intellectually and creatively gifted young man aged 14 years, diagnosed with dyslexia and ADHD was talking with his coach, Lindy.

> Lindy: *In which of your classes does the learning environment and curriculum come together for you and why do you think it is working?*
>
> Michael: *It is in my favourite subjects, Maths and Drama. It is all about the relationship with the teachers. Though their styles of teaching are completely different they both involve a high level of humour with casual but obvious intentions.*

TABLE 11.11   Michael's reflections on his class learning environment and curriculum

In Maths I love …	How this pedagogy works with his learning profile
The use of ACRONYMS, e.g. BIDMAS stands for Brackets, Indices, Division/Multiplication, Addition/Subtraction.	Working memory deficits with ADHD. An aid for recall.
When part-way through a topic Ms M puts 3 questions on the board that we attempt and then have to explain to the class or to her (Formative assessment)	Proven application of knowledge of the sequential steps in a maths solution. Demonstrates understanding before moving on in the topic indicating progress toward mastery of the topic.

Textbook work	Enjoys 'self-teaching' once confident that he has the Remembering, Understanding and Applying levels covered in each topic. He likes to challenge himself with problems that relate to the higher order levels of the Anderson & Krathwohl (2001) taxonomy and he does this intuitively.
In Drama I love ...	
The flexibility. It is so student-centred with improvisation, group (formative) *assessment & peer evaluation,*	Feeds his creative gifts in Drama and his need for self-expression
It is a balancing act of fun and targeted work, but she pulls it off.	An excellent trusting relationship between teacher and students, fully appreciated by him.

Part C

More on theories of curriculum differentiation

The work of Tomlinson and McTighe & Wiggins is complementary and deeply grounded in talent development. The two theories amalgamate well to meet the needs of the 2e student. Upon a teacher's comprehensive knowledge of each student's learning profile (Tomlinson's approach to CD) is applied the authentic pedagogy standards of higher-order thinking, deep-knowledge approaches and connections to the world beyond the classroom, (contained in the UbD framework).

Wiggins & McTighe (2011) developed Understanding by Design (UbD) as a curriculum design approach emphasising that big questions, the important principles of the world that lead to meaningful, transferable learning, should be used to organise curriculum standards so that learning endures. Vast arrays of content should not drive curriculum and this is particularly true for gifted students. Teachers can work out how to organise, store, retrieve and apply it to deep, important questions.

UbD claims to be research based but you will not find randomised controlled trials that have tested it because it is impossible to control and isolate for variables exclusively in the classroom setting. I would prefer to call it a *theoretical framework* firmly embedded in the cognitive psychology research into learning and cognition which emphasises:

- curricular planning
- developing deep student understanding and transfer of learning through the teaching of generalised principles rather than rote memory of knowledge
- teaching understanding which is demonstrated through:
  the capacity to explain, interpret, apply, shift perspective, empathise and self-assess
- curriculum which is planned 'backwards' from overarching, long-term desired results
- ensuring that learning actually happens, not just 'teaching'
- regular review and continual improvement in student achievement and teacher craft.

UbD instructs teachers to:

- identify desired results first
- determine assessment evidence
- plan learning experiences and instruction (see
  McTighe & Wiggins, ASCD website, Understanding by Design Framework).
- consider and self-assess the key elements and logic of a learning plan by using the

WHERETO acronym:

*W*here: ensuring that the student sees the big picture, has answers to the Why? questions, and knows the final performance demands as soon as possible.

*H*ook: getting the student interested immediately in the idea and issues of the unit, engaging the student in thought-provoking experiences/challenges/questions at the heart of the unit.

*E*quip & *E*xperience: providing the student with the tools, resources, skill, and information needed to achieve the desired understanding; experiencing the big ideas as real, important.

*R*ethink: taking the unit deeper by shifting perspective, considering different theories, challenging prior assumptions, introducing new evidence and ideas, etc. Also: providing the impetus for an opportunity to revise prior work, to polish it.

*E*valuate: ensuring that students get diagnostic and formative feedback, and opportunities to self-assess and self-adjust.

*T*ailor: Personalise the learning through differentiated assignments and assessments, as appropriate, without sacrificing rigour/validity.

*O*rganize: Sequence the work to suit the understanding goals (thus, often questioning the flow provided by the textbook, which is typically organized around discrete topics).

(Wiggins (2006) UbD in a Nutshell, p. 4)

In differentiated lessons, motivation for learning is built by the learning intentions and success criteria being very clear so that students (eventually!) take ownership of their learning and production of work.

Be wary of the claims of educational theories and schemes

1. Universal Design for Learning (UDL)

Universal Design for Learning (UDL) claims that it 'meets the needs of all with universal design for learning' www.novakeducation.com. Thibodeau (2021) explains the philosophy here: www.novakeducation.com/blog/the-science-and-research-behind-the-udl-framework.

It provides for diversity by supplying a wide range of tools, especially technology, from which students can choose to learn and present information. See https://f.hubspotusercontent00.net/hubfs/7288705/Resources/UDL-Special-Ed-Inforgraphic-Novak%20Education.png.

One resource, the *Teacher's Guide to UDL* https://info.novakeducation.com/udl-teachers-guide states, 'If UDL is to be effective, students will have to understand how to self-regulate, collaborate effectively and use scaffolds available to them', suggesting that lessons may need to be designed to teach collaboration, initially. The infographic *UDL & Special Education* suggests that 'UDL helps both general education and special education providers address barriers to learning' but I could not find any suggestions for how to help students who are not self-regulated, which would include the 10% of students who have attention deficit difficulties. Morin on readingrockets.org praises the role of UDL, saying it 'doesn't specifically target kids with learning and attention issues. But it can be especially helpful for the 1 in 5 kids with these issues – including those who have not been formally diagnosed. It can also be very helpful for English language learners'. How does UDL achieve this?

Many excellent principles, in common with CD, are proposed on the website of Novak who is a purveyor of UDL resources and professional development. However, Murphy (2021) found that the effectiveness of the theory has not been proven and that 'there are no grounds for UDL implementation plans to be framed as 'evidence-based' decisions (p. 7).' It would appear that the reference to neuroscience is theoretical. CAST, the non-profit organisation that created UDL, publishes its own materials.

The focus of UDL is clearly not on the individual needs of students but on the expected variability of all students. Meyer et al (2014) quoted in Murphy (2021) state 'we don't even need to know our particular students to plan for the range of variability in a given dimension' (p. 9). While it is true that prevalence rates give us predictability around the variable nature of students in schools, this statement runs counter to the research on neurodevelopmental disorders and the need to address individual differences through personalised knowledge and using direct, explicit instruction for basic skills. It is also at odds with Tomlinson's principles of curriculum differentiation founded in a deep knowledge of each student and her learning needs.

'The claim that students know best and can self-select to activities that best suit their learning style has been resoundingly rejected as a neuromyth' (Murphy, 2021, p. 9).

I hope I have proven the veracity of this statement throughout this book.

2. 'Learning Styles'

In the literature on UDL there is reference to students making learning choices according to learning style preferences. There is a big difference between an understanding of what barriers exist for students in their learning profiles and the numerous 'learning styles' theories that have been popular in schools. A student who has poor auditory processing skill which presents as a learning difficulty should be offered visual means such as a chart or prompt to assist her to understand instructions. This is very different from a stated learning preference for 'visual' means of learning. Boysen (2021) claims that UDL and learning styles theories have similar problems in their premises and theory with neither having strong research evidence that learning is increased and that both theories rely on 'overgeneralisations of neuroscience research (abstract)'. Whitman (2023) states that there is no empirical research that shows matching a student's learning style preference to a means of instruction has any benefit in learning outcomes largely because these preferences are self-reported and unreliable. It is a 'neuromyth' that continues despite no founding evidence. Pashler, McDaniel et al. (2009) concluded, in a very comprehensive, creditable analysis of the literature that:

The contrast between the enormous popularity of the learning-styles approach within education and the lack of credible evidence for its utility is, in our opinion, striking and disturbing. If classification of students' learning styles has practical utility, it remains to be demonstrated (p. 117).

It is rather concerning that this conclusion was reached in 2009 but the sale of Learning Styles Inventories and related commercial products has continued to this day.

3.   'Multiple intelligences'

Howard Gardner, psychologist, developed his Multiple Intelligences (MI) theory in 1983. In an interview by Strauss for the Washington Post in 2013 he was adamant that his theory had become conflated with the concept of learning styles, but it was never meant to be. Rather, MI theory was a considered alternative to the idea of *g*, the one single, central intelligence in all people that can be measured with an IQ test. Unfortunately, MI was oversimplified and teachers were being asked to accommodate the preferences of students with nine different 'intelligences', among them *spatial, linguistic, musical-rhythmic* in their lessons. In this interview he clarified that teaching should be individualised as much as possible and that by 'pluralising' lessons or teaching them through a variety of means; stories, diagrams, role play etc, that all students will come to understand concepts and ideas well.

   'Multi-sensory' modes of instruction, auditory, visual and kinesthetic, for all students particularly in the early stages of education, is recommended for promoting memory, wide understanding and enjoyment in learning.

Conclusion

This chapter has aimed to assist you to set priorities in your planning time for a differentiated curriculum. We have comprehensively worked through two student profiles, drawing from them a process for how to decipher and interpret 2e students' strengths and needs, bringing confidence in how to put together an effective ILP. By managing the learning environment of your classroom to accommodate the 2e student, benefits accrue for the whole class. Framed in this way, the time spent to adjust for disabilities flows over into advantages for the whole class in terms of classroom culture, acceptance and collaboration between students.

   When it comes to the claims of curriculum model makers you are encouraged to be discerning and critical in your reading, always checking how their approaches would support or fail to address your students' needs.

   If you are a School Principal or a Professional Learning Leader then you have input here on where to take your staff to increase their capacity, resourcing and collaborative skills to build manageable curriculum differentiation in every classroom.

   The resources and references following will help you further in your quest to meet the needs of your 2e students and the whole class.

'Go to' resources

ACER Teacher magazine.

Hattie (2019) Barometer of influence – Infographic https://visible-learning. org/2022/01/hatties-barometer-of-influence-infographic/

Joshua, A. (2006) *Enrichematics* (3rd edn) Books 1–6, Longman Cheshire Pty Ltd, Australia.
Revised Edition, 2006, first published 1991. This series is invaluable for the teaching of 2e students in mathematics.

Kolber, S. (2022) Teaching techniques – six ways to use Instructional video, ACER teacher magazine www.teachermagazine.com/au_en/articles/teaching-techniq ues-six-ways-to-use-instructional-video.

Kolber, S. (2020) Course 4: Different Forms of Instructional Video Use of instructional video capitalising on teacher skills learned during remote learning.
See this YouTube video explaining some uses of instructional video in the classroom:
www.teachermagazine.com/au_en/articles/teaching-techniques-six-ways-to-use-instructional-video
1. Screen capture ->recording of everything on your screen
Programs to use: Online Broadcast Software,
MS Power Point (drawing on the screen as you go)
Webcam (in-device)

2. Document camera or video overlooking your work
Boards: camera at eye-level, pre-prepare whiteboard content and speak to it using a lapel microphone.
Light boards

3. Classroom observation or video-on-demand

4. Green screen – technically demanding but might be a great whole-school innovation.

Pickett (2022) Video: Supporting students with additional needs – using task slips. See www.teachermagazine.com/au_en/articles/video-supporting-stude nts-with-additional-needs-using-task-slips

Colorado Dept. of Education, Office of Gifted Education
Level 1: An Introductory Resource Book. See www.cde.state.co.us/gt/level_1_resource _handbook_4th_edn_1-17-17
Level 2: Twice-Exceptional Students, Gifted Students with Disabilities, Level 2, 2nd edition, 2009. See www.cde.state.co.us/sites/default/files/documents/gt/downl oad/pdf/level2_edplanthroughproblemsolvingmodel.pdf

InclusionED
Setting up for success: Let's learn together PDF. Available at:
www.inclusioned.edu.au/media/1142

McCabe, J. (2022) YouTube channel episode: You Have So much Potential (ft. Twice Exceptional) www.youtube.com/watch?v=qa5v1a2H-xs

NCCD portal Classroom Adjustments: ADHD (podcast)
See www.nccd.edu.au/professional-learning/classroom-adjustments-adhd

NSW Department of Education website
Curriculum Differentiation – an effective summary of Tomlinson's work
See   https://education.nsw.gov.au/teaching-and-learning/professional-learning/ teacher-quality-and-accreditation/strong-start-great-teachers/refining-practice/ differentiating-learning

NSW Department of Education website
Creating units of work
See   https://education.nsw.gov.au/teaching-and-learning/learning-from-home/ teaching- at-home/teaching-and-learning-cycle/planning/creating-units-of-work
Differentiation Adjustment Tool
See   https://education.nsw.gov.au/teaching-and-learning/high-potential-and-gif ted-education/supporting-educators/implement/differentiation-adjustment-strateg ies#Adjustment:1
Curriculum planning for every student – introductory webinars
See   https://education.nsw.gov.au/teaching-and-learning/curriculum/planning- programming-and-assessing-k-12/curriculum-planning-for-every-student-intro ductory-webinars

The Renzulli Center for creativity, gifted education and talent development. This offers professional learning online on a variety of topics for gifted/high potential learners and 2e students.

Free online courses from the University of Connecticut. See https://gifted.uconn. edu/events-2021-22/
Renzulli Learning
This is a commercial website offering tools about how to personalise learning for students. There is a free trial opportunity on the website. See https://renzullilearn ing.com.

Tomlinson, C (2017) *How to Differentiate Instruction in the Academically Diverse Classroom*, ASCD, Alexandria, Virginia. See https://files.ascd.org/staticfiles/ascd/ pdf/siteASCD/publications/books/HowtoDifferentiateInstructioninAcademical lyDiverseClassrooms-3rdEd.pdf

Tomlinson & Imbeau (2010) *Leading and Managing a Differentiated Classroom* (2nd edn), ASCD, Alexandria, Virginia. See https://files.ascd.org/pdfs/publications/books/Leading-and-Managing-A-Differe ntiated-Classroom-2ed-sample-pages.pdf
This book gives practical advice, activities and strategies on how to build community in the classroom, how to create a conducive classroom environment for differentiation including routines for managing different work programmes and how to use non-verbal cues. A useful toolkit is included.

Wiggins (2006) *UbD in a Nutshell.*
See https://jedc.org/stemak/sites/default/files/ubdnutshell.pdf.

Zaccaro, E. (2006) *Becoming a Problem-Solving Genius: A Handbook of Maths Strategies,* Hawker Brownlow Education, Australia.

References

American Psychiatric Association. (2022). *Diagnostic and Statistical Manual of Mental Disorders* (5th edn, Text Revision). Washington, DC: American Psychiatric Association.

Amran, H. A., & Majid, R. A. (2019). Learning strategies for twice-exceptional students. *International Journal of Special Education, 33*(4), 954–976.

Anderson, L. W., & Krathwohl, D. R. (2001). *A Taxonomy for Learning, Teaching, and Assessing: A Revision of Bloom's Taxonomy of Educational Objectives.* New York: Longman.

Assouline, S., Foley Nicpon, M. & Colangelo, N., & O'Brien, M. (2008). The Paradox of Twice-Exceptionality: Packet of Information for Professionals (2nd edn) (PIP-2). Retrieved from The University of Iowa, College of Education, Belin-Blank Center for Gifted Education and Talent Development. https://belinblank.education.uiowa.edu/research/docs/pip2.pdf

Bloom, B. S., & Krathwohl, D. R. (1956) *Taxonomy of Educational Objectives: The Classification of Educational Goals.* Handbook I: Cognitive Domain. New York, NY: Longmans, Green (may be of historical interest)

Bouwer, R.,& Dirkx, K. (2023) The eye-mind of processing written feedback: Unravelling how students read and use feedback for revision. *Learning and Instruction, 85*(1), 101745. https://doi.org/10.1016/j.learninstruc.2023.101745

Bower, M. (2012). An ability approach to within-class curriculum differentiation using student response systems and web 2.0 technologies: Analysing teachers' responsiveness. *Themes in Science and Technology Education, 5*(2), 5–26.

Boysen, G. A. (2021). Lessons (not) learned: The troubling similarities between learning styles and universal design for learning. *Scholarship of Teaching and Learning in Psychology.* Advance online publication. https://doi.org/10.1037/stl0000280

Brulles, D., & Winebrenner, S. (2019) *The Cluster Grouping Handbook: A Schoolwide Model: How to Challenge Gifted Students and Improve Achievement for All.* Minneapolis, MN: Free Spirit Publishing Inc., Revised edition.

Çakır, H., & Cengiz, Ö. (2016) The use of open ended versus closed ended questions in Turkish classrooms. *Open Journal of Modern Linguistics, 6,* 60–70. doi: 10.4236/ojml.2016.62006

Capern, T., & Hammond, L. (2014). Establishing positive relationships with secondary gifted students and students with emotional/behavioural disorders: Giving these diverse learners what they need. *Australian Journal of Teacher Education, 39*(4). http://dx.doi.org/10.14221/ajte.2014v39n4.5

Caram, C. A., & Davis, P. B. (2005). Inviting student engagement with questioning. *Kappa Delta Pi Record, 42*(1), 18–23. http://dx.doi.org/10.1080/00228958.2005.10532080

Chin, C. (2007). Teacher questioning in science classrooms: Approaches that stimulate productive thinking. *Journal of Research in Science Teaching, 44,* 815–843. http://dx.doi.org/10.1002/tea.20171

Coleman, M. R. (2003). Exploring secondary options: Four variables for success. *Gifted Child Today, 26*(1), 22–24. https://doi.org/10.4219/gct-2003-87

Coleman, M. R., & Gallagher, S. (2015). Meeting the needs of students with 2e: It takes a team. *Gifted Child Today Magazine, 38*(4), 252–254. https://doi.org/10.1177/1076217515597274

Coleman, M. R., & Johnsen, S. K. (2021). *RtI for Gifted Students: A CEC-TAG Educational Resource* (1st edn). Abingdon: Routledge. https://doi.org/10.4324/9781003237785

Dawson, P., & Guare, R. (2012). *Coaching Students with Executive Function Deficits*. New York: Guilford Press. (Appendix 4, 176–177.)

Dweck, C. S. (2006). *Mindset: The New Psychology of Success*. London: Random House.

Eysink,T. H., Hulsbeek, M., & Gijlers, H. (2017). Supporting primary school teachers in differentiating in the regular classroom. *Teaching and Teacher Education, 66*, 107–116. https://doi.org/10.1016/j.tate.2017.04.002

Foley Nicpon, M., Allmon, A., Sieck, B., & Stinson, R. D. (2011). Empirical investigation of twice-exceptionality: Where have we been and where are we going? *Gifted Child Quarterly, 55*(1), 3–17. https://doi.org/10.1177/0016986210382575

Gibbs, K., & Beamish, W. (2021). Conversations with Australian teachers and school leaders about using differentiated instruction in a mainstream secondary school. *Australian Journal of Teacher Education, 46*(7). http://dx.doi.org/10.14221/ajte.2021v46n7.6

Gilman, B. J., Lovecky, D. V., Kearney, K., Peters, D. B., Wasserman, J. D., Silverman, L. K., … Rimm, S. B. (2013). Critical issues in the identification of gifted students with co-existing disabilities: The twice-exceptional. *SAGE Open, 3*(3), 215824401350585–. https://doi.org/10.1177/2158244013505855

Gierczyk, M., & Hornby, G. (2021). Twice-exceptional students: Review of implications for special and inclusive education. *Education Sciences, 11*(2), 1–10. https://doi.org/10.3390/educsci11020085

Hattie, J., & Zierer, K. (2017). *10 Mindframes for Visible Learning: Teaching for Success*. London & New York: Routledge.

Hattie, J., & Zierer, K. (2019). *Visible Learning Insights* (1st edn). London: Routledge. https://doi.org/10.4324/9781351002226

Ireland, C., Bowles, T., Brindle, K., & Nikakis, S. (2020). Curriculum differentiation's capacity to extend gifted students in secondary mixed-ability science classes. *Talent, 10*(1), 40–61. https://doi.org/10.46893/talent.758527

Jackson, J., & Endekov, Z. (2019). *Achieving Our Educational Goals: A Declaration for System Transformation*. Report to the Mitchell Institute, Victoria University. www.vu.edu.au/sites/default/files/achieving-educational-goals-a-declaration-for-system-transformation-mitchell-institute.pdf

Jeweler, S., Barnes-Robinson, L., Shevitz, B. R., & Weinfeld, R. (2008). Bordering on excellence: A teaching tool for twice-exceptional students. *Gifted Child Today, 31*(2), 40–46. https://files.eric.ed.gov/fulltext/EJ789920.pdf

Johnsen, S. K., Fearon-Drake, D., & Wisely, L. W. (2020). A formative evaluation of differentiation practices in elementary cluster classrooms. *Roeper Review, 42*(3), 206–218. https://doi.org/10.1080/02783193.2020.1765921

Kanevsky, L. (2011). Deferential differentiation: What types of differentiation do students want? *Gifted Child Quarterly, 55*(4), 279–299. https://doi.org/10.1177/0016986211422098

King-Sears, M. E. (2008). Facts and fallacies: Differentiation and the general education curriculum for students with special educational needs. *Support for Learning, 23*(2), 55–62. https://doi.org/10.1111/j.1467-9604.2008.00371.x

Kolber, S. (2022) Teaching techniques—Six ways to use Instructional Video. *ACER Teacher Magazine*. www.teachermagazine.com/au_en/articles/teaching-techniques-six-ways-to-use-instructional-video

Levykh, M. G. (2008). The affective establishment and maintenance of Vygotsky's zone of proximal development. *Educational Theory, 58*(1), 83–101. http://dx.doi.org/10.1111/j.1741-5446.2007.00277.x

Lindner, K. T., Alnahdi, G. H., Wahl, S., & Schwab, S. (2019). Perceived differentiation and personalization teaching approaches in inclusive classrooms: Perspectives of students and teachers. *Frontiers in Education 4*(58). https://doi.org/10.3389/feduc.2019.00058

Logan, B. (2011). Examining differentiated instruction: Teachers respond. *Research In Higher Education Journal, 13*. www.aabri.com/manuscripts/11888.pdf

Lopez, S. J., & Louis, M. C. (2009). The principles of strengths-based education. *Journal of College and Character*, *10*(4). https://doi.org/10.2202/1940-1639.1041

Mahoney, J., & Hall, C. (2017). Using technology to differentiate and accommodate students with disabilities. *E-Learning and Digital Media*, *14*(5), 291–303. https://doi.org/10.1177/2042753017751517

Margari, L., Buttiglione, M., Craig, F., Cristella, A., de Giambattista, C., Matera, E., Operto, F., & Simone, M. (2013). Neuropsychopathological comorbidities in learning disorders. *BMC Neurology*, (*13*)198. https://doi.org/10.1186/1471-2377-13-198

Masi, L., & Gignac, M. (2015). ADHD and comorbid disorders in childhood psychiatric problems, medical problems, learning disorders and developmental coordination. *Clinical Psychiatry*, *1*(1), 1–9. www.primescholars.com/articles/adhd-and-comorbid-disorders-inc hildhoodpsychiatric-problems-medicalproblems-learning-disordersand-developmental-coordina-104677.html. Retrieved 5 November 2023.

McTighe, J., & Wiggins, G. *Understanding by Design Framework*. Alexandria, VA: ASCD. https://files.ascd.org/staticfiles/ascd/pdf/siteASCD/publications/UbD_WhitePaper0312.pdf Retrieved 26 July 2023

Mofield, E. L. (2020). Benefits and barriers to collaboration and co-teaching: Examining perspectives of gifted education teachers and general education teachers. *Gifted Child Today*, *43*(1), 20–33. https://doi.org/10.1177/1076217519880588

Moody, C. J. (2014). *Expert-Recommended Strategies for Teaching the Twice-Exceptional Student in the General Education Classroom* (Doctoral dissertation, University of La Verne).

Morin, A. www.readingrockets.org/topics/assistive-technology/articles/universal-design-learn ing-udl-what-you-need-know#learning-and-attention-issues-and-udl Retrieved 26 July 2023.

Pashler, H., McDaniel, M., Rohrer, D., & Bjork, R. (2008). Learning styles: Concepts and evidence. *Psychological Science in the Public Interest*, *9*(3), 105–119. https://doi.org/10.1111/j.1539-6053.2009.01038.x

Reis, S. M., & Renzulli, S. J. (2021). Parenting for strengths: Embracing the challenges of raising children identified as twice exceptional. *Gifted Education International*, *37*(1), 41–53. https://doi.org/10.1177/0261429420934435

Reis, S. M., Renzulli, S. J., & Renzulli, J. S. (2021). Enrichment and gifted education pedagogy to develop talents, gifts, and creative productivity. *Education Sciences*, 11(10), 615. https://doi.org/10.3390/educsci11100615

Roth, D. (2007). Understanding by design: A framework for effecting curricular development and assessment. *CBE—Life Sciences Education*, *6*(2), 95–97. https://doi.org/10.1187/cbe.07-03-0012

Strauss, V. (2013). Howard Gardner: 'Multiple intelligences' are not 'learning styles.' Retrieved from www.washingtonpost.com/blogs/answer-sheet/wp/2013/10/16/howard-gardner-multiple-intelligences-are-not-learning-styles/

Thibodeau, T. (2021, June 6). *The Science and Research Behind the UDL Framework*. www.nov akeducation.com/blog/the-science-and-research-behind-the-udl-framework

Tomlinson, C. A. (2000). Differentiation of instruction in the elementary grades. ERIC Digest. https://files.eric.ed.gov/fulltext/ED443572.pdf

Tomlinson, C. A. (2017) *How to Differentiate Instruction in the Academically Diverse Classroom*. Alexandria, VA: ASCD.

Tomlinson, C. A., & Strickland, C. A. (2005). *Differentiation in Practice: A Resource Guide for Differentiating Curriculum, Grades 9-12*. Alexandria, VA: ASCD.

Tomlinson, C. A., Moon, T. R., & Imbeau, M. B. (2013). *Assessment and Student Success in a Differentiated Classroom*. Alexandria, VA: ASCD. https://files.ascd.org/staticfiles/ascd/pdf/siteASCD/publications/assessment-and-di-whitepaper.pdf

Troxclair, D. (2000). Differentiating instruction for gifted students in regular education social studies classes. *Roeper Review*, *22*(3), 195–198. https://doi.org/10.1080/02783190009554033

VanTassel-Baska, J. (Ed.). (2021). *Talent Development in Gifted Education: Theory, Research, and Practice* (1st ed.). Routledge. https://doi.org/10.4324/9781003024156

Westwood, P. (2018). *Inclusive and Adaptive Teaching: Meeting the Challenge of Diversity in the Classroom* (2nd ed.). Routledge. https://doi.org/10.4324/9781351061261

Whitman, G. M. (2023). Learning styles: Lack of research-based evidence. *The Clearing House: A Journal of Educational Strategies, Issues and Ideas, 96*(4), 111–115, http://dx.doi.org/10.1080/00098655.2023.2203891

Wiggins, G., & McTighe, J. (2011). *The Understanding by Design Guide to Creating High-Quality Units.* Alexandria, VA: ASCD.

Winebrenner, S. (2003). Teaching Strategies for Twice-Exceptional Students. *Intervention in School and Clinic*, 38, 131–137. https://doi.org/10.1177/10534512030380030101

Wilkinson, S. D., & Penney, D. (2014). The effects of setting on classroom teaching and student learning in mainstream mathematics, English and science lessons: A critical review of the literature in England. *Educational Review, 66*(4), 411–427. https://doi.org/10.1080/00131911.2013.787971

Willard-Holt, C., Weber, J., Morrison, K. L., & Horgan, J. (2013). Twice-exceptional learners' perspectives on effective learning strategies. *Gifted Child Quarterly, 57*(4), 247–262. https://doi.org/10.1177/0016986213501076

Wilson, L. O. (2016). Anderson and Krathwohl Bloom's Taxonomy Revised Understanding the New Version of Bloom's Taxonomy https://quincycollege.edu/wp-content/uploads/Anderson-and-Krathwohl_Revised-Blooms-Taxonomy.pdf

Wu, E. H. (2013). The path leading to differentiation: An interview with Carol Tomlinson. *Journal of Advanced Academics, 24*(2), 125–133. https://doi-org.rp.nla.gov.au/10.1177/1932202X13483472 PDF is downloadable from ResearchGate.

Yeager, D. S., & Dweck, C. S. (2020). What can be learned from growth mindset controversies?. *American Psychologist, 75*(9), 1269–1284 https://doi.org/10.1037%2Famp0000794 PDF is downloadable from the National Library of Medicine website www.ncbi.nlm.nih.gov/pmc/articles/PMC8299535/pdf/nihms-1643736.pdf

Longitudinal case studies

Following up on

Sophie

... from Chapter 11

In the Higher School Certificate (school leaving exam) Sophie gained three Band 6 levels – the highest attainable – in Biology, Design and Technology and Business Studies and two Band 5 levels in Maths Advanced and English Advanced. Sophie was nominated for SPACE, a prestigious exhibition of top achieving HSC works for her Design and Technology major work as well as making the Distinguished Achievers List for that subject. When combined with school assessments it translated to an ATAR 90. The university commuted it to an ATAR 95 which meant she gained entry into her course of first preference, Bachelor of Design in Architecture.

Recently she enquired of her mother: 'How come I am finding it easy, Mum?'

Even though she was already in Year 6 when her co-morbid diagnosis of ADHD (PIP) was made, it is relatively early to gain intervention prior to secondary school. Sophie is bright and articulate and she learned the metacognitive language required to explain her SLD and attention problem to her teachers with polite directions for the adjustments that worked for her. Teachers were able to accommodate her needs while maintaining high expectations for her performance.

Her IQ was never re-assessed but I am certain that the lower-than-expected Full Scale score of 120 was calculated because of the 'masking effect' of her learning disabilities. The General Ability Index (GAI) was not calculated by the psychologist. Without doubt, Sophie is an intellectually and creatively gifted person who could not show what she knew in her early assessments.

Interview with Sophie

Sophie reflected on her learning history:

If you could tell your teachers about the best ways to teach the young Sophie, what would you say?

DOI: 10.4324/9781003404972-15

*I needed **individual smaller due dates** instead of one large due date with **smaller goals** to work towards, so I didn't fall behind and therefore **didn't feel overwhelmed by the large task** ahead. I therefore wouldn't need to concentrate for a long period of time on the same project as it was broken down into mini projects. Even if I wrote out the smaller goals myself, I **needed someone to keep me accountable** and make sure I stuck to them otherwise I would tell myself I could do it later with no consequences. I also would say having **previous examples of work (visual aspects were always very helpful)** would help as otherwise I wouldn't know where to start and I would become overwhelmed and doubt whether what I was doing was right.*

You are enjoying success now. What happened to turn around your school achievement earlier in your time at school?

*I think overall there was a lot of support along the way. I think in primary school being in reading support until Year 4 was important. At high school, having the support from the Learning Support department, being diagnosed with ADHD, private tutoring and other health professional support. Also **knowing through that support, I had the ability but just needed to find my way to access it and then learn how to execute tasks.***

Was there any particular person or program that taught you what you needed to know?

*I wouldn't say there was only one person or thing. My mum was amazing. By experimenting with ways I thought would help me I found things that work for me such **as listing out everything I needed to do** and then only focusing on the one chosen thing. I figured out that **small goals over the many weeks before an assessment was due** was very helpful through my Design and Technology class as that was how our classes functioned, especially in Year 12. In each class there was feedback on what we had worked on, which is how I started to realise what helped me be more productive and not to fall behind. I think figuring out little things like that from classes helped me start to figure out what helped.*

What challenges do you continue to face in your university course and in life?

I have always struggled with procrastination. I start doing something then I start doing something else and then jump around between 20 things I had to do before becoming overwhelmed and stopping altogether. This is true in all aspects of life but especially for Uni. If I miss a checkpoint I begin to fall behind and I struggle to get back ahead and that's when it becomes overwhelming.

What goals do you have for your working life?

*I don't think I could sit behind a desk and work, so a goal is to either be **working out-side** or in a job where I move a lot and not in an office job. I prefer to be more **creative and moving** as it keeps my brain working and excited instead of sitting down in front of a computer, working on something that wouldn't excite me and I would tend to lose* *concentration especially if it isn't a creative project. Preferably I would like to work **close to architecture** which is what I am studying as that checks my boxes in terms of being creative and not being in a stagnant workspace.*

Do you have other goals that you would be happy to share?

*I would **love to work for myself one day** to be in control of what I do as I find it harder to interpret or understand someone else's ideas and what their goals are especially if they differ from mine which can interfere with my productivity.*

What are the key factors that have allowed you to come through some tough challenges to arrive where you are?

*I find having **at least one friend in your class that you can match work with** has helped me when I have not been motivated to do any work. This gives me a goal to get to if I am struggling to give myself goals or there are none set by teachers.*

The goal of this book is for teachers and parents to understand 'the twice-exceptional student'. Do you have insights or suggestions that you would like to share with this potential audience?

***Be patient.** I struggled to do at-home tasks such as cleaning my room or doing other chores. Obviously, it's not an excuse to not do them but please don't get mad or annoyed and take it out on them if you don't understand why they can't perform a simple task. It can be quite difficult. **Give gentle encouragement** or **offer help** or allow the task to be done later, in their own time. In the classroom, **setting out smaller goals for them to achieve, holding them accountable and providing positive reinforcement** makes big assessments or tasks seem so much less overwhelming and provides achievable goals and keeps them up to date and not falling behind. However, don't single them out: either do it subtly for the kid (e.g., you could email them individually) or do it for the whole class and make sure that they are keeping up to date.*

Following up on Liam with contributions from his mother, Beverley ... from Chapter 6

Liam has begun several courses at university but each time he found that he could not sustain interest in the course because sitting in lecture halls or on zoom, listening without doing, is unbearable for him.

Through his interest in martial arts where he teaches young children, he was offered a job with a local Occupational Therapist. She has become a great friend who believes in him and he loves working with the science of the field and the children who come to the practice. 'They are just like me!' Liam is a very popular teacher and assistant therapist.

Interview with Liam

At around what age or stage of school did you realise that your brain operated differently from the children around you?

*Very early on in K/Yr1 I remember walking around thinking 'I have to squint my eyes so they think I am smart'. Round Year 1 I was worried about kids' perceptions of me. It felt like I was **picking up cues more quickly than others**.*

How did you think and learn differently from most other children in your cohort?

I have no idea! I cannot learn by being told something. I have to do it: actively participating. If it is not interesting, I will never remember it but I love Dungeons and Dragons. I have been running a game for 4 years after spending months just reading all about it. I need to be knowledgeable about it, friendly, not overly competitive.

I am a 'researchaholic' about space engineering and the way the universe works but I can't manage the expectations of university. I don't want to only read and write about it; I want to do it. I have trouble formulating my ideas into an essay. I may keep it as a hobby. I don't commit to too many things.

If you could tell your teachers about the best ways to teach the young Liam, what would you say?

*Some teachers did not get me at all. I had a Maths teacher in Year 12 when my (ADHD) medication was being adjusted but I had holes in my knowledge. Yet, I got 90% without working. This one teacher was a mentor. He **understood that I needed to do things at my own pace.** I went ahead till I became bored so then he could help the other students.*

I had 3–4 teachers who intuitively understood. They let me be interested in science materials and have fun. I have spent my whole life trying to work out ADHD. If I am not enjoying something I won't be able to do it. I had fun in those classes and it worked. I have more control now and I do much better, but not then.

I was the worst kid in primary school! I was sent to other classes because I was so bad but sometimes that teacher engaged with me and had fun. I often found more understanding there.

Inflexible, strict teachers evoked responses in me that were sometimes bizarre.

Please tell me about your school experience, that is, about the 'highs' and the 'lows'.

I would get into so much trouble for being angry and sometimes erratic. But I loved it when a teacher gave me great fun with Maths or Science, like Fibonacci numbers.

What goals do you have for your working life?

Teaching martial arts is amazing but I am never fully aware of myself at the time.

I am an OT assistant & loving it. I want to go into OT. Perhaps I will study to gain my full qualifications in this field. I work part-time because I find it hard to work full-time.

Do you have other goals that you would be happy to share?

> *No. It's very 'ADHD' to 'go with the wind'. Be happy and have everyone else around me happy. That's it.*

What are the key factors that have allowed you to come through some tough challenges to arrive where you are?

> *Parents were helpful. The best people that brought me through hard times have been those good teachers who 'got' me. They **helped me to keep it together** and never go too far off the edge **until I worked out how to manage my chaos**. I see others getting into drugs and alcohol. I promised myself not to swear as a small child and I kept strictly to that promise.*

Reflections from Liam's mother, Beverley

Liam's mother, Beverley, a nurse educator, was a passionate advocate for her son. She confided that writing about the struggles was a very emotional experience that re-kindled some anger about how her son was misunderstood at school. If some teachers could manage to understand him, why couldn't they all? She has put her reflections of managing Liam's time in school very candidly, to offer help to teachers.

It would have made such a difference if Liam's giftedness and learning disability had been diagnosed early!

In his early years at school, teachers had a 'love 'or 'hate' relationship with Liam based on whether they understood his creativity or not e.g. all his creative teachers loved him.

In kindergarten, I was invited to a meeting with his teacher to talk about Liam's behaviour. The teacher showed me one of his drawings of a lake, with a city in the background with smoke stacks, birds falling out of the sky, all in dark colours and then scribbles all over the page. The teacher said, 'he has scribbled all over his drawing'. I went limp (as I write, it brings me to tears) with the realisation of how misunderstood Liam was from the beginning at school. I responded to the teacher that the scribbles were pollution. The drawing was a direct replica of a picture in a book we had at home.

Towards the end of Term 1, kindergarten, I was called to a meeting to discuss Liam's behaviour. At the meeting was the K-2 principal, school counsellor, kindergarten teacher, my husband and I. They were considering expelling him from school because he had gone into the kindergarten teacher's resource room and urinated on the bookshelves. When I asked Liam what had happened, he said he had followed another child into the classroom, he saw the teacher's desk and it made him so angry thinking about the teacher that he urinated on the bookshelves. This was the beginning of Liam demonstrating frustration and anger in unexpected, surprising ways.

There were so many key issues that the **schools just did not understand**. ADHD is considered a behaviour problem rather than a neurodevelopmental condition. It sends messages to other children in the class that a child with ADHD is 'naughty' rather than having a learning difficulty which leads to social isolation as children withdraw from playing with the ADHD child and other children's parents do not encourage their child to play with the ADHD child. The negative messaging that the child gets impacts his self-esteem.

The day I medicated Liam he stopped doing his drawings, saying that he couldn't see his pictures anymore. I felt torn between stifling his creativity and medicating him to be able to sit and be calm in class so that he could be managed by the teacher, not get into trouble, not have the social implications of being different and the negative messaging to his self-esteem that he is 'bad' and different which have impacted his long-term mental health. This torn feeling is highlighted by the fact that, when medicated, Liam looked unanimated and less interested in the world. He was definitely not his former alert self. Medication can also impact a child's appetite which requires careful management, so the child's growth is not impeded. As he grew older and could manage his own medication, he chose to medicate himself so he could maintain focus in the 'boring lectures' (as he describes them) and to write his assignments.

The provision of adjustments such as scribes and computers would have assisted Liam as he has a ligament laxity that prohibited him from writing for long periods, his brain would run ahead of his ability to write and he'd lose his thought pattern. He would write without leaving any spaces because he didn't want to lose his thoughts!

Liam was struggling at school with writing. In Year 7, he had only attained a Year 3 level in writing and he continues to avoid writing. We tutored him in English for the HSC. After the first lesson he came out, threw his hands in the air ('Hallelujah' moment) and he said, 'That is what I need!' He was able to go at a faster pace because he had the understanding and insight while the 1:1 tutor could support his writing structure.

Whenever Liam was encouraged to show his creativity he thrived and wherever a teacher kept a calm, safe environment Liam could feel secure, able to self-regulate and be settled enough to learn.

The schools could have helped our family to take the pressure off home life and parenting

The main difficulty we experienced was trying to determine what learning disability Liam had and discovering that he was gifted. If this was better identified early in the school environment it may have avoided time consuming, costly assessments and stress involved as we tried to navigate the education and health systems to determine what Liam needed.

It is too late to wait until Year 5 opportunity class, to nurture gifted children's talents. They have often disengaged by then and they don't want to move schools and leave their friends. Sporting scouts look for sporting talented children as soon as they enter sporting teams and offer them development camps. Why do we not do this with academically talented kids?

It is expensive, time consuming and difficult to navigate the health and education systems. If allied health professionals such as occupational therapists, psychologists and speech pathologists were on site working alongside the teachers and learning support teams it would be so much easier for parents.

Reflections from Eleni

Eleni is a high-achieving student who is currently at university studying Motion Graphics specifically working on movie and TV titles. She has creative talent in Art. She first noticed that she worked slower than other students in Year 2 or 3. As she grew older, probably around Year 6, she started to realise that it took her a vast amount of effort and time to complete the same tasks as everyone else. This was extremely frustrating. Eleni was eventually diagnosed with SLD dyslexia in Reading accuracy, rate and fluency and with impairment in Mathematics in accurate or fluent calculation. She experiences the challenges that arise from processing information at a slower speed than her intellectual peers.

Eleni is a socially responsible and brave young person who has spoken along with me at public presentations on dyslexia bringing valuable lived experience to the audience.

Eleni, you are enjoying success now. What happened to turn around your school achievement?

> *I am enjoying success now* (she says, laughing). *But it looks very different to what is generally defined as success because I'm at university working very hard. For me, around Year 10 was when my school achievements started to go up. Being able to pick the subjects I wanted to do really helped me. I was dedicated to my studies and spent practically every day studying because that was what I needed to do in order to achieve the same results as everyone else. I started being 'obsessive' with my studies from Year 10 and I motivated myself by knowing that once I finished school I could then live my life however I wanted to. I showed my teachers that I was dedicated and explained my learning disabilities to them. Throughout my schooling there were a few special teachers, like my Art teacher, who really helped me and saw how much effort I put in regardless of my grades. Because they saw potential in me it enabled me to power through the challenges I had to face and prove that I could achieve. I also had a few external tutors and mentors who definitely helped me show my ability. In Years 11 and 12 I did three creative major works, plus English and Maths. Being able to specialise in creative subjects in my final years helped immensely. I don't fundamentally believe that getting good grades is as important as the amount of pressure put on them. I was lucky that my parents were always focused on me doing my best. This mentally really helped me throughout my final schooling years. I think the main thing that turned my school achievements around was accepting that I would have to put more time and effort into my work compared to other students.*

What are the key factors that have allowed you to come through some tough challenges to arrive where you are?

The key factors are having a supportive and understanding family, having a really strong work ethic, being resilient and always remembering why I was working towards whatever it was I wanted to achieve.

If you could tell your teachers about the best ways to teach the young Eleni, what would you say?

I would say that teachers should have a lot of patience and time for children with learning disabilities as it can take a few different ways of explaining something before they under-stand. Not all teachers have the time or effort required for this but there is nothing worse, as a young child, than seeing the frustration in your teacher because you don't understand. Think of it as though you are trying to decode what someone is asking you to do but it's in your second language and you have to try to explain to them in that language what you don't understand. I would say that for me the best thing a teacher could do is be extremely clear in what they want from a task in clear dot points so that I can understand what I need to do. Also, providing the student with a lesson plan can help them prepare themselves mentally for what will be covered. I think that teachers shouldn't just rely on exams and text as the basis for assessing understanding. Having a conversation with the teacher is a much more engaging way to assess if the student understands something. The downside to exams and quizzes is that it is purely just assessing memory which can be detrimental to students who have learning disabilities as they often have memory issues as well.

The goal of this book is for teachers and parents to understand 'the twice–exceptional student'. Do you have insights or suggestions that you would like to share with this potential audience?

I think the most helpful advice I could give is to spend the time it requires with these students to enable them to believe in themselves, if nothing else. Try to adjust the curric-ulum and talk to the students with respect when trying to understand what will work best for them to succeed.

There is a clear and resounding message:

Reflections from Darcy

I will let Darcy, a profoundly gifted student with ADHD, currently in Year 9, be the last student voice to you:

Connect the topics to each other and to the whole of life while keeping the integrity of the discipline. Teachers who demonstrate their own level of enquiry and allude to the big picture, inspire me.

   Don't feel that students are not thinking if they don't give you what you expect. Don't get angry with them for not fulfilling your expectations as other children might. Look for ways to intrigue and challenge them.

   Extend students but if they are not getting work in, don't give up on them.

Motivation comes in the areas of interest. I just can't make myself think about something when there is no interest for me!

Sometimes tweak projects so they meet your criteria but so they suit particular students' ways of thinking and their interests.

Allow us to tell you what we need. It took to Year 6 before I could speak up & give feedback to my teachers. Assume the student is being authentic and sincere even if she can't meet submission deadlines and don't stop giving appropriate opportunities!

To the teachers …

To you, the undertrained, under-resourced, extraordinary people that you are … Thank you for your courage, your pro-activity to fill in the gaps in your professional knowledge for the 2e student and your care of them when they are so often misunderstood and overlooked. You can have no foreknowledge of where each student will take his efficacy. Teaching to enhance the outcomes of a young person's life toward self-fulfillment and meaningful societal contribution is most often a high yielding investment and, indeed, a privilege.

Our profession is potentially the most noble of all.

Glossary

Acceleration   Progression through school grades at a faster pace than usual. It can encompass grade skipping or one of many options in the process.

Adjustments   Changes made to a student's program and determined based on the functional impact of a disability on the student's learning, rather than a particular diagnosis of disability.

Affective   Connected to the emotions.

Anxiety disorder   Excessive worry that begins to affect a person's life and prevents engagement with normal activity. It can be in the form of a generalised anxiety disorder, social anxiety, panic disorder, agoraphobia or specific phobias.

Asynchronous development   Where a gifted student's intellectual abilities develop before the emotional, physical or social aspects and the student can be frustrated by not being able to communicate or demonstrate her advanced ideas.

Attention Deficit Hyperactivity Disorder (ADHD)   A neurodevelopmental condition of attention that indicates differences in brain development and potentially inhibits not only the learning but also the life outcomes of a child.

Autism Spectrum Disorder (ASD)   A condition that affects how a person thinks, feels, interacts with others, and experiences their environment. It is a lifelong disability that starts when a person is born and stays with them into old age. Every autistic person is different to every other. This is why autism is described as a 'spectrum'. (See https://www.autismspectrum.org.au/about-autism/what-is-autism).

Automatisation   The action or process of making behaviour, language, etc., automatic, habitual, or producible without conscious thought.

Behavioural disorder   Disruptive behaviours that are uncommon for the child's age at the time and persist over time or are severe.

Cognitive   Connected with thinking or conscious mental processes.

Cognitive load (theory)   When the brain is working with new information from the environment, the working memory is limited in both capacity and duration. We can process about 3–4 items and hold new items in working memory for only about 20 seconds. The application of this theory is particularly relevant to students with learning difficulties and attention problems where working memory may be reduced.

Co-morbidity   More than one co-existing condition impacting at once.

Conduct disorder   A behavioural disorder where symptoms from this list: aggression to animals or people, destruction of property, deceitfulness, theft or rule violations are present (DSM-5-TR).

Curriculum compacting   Reducing time spent on grade curriculum by the advanced student in order to allow time for enrichment, extension work or independent study.

Developmental Co-ordination Disorder (DCD)   A neurodevelopmental disorder involving reduced capacity to execute motor skills in either fine or gross motor skills or both.

Differentiation   The response that a teacher makes to an individual student's learning needs, by changing the content, process, product and/or learning environment of lessons.

Disability   As used in Australian legislation, includes physical, intellectual, psychiatric, sensory, neurological and learning disabilities. (It also includes physical disfigurement and the presence in the body of disease-causing organisms, such as the HIV virus.)

[Author note: This book only refers to the physical, sensory, neurological and learning types.]

Dyscalculia   An innate difficulty in learning or comprehending mathematics. Students with dyscalculia have trouble understanding numbers, learning how to manipulate numbers, learning mathematical facts and a number of other related difficulties.

Dysgraphia   A specific learning disability where a child's spelling and/or written grammatical or punctuation work are weaker than expected. See also *motor dysgraphia*.

Dyslexia   Dyslexia is a specific learning disability that is neurobiological in origin. It is characterised by difficulties with accurate and/or fluent word recognition and by poor spelling and decoding abilities. These difficulties typically result from a deficit in the phonological component of language that is often unexpected in relation to other cognitive abilities and the provision of effective classroom instruction. Secondary consequences may include problems in reading comprehension and reduced reading experience that can impede growth of vocabulary and background knowledge.

Effect size (ES)   Indicates the size of an experimental effect indicating its relative strength as an educational intervention.

Enrichment   Curriculum material used with advanced or high potential students that explores greater depth in a subject or takes in affiliated material that may not be covered by the majority of a class.

Executive function   A set of skills involving planning, self-regulation and metacognition among other aspects of cognitive, brain development

Extension   Curriculum material that is substantially more challenging than that covered by the majority of a cohort but is not accelerated content from the grade above.

Gifted students   Those whose potential significantly exceeds that of students of the same age in one or more domains: intellectual, creative, social-emotional, and physical. This is considered to be those students whose ability is above the 90th percentile, that means the top 10% of age peers across the country.

High-potential students Those whose potential exceeds that of students of the same age in one or more domains: intellectual, creative, social-emotional and physical.

Hyperactivity Unusual or abnormal level of activity in physical movement, impulsive behaviour or distractibility.

Hyperfocus An intense state of sustained or selective attention which can actually be a symptom of ADHD.

Hyperlexia When a child starts reading early beyond age expectations but may not understand or comprehend meaning at the same level. It may or may not be associated with autism.

Imputed disability An undiagnosed disability that the school team considers a student to have that is having a functional impact on their learning.

Intervention The action of becoming intentionally involved in a difficult situation, in order to improve it or prevent it from getting worse.

Learning difficulty Problem with learning from a variety of causes including absenteeism from school, an educational setting that does not suit their needs, English is their second language, visual or auditory acuity weaknesses or behavioural, emotional or psychological problems.

Learning disability A diagnosable disorder of learning including Specific Learning Disorder.

Learning profile A comprehensive understanding of a student's strengths and underlying conditions.

Legislation A law or set of laws suggested by a government and made official by a parliament.

Metacognition Thinking about the type of thinking required to perform a task or to progress in academic performance.

Motor dysgraphia A specific learning disorder in which handwriting difficulties, particularly involving letter-formation, make the process slow and the product illegible.

Motor planning Organising the body to perform actions.

Neurodevelopmental disorder Disorders of early brain development are often called neurodevelopmental disorders and include autism spectrum disorder (ASD), motor disability, learning disabilities (e.g. dyslexia), and attention deficit hyperactivity disorder (ADHD).

Neurodiversity People have different ways of perceiving and interacting with the world. This concept allows for the neurological conditions that people have but frames them as a variation of normal brain functioning with identifiable strengths. The term was first used by Judy Singer, an Australian sociologist, in the 1990's.

Norm-referenced test A standardised test that compares a student's performance with others of the same age and has been piloted on a sample population to give it validity and reliability.

Oppositional Defiant Disorder (ODD) A disorder where symptoms involving anger, irritability, defiance, argumentativeness and vindictiveness are evident. It is often co-morbid with ADHD.

Pedagogy   A strategy for educational instruction considering the interactions that will take place in the process and the learners for whom it is intended.

Phonemic awareness   The ability to identify and manipulate phonological elements in spoken words.

Phonics check   The Year 1 Phonics Screening Check assesses how students blend sounds together to read a word. It consists of 40 words both real and made up.

Pseudoword   A non-word used in phonic tests to check a child's capacity to decode without the prompt of meaning.

Qualitative screener   Checklist, brief test or list of questions to identify student characteristics without the precision of a quantitative assessment.

Quantitative assessment   A standardised test that concentrates on the generation of numerical data allowing the calculation of percentiles for comparison within the student population.

Remediation   The process of improving or correcting a situation e.g. poor reading skills.

Self-esteem   The sense of value and perception held about oneself.

Self-efficacy   The belief one has about one's capacity to complete the tasks necessary for a particular outcome.

Specific Learning Disorder (SLD)   A neurodevelopmental condition that affects aspects of academic learning in reading, written expression and mathematics.

SPELD NSW   Specific Learning Difficulties Association of NSW. It is federated with the associations from other states through the national association, AUSPELD.

Talent development   The process of turning potential into talent or high achievement in a specific domain or subject.

Tic Disorders   Neurodevelopmental disorders with motor (body movement) and vocal (sound) tics which are involuntary muscle movements.

Twice-exceptional student   One who is gifted in one or more of the domains of human ability yet has at least one co-existing disability which can be in the area of a specific learning disability or an emotional, physical or other disorder.

Underachievement   When the estimated or assessed intellectual potential of a student is not being realised into the expected level of academic results.

Visuo-manual coordination   This includes the actions of reaching for objects or catching a ball.

Visuospatial working memory   This is a component of working memory responsible for the holding of information about the visual characteristics of an object, its textures and colour and for the location of features in space, for example, particular buildings, furniture and personal items.

Whole word reading   A method of teaching reading that emphasises the recognition of whole words not the sounds within those words.

Milton Keynes UK
Ingram Content Group UK Ltd.
UKHW011529071224
451979UK00017B/188